WOMEN OF COLOR AND SOUTHERN WOMEN:

A BIBLIOGRAPHY OF SOCIAL SCIENCE RESEARCH, 1975 TO 1988

Annual Supplement, 1990

Edited by

Andrea Timberlake

Lynn Weber Cannon

Rebecca F. Guy

Elizabeth Higginbotham

Printed in the United States of America

International Standard Serial Number 1054-1969
Library of Congress Catalog Card Number 90-656447

ISBN 0-9621327-2-1

A publication from *The Research Clearinghouse and Curriculum Integration Project on Women of Color and Southern Women*, Lynn Weber Cannon, Project Director, Center for Research on Women, Memphis State University, Memphis, TN 38152

Supported in part by a grant from the Fund for the Improvement of Post-Secondary Education and contributions from the Office of Planning and Public Service, the College of Arts and Sciences, the Department of Sociology and Social Work, Memphis State University, Memphis, TN 38152

CONTENTS

INTRODUCTION

Women of Color and Southern Women: A Bibliography of Social Science Research, 1975 to 1988. Annual Supplement, 1990 is the second annual supplement to the original bibliography produced by the Center for Research on Women at Memphis State University. Presented here are approximately 900 references drawn from the 1200 citations newly added to our Research Clearinghouse on Women of Color and Southern Women. The Research Clearinghouse is an on-line database of 5,500 bibliographic citations to current (published or produced since 1975) social science scholarship on these two groups. Citations cover books, non-print media, chapters in books, published papers, and unpublished works such as doctoral dissertations, working papers or papers presented at meetings.

These references were obtained from several sources. Center staff regularly review journals, periodicals, newsletters, books, abstracts, vitae, publishing house brochures and proceedings from pertinent research forums. Our National Advisory Board members, representing various disciplines, send materials to review for possible inclusion in the database. Also, approximately 200 scholars conducting research on southern women and women of color are included in our Human Resource File and submit their work for examination. In addition to alerting us to new materials, our National Advisory Board and Human Resource File scholars help in other ways, too: they distribute Center materials at professional meetings, encourage others to submit works to us and to use the Clearinghouse and other Center resources.

The format of the supplement is the same as the previous bibliographies with six major subject headings: culture, education, employment, family, health and political activism/social movements. Under each of these headings, the racial ethnic categories are: African American, Asian American, Latina, Native American, Southern and comparative research on Women of Color. The South is defined to include Washington, DC and the following states: Alabama, Arkansas, Florida, Georgia, Kentucky, Louisiana, Maryland, Mississippi, North and South Carolina, Tennessee, Texas, Virginia and West Virginia. Both a keyword index and a first-author index are included.

Highlights in this edition are the inclusion of numerous non-print media listings and many new citations to research about Native American women. Non-print media (movies, slide presentations, film strips, etc.) can be important learning tools which enhance a classroom lecture or detail a public talk. We think you will find them beneficial. Dr. Helen Bannan of Florida Atlantic University, one of the Center's advisory board members, contributed an extensive bibliography on Native Americans to the Research Clearinghouse early in 1990; most of it has been incorporated into this volume, increasing our listing of works on that group by over a third from last year. And finally, we worked diligently to eliminate unnecessary duplicates.

Each citation is accompanied by keywords used to describe, identify and define the content of the work. These keywords are taken from *A Women's Thesaurus*, Mary Ellen Capek, ed. (New York: Harper and Row, 1987) and our own racial ethnic descriptor list. A sample citation section and the list of racial descriptors, both specific and general, follow this introduction.

Acknowledgements

Members of our National Advisory Board are: Margaret Andersen, Maxine Baca Zinn, Helen Bannan, Kathleen Berkeley, Rosie Bingham, William Boone, Elsa Barkley Brown, Esther Ngan-Ling Chow, Earnstein Dukes, Joe R. Feagin, Mary Fredrickson, Cheryl Townsend Gilkes, Jacquelyn Hall, Rhoda Johnson, Jacqueline Jones, Julianne Malveaux, Vicki Mays, Sandra Morgen, Leith Mullings, Pamela Palmer, Jacqueline Pope, Clara Rodriguez, Vicki Ruiz, Sheryl Ruzek, Carol Stack, Rosalyn Terborg-Penn, Sarah Watts and Ruth Zambrana. We appreciate their counsel and suggestions. The scholars of the Human Resource File are acknowledged for allowing us to include their work and for making themselves available for contact by users of the database.

As in previous years, much work of the Clearinghouse has been carried out by the Center's graduate assistants and work study students. The students who have most recently worked on this Clearinghouse project are: Michael Buchenroth, Kristin Claar, Melissa Connelly, Dinah Dickerson, Mary Beth Snapp, Wyatt Treat and Maria Ogle. Center secretaries, Patricia Jackson, Mia Reddick, and Jo Ann Ammons, the technical clerk, have provided support for this and all Center activities.

Andrea Timberlake *Rebecca F. Guy*

Lynn Weber Cannon *Elizabeth Higginbotham*

Memphis, Tennessee

1991

SAMPLE CITATIONS

BOOK: single author

citation number — author — keywords

0006 **Bethal, Elizabeth R.**
(1981) Promiseland: A Century of Life in a Negro Community. Philadelphia, PA: Temple University. pp. 318.
History/ People of Color/ Social Environment/ Cultural Heritage/ Coping Strategies/ South Carolina/ Resistance

BOOK: two or more authors

publication date — second & third authors — publisher information

0183 Rodriguez, Clara E.
Korrol, Virginia S. and Alers, Jose O. (1984) The Puerto Rican Struggle: Essays on Survival in the U.S. (2nd edition). **Waterfront Press, Maplewood, NJ. 07040.** pp. 151.
Puerto Rican/ Survival Strategies/ Women of Color/ Latina/ Cultural Heritage/ Family/ Acculturation/ Support Systems

PUBLISHED ARTICLE: one or more authors

journal title & volume information

0345 Baranowski, T.
Bee, D. E., Rassin, D. K., et al. (1983) "Social Support, Social Influence, Ethnicity and the Breast Feeding Decision." **Social Science and Medicine 17:21:pp. 1599-1611.**
Infant Care/ Health Care/ Ethnicity/ Racial Factors/ Women of Color*/ Support Systems/ Cultural Influences/ Breast Feeding

UNPUBLISHED: dissertation

date degree conferred — university conferring degree — dissertation abstracts international information

0514 Mansfield, Betty
(1980) "That Fateful Class: Black Teachers of Virginia Freedmen, 1861-1882." Dissertation: **Catholic University of America**, Washington, D.C. pp. 391. **DAI 41(02A)773.**
African Americans/ People of Color/ Social History/ 19th Century/ Education/ Teachers/ Virginia/ South

UNPUBLISHED: paper presented/working paper

0587 Fong, Pauline L.
(1976) "Economic Status of Asian Women."
conference — **Presented: Advisory Council on Women's Educational Programs. San Francisco, CA.**
Asian American/ Women of Color/ Economic Status/ Education/ Employment

0421 Brewer, Rose M.
(1987) "Troubled Passage: Labor, Family Formation and the Young Black Working Class."
Author: Department of Sociology, University of Minnesota, Minneapolis, MN. 55455. — author's current address
Presented: American Sociological Association, Chicago, IL.

CHAPTER IN A BOOK

0447 Eckford, Elizabeth
(1981) "The First Day: Little Rock, 1957." in — chapter title
book title — **Growing Up Southern. Chris Mayfield.** — book author
New York: Pantheon. pp. 257-261.
African American/ School Desegregation/ Education/ Civil Rights Movement/ South/ Arkansas/ Race Relations/ People of Color

RACIAL/ETHNIC DESCRIPTOR LIST

- African American
- African Caribbean
- Arab
- Asian
  - Asian Pacific
  - Chinese
  - Filipino
  - Japanese
  - Korean
  - Vietnamese
- Asian American
  - Asian Pacific American
  - Chinese American
  - Filipino American
  - Japanese American
  - Korean American
  - Vietnamese American
- Cajun
- Caribbean
- Caribbean American
- Chicanos
- Creole
- Hawaiian
- Latina
  - Chicana
  - Cuban
  - Cuban American
  - Mexican
  - Puerto Rican
- Latinos
- Native American
  - Aleuts
  - Algonkian
  - Apache
  - Arikara
  - Blackfeet
  - Cherokee
  - Cheyenne
  - Chippewas
  - Comanche
  - Crees
  - Creeks
  - Ditdahts
  - Eskimos
  - Hidatsa
  - Hopi
  - Hupa
  - Huron
  - Inupiat
  - Iroquois
  - Makahs
  - Manitous-Naskapi
  - Micmac
  - Mohawk
  - Navaho
  - Okanogan
  - Paiute
  - Plains
  - Powhatans
  - Pueblo
  - Seminole
  - Shoshone
  - Sioux
- Pacific Islanders
- People of Color*
- Sikhs
- Women of Color*

PARTIAL LIST OF SOURCES REVIEWED

JOURNALS/MAGAZINES:
American Anthropologist
American Journal of Sociology
American Indian Quarterly
American Sociological Review
American Visions
Birth Gazette
Catalyst
Children's Advocate
Contemporary Sociology
El Palacio
Feminist Issues
Feminist Studies
Feminist Teacher
Frontiers
Gender and Society
Hispanic Journal of Behavioral Sciences
Insight
Intercambios Femeniles
Internatl. Migration Review
Journal of American History
Journal of Health and Social Behavior
Journal of Ethnic Studies
Journal of Social & Behavioral Sciences
La Red/The Net
Living Blues
Phylon
Psychology of Women Quarterly
Radical America
Radical Teacher
Sage: A Scholarly Journal of Black Women
Signs: A Journal on Women in Culture and Society
Sociology of Education
Social Forces
Social Problems
Social Science Quarterly
Sociological Spectrum
Sociological Inquiry
Southern Exposure
Southern Sociologist
Teaching Sociology
Western Historical Quarterly
Women's Studies Quarterly

NEWSLETTERS/NEWSPAPERS/ OTHER:
Afro Scholar
Belles Lettres
Bureau of Labor Statistics News
Congressional Caucus for Women's Issues
Feminist Collections (U. of Wisc.)
Footnotes (ASA Newsletter)
Ford Foundation Letter
Interracial Books for Children Bulletin
NWSA-Perspectives
On Campus With Women
National Committee on Pay Equity
Minorities and Women in Business

Psychology of Women Newsletter
Sojourner: The Women's Forum
SE Women's Studies Assn Newsletter
Southern Feminist
Span Speaking Mental Health Research Ctr. Newsletter
SWS Network
The Unfinished Agenda
Women's Review of Books

AUXILIARY SOURCES

AAUW Journal
Akwesasne Notes
Am. Indian Law Review
Bureau of Am. Ethnology Bulletin
California History
Chronicles of Oklahoma
Ethnology
Ethos
Immigration History Newsletter
Integrated Education
Journal for Scientific Study of Religion
J. of Am. Ethnic History
Journal of Am. Indian Education
J. of Educational Psychology
J. of Educational Research

The Center for Research on Women is a member of the National Council for Research on Women and regularly receives and reviews newsletters from member centers.

CULTURE

African American

0001 Armitage, Susan H.
Wilbert, Deborah Gallacci. (1988) "Black Women in the Pacific Northwest: A Survey and Research Prospectus." in Women in Pacific Northwest History: An Anthology. Karen J. Blair (ed.). Seattle: University of Washington Press. pp. 136-151.
Women of Color/ African American/ Pacific/ Northwest/ Women's History

0002 Beard, Linda Susan
(1989) "Daughters of Clio and Calliope: Afro-American Women Writers as Reclamation and Revisionist Herstorians." Psychohistory Review 17(Spring):pp. 301-43.
Women of Color/ Curriculum Integration/ African American/ Women's Culture/ Writers/ Herstory/ Revisionism/ Women's History

0003 Bell, Suzanne Comer
(1989) "Epaminondas: The African American Silly Son." Southern Folklore 46:3:pp. 221-237.
Women of Color/ African American/ Cultural Heritage/ Oral Tradition/ Folk Literature/ Storytelling

0004 Berkeley, Kathleen C.
(1989) "Days of Jubilo and Sorrow: Black Women's Quest for Freedom in the Post Civil War South." Presented: Southern Anthropological Society Meeting, Memphis, TN.
Minority Experience/ Women's History/ Freedom/ Agriculture/ Families/ Violence/ Economic Value of Women's Work/ Communities/ Wives/ African American/ Mothers/ Women of Color

0005 Blackburn, Regina
(1989) "In Search of the Black Female Self: African American Women's Autobiographies and Ethnicity." in Women's Autobiography Essays in Criticism. Estelle C. Jelinek (ed.). Bloomington, IN: Indiana University Press.
Women of Color/ Self Concept/ African American/ Self Esteem/ Identity/ Ethnicity/ Self Actualization/ Autobiographies

0006 Blee, Kathleen M.
Tickamyer, Ann. (1987) "Black-White Differences in Mother to Daughter Transmission of Sex-Role Attitudes." Sociological Quarterly 28(Summer):2:pp. 205-222.
Women of Color/ Socialization/ African American/ Women's Culture/ European American/ Sex Roles/ Attitudes/ Mother Daughter Relationships

0007 Boyd, Julia A.
(1990) "Ethnic and Cultural Diversity: Keys to Power." Women and Therapy

9:1,2:pp. 151-167.
Women of Color/ Feminist Therapy/ Asian American/ Mental Health/ African American/ Crosscultural Studies/ Ethnic Diversity/ Psychotherapy/ Dominant Culture/ Feminist Therapists/ Racial and Ethnic Differences/ Social Psychology

0008 Boylan, Anne M.
(1986) "Reclaiming the Early History of Black Women's Organizations." Presented: Research on Racism Series, University of Delaware.
Women of Color/ Voluntary Organizations/ African American/ Women's History/ Women's Studies/ Women's Organizations/ Clubs/ Women's Culture

0009 Bracey, John H., Jr.
Meier, A. (eds.). (1990) Black Studies Research Resources. Bethesda, MD: University Publications of America.
People of Color/ Legislation/ Laws/ African Americans/ Leadership/ Research Resources/ History/ Collections/ Working Papers/ Culture/ Journals/ South

0010 Brown, Diane Robinson
Gary, Lawerence E. et al. (1984) "Pathways: A Study of Black Informal Support Networks." Available: Institute for Urban Affairs and Research, Washington, DC 20008.
People of Color/ Networks/ African Americans/ Coping Strategies/ Support Systems/ Culture

0011 Brown, Elsa Barkley
(1989) "African American Women's Quilting." SIGNS: Journal of Women in Culture and Society 14(Summer):4:pp. 921-929.
Women of Color/ African American/ Quilting/ Culture/ Women's Groups/ Diversity

0012 Bullard, Robert D.
(1989) In Search of the New South: The Urban Black in the 1970's and 1980's. Tuscaloosa, AL: University of Alabama Press. pp. 232.
People of Color/ Social Change/ African Americans/ Migration/ South/ Culture/ History/ Urban Areas

0013 Burnham, Dorothy
(1983) "Black Women as Producers and Reproducers for Profit." in Woman's Nature: Rationalizations of Inequality. Marian Lowe and Ruth Hubbard (ed.). New York: Pergamon Press. pp. 29-38.
Women of Color/ African American/ History/ Slavery/ Sexuality/ Economic Factors/ Population Distribution/ Reproduction Exploitation/ Fertility/ Women's Culture

0014 Butler, Anne M.
(1989) "Still in Chains: Black Women in Western Prisons, 1865-1910." Western Historical Quarterly 20(February):pp. 19-35.
Women of Color/ Prisons/ Prisoners/ African American/ 19th Century/ West/ Criminal Justice/ Women's Culture/ Women's History/ Incarceration

0015 Cannon, Katie G.
(1988) Black Womanist Ethics. Atlanta, GA: Scholars Press.
Women of Color/ Social Values/ African American/ Philosophy/ Ethnicity/ Womanism/ Women's Culture

0016 Carawan, Guy
Carawan, Candie. (1989) Ain't You Got a Right to the Tree of Life?: The People of Johns Island, South Carolina - Their Faces, Their Words, and Their Songs. Athens,

GA: University of Georgia Press. pp. 256.
People of Color/ Culture/ African Americans/ History/ South Carolina/ Life Styles/ Songs/ Music/ Literature

0017 Cauthern, Cynthia
(1979) "900 Black Lesbians." Off Our Backs 9(June):pp. 12.
Women of Color/ Women's Culture/ African American/ Lesbian Studies / Homosexuality/ Life Styles

0018 Cody, Cheryll Ann
(1987) "There Was No 'Absalom' on the Ball Plantations: Slave Naming Practices in the South Carolina Low Country, 1720-1865." The American Historical Review 92(June):3:pp. 563-596.
People of Color/ Name Rights/ African Americans/ Slavery/ South/ South Carolina/ History/ 18th Century/ Slave Names/ Cultural Influences/ Plantations

0019 Collins, Patricia Hill
(1987) "The Meaning of Motherhood in Black Culture and Black Mother/Daughter Relationships." SAGE: A Scholary Journal on Black Women 4(Fall):2:pp. 4-11.
Women of Color/ Racial Discrimination/ African American/ Motherhood/ Parent Child Relationships/ Parenting/ Mothers/ Images of Women/ Cultural Influences

0020 Collins, Patricia Hill
(1989) "Black Women as Agents of Knowledge." Presented: American Sociological Association Annual Meeting, San Francisco, CA.
African American/ Cultural Heritage/ Women of Color/ Agents/ Knowledge/ Women's History/ Women's Culture

0021 Cuciti, Peggy
James, Franklin. (1990) "A Comparison of Black and Hispanic Poverty in Large Cities of the Southwest." Hispanic Journal of Behavioral Sciences 12(Feb.):1:pp. 50-75.
African Americans/ Latinos/ People of Color/ Comparative Studies/ Poverty/ Urban Areas/ Southwest/ Crosscultural Studies

0022 Cummings, Melbourne S.
(1988) "The Changing Image of the Black Family on Television." Journal of Popular Culture 22(Fall):pp. 75-87.
People of Color/ Communications/ African Americans/ Mass Media/ Image/ Stereotypes/ Popular Culture/ Social Attitudes/ Family

0023 Dash, Julie
(1982) "Illusions." Distributor: Women Make Movies, Inc., 225 Lafayette St., Suite 212, New York, NY 10012. Phone: (212) 925-0606 or Fax: (212) 925-2052.
African American/ Social Attitudes/ Women of Color/ Cultural Identity/ Images of Women/ Media Stereotyping/ False Dichotomies/ Social Identity/ Social Adjustments

0024 Davis, Richard
(1987) "The Legacy of Poverty: Cultural Survivals in Black Middle Class Families." Presented: Sociological Research Symposium, Richmond VA.
African Americans/ People of Color/ Poverty/ Socioeconomic Status/ Middle Class Families/ Survival Strategies

0025 Eckardt, Arthur Roy
(1989) Black-Woman-Jew: Three Wars for Human Liberation. Bloomington, IN: Indiana University Press. pp. 240.
African American/ Human Rights/ Jewish/ Women of Color/ Cultural Heritage/ Antisemitism/ Discrimination/ Social Bias

0026 Eho, E.
(1986) "Changes in the Image of African Women - A Celebration." Phylon 47(September):3:pp. 210-218.
Women of Color/ Women's Culture/ African American/ Images of Women/ Social Change/ Social Perception/ Empowerment

0027 Film & Video Library
(1980) "That Rhythm, Those Blues." Distributor: Film & Video Library, University Library, University of Michigan, 400 Fourth St., Ann Arbor, MI 48103-4816. Phone: (313) 764-5360 or 1-800-999-0424.
People of Color/ Music/ Blues/ African Americans/ Music History/ South/ Culture/ Musicians

0028 Film & Video Library
(1988) "Alice Walker: A Portrait in the First Person." Distributor: Film & Video Library, University Library, University of Michigan, 400 Fourth St., Ann Arbor, MI 48103-4816. Phone: (313) 764-5360 or 1-800-999-0424.
Women of Color/ Race Relations/ African American/ Family Relations/ Alice Walker/ Struggles/ Culture/ Class/ Life Styles/ Social Mobility/ Poverty/ Social Status

0029 Film & Video Library
(1981) "Maya Angelou." Distributor: Film & Video Library, University Library, University of Michigan, 400 Fourth St., Ann Arbor, MI 48103-4816. Phone: (313) 764-5360 or 1-800-999-0424.
Women of Color/ Culture/ African American/ Self Concept/ Maya Angelou/ Life Histories/ South/ Arkansas

0030 Folb, Edith A.
(1988) "Black Vernacular Vocabulary: A Study of Intra/Intercultural Concerns and Usage." Available: University of California at Los Angeles Center for Afro-American Studies, Los Angeles, CA 90024-1545. pp. 53.
People of Color/ Sociolinguistics/ African Americans/ Racial and Ethnic Differences/ Language/ Speech/ Cultural Heritage/ Cultural Influences

0031 Forbes, Jack D.
(1984) "Mulattoes and People of Color in Anglo-North America: Implications for Black-Indian Relations." The Journal of Ethnic Studies 12(Summer):pp. 17-61.
People of Color/ Social Relations/ African Americans/ Interracial Relations/ Native Americans/ Ethnic Studies/ Mulattoes

0032 Forbes, Jack D.
(1988) Black Africans and Native Americans: Color, Race and Caste in the Evolution of Red-Black Peoples. New York: Blackwell. pp. 345.
Women of Color/ Racial Stratification/ People of Color/ History/ Native Americans/ Culture Conflict/ African Americans/ Colonization/ Interracial Relations/ Imperialism/ Race Relations

0033 Fox-Genovese, Elizabeth
(1990) "Between Individualism and Fragmentation: American Culture and the New Literary Studies of Race and Gender." American Quarterly 42(March):1:pp. 7-34.
Women of Color/ Feminist Criticism/ African American/ Literary Criticism/ American Studies/ Race, Class and Gender Studies/ Literature/ Cultural Influences

0034 Gavins, Raymond
(1989) "North Carolina Black Folklore and Song in the Age of Segregation: Toward Another Meaning of Survival." North Carolina Historical Review

66(November):pp. 412-442.
People of Color/ Oral Tradition/ South/ North Carolina/ Segregation/ African Americans/ Survival Strategies/ Folk Literature/ Songs/ Music/ Cultural Heritage

0035 Gwin, Minrose C.
(1989) "A Theory of Black Women's Texts and White Women's Readings or . . . the Necessity of Being Other." NWSA Journal 1:1.
Women of Color/ Cultural Heritage/ African American/ Racial Diversity/ Literature/ Images of Women/ Curriculum Integration/ Identity/ Culture/ European American

0036 Handy, Antoinette D.
(1983) The International Sweethearts of Rhythm. Metuchen, NJ: Scarecrow Press. pp. 258.
Jazz/ Musicians/ Race Relations/ African American/ Gender Differences/ Women of Color/ Racial and Ethnic Differences/ Biographies/ Music/ Employment/ Race, Class and Gender Studies

0037 Harrison, Algea O.
(1987) "Images of Black Women." in The American Woman, 1987-88. Sarah E. Rix. (ed.). New York: W. W. Norton & Co. pp. 257-261.
Women of Color/ Self Concept/ African American/ Race, Class and Gender Studies/ Images of Women/ Women's Culture/ Media Stereotyping/ Stereotypes/ Traditional Family

0038 Hernton, Calvin C.
(1990) The Sexual Mountain and Black Women Writers. New York: Anchor. pp. 192.
Women of Color/ Social Influences/ African American/ Racial Factors/ Writers/ Authors/ Literature/ Literary Criticism/ Women's Culture

0039 Hughes, Michael
Demo, David H. (1989) "Self-Perceptions of Black Americans: Self-Esteem and Personal Efficiency." American Journal of Sociology 95(July):1:pp. 132-159.
African Americans/ Racial and Ethnic Differences/ People of Color/ Self Perception/ Psychological Needs/ Self Esteem/ Racial Discrimination

0040 Hughes, Michael
Hertel, Bradley R. (1990) "The Significance of Color Remains: A Study of Life Chances, Mate Selection, and Ethnic Consciousness among Black Americans." Social Forces 68(June):4:pp. 1105-1120.
Cultural Identity/ Life Styles/ Women of Color/ Image/ Attitudes/ African Americans/ Economic Factors/ Marriage/ Social Perception/ Ethnicity/ Consciousness/ Married Couples/ Racial Discrimination/ Skin Color/ Complexion/ Perceptual Bias

0041 Hurtado, Aida
(1989) "Relating to Privilege: Seduction and Rejection in the Subordination of White Women and Women of Color." SIGNS: Journal of Women in Culture and Society 14:4:pp. 833-855.
African American/ Black Feminism/ Women of Color/ Structural Discrimination/ Feminism/ Racial Discrimination/ Sex Discrimination/ Privilege/ Exploitation/ Minority Experience/ Subordination of Women/ Women's Culture

0042 Jacobs, Sylvia M.
(1986) "Say Africa When You Pray: The Activities of Early Black Baptist Women Missionaries among Liberian Women and Children." SAGE: A Scholary Journal on Black Women 3(Fall):pp. 16-21.
Women of Color/ Missionaries/ African American/ Religions/ Baptists/ Churches/ Women's Culture

0043 Jennings, Thelma
(1990) "Us Colored Women Had To Go through a Plenty: Sexual Exploitation of African-American Slave Women." Journal of Women's History 1(Winter):3.
African American/ Women of Color/ History/ Women's Culture/ Slavery/ Sexual Exploitation/ Sexual Oppression/ Sexual Violence

0044 Jones-Jackson, Patricia
(1989) When Roots Die: Endangered Traditions on the Sea Islands. Athens, GA: University of Georgia Press. pp. 224.
Women of Color/ Culture/ African American/ Tradition/ South Carolina/ Cultural Heritage/ Georgia/ Life Styles/ South East

0045 King, Deborah Karyn
(1987) "In Dialogue with our Mothers: Black Women's Tradition of Struggle and Survival." Presented: Series on Women's Culture, Middlebury College, Middlebury, VT.
Women of Color/ Survival Strategies/ African American/ Traditions/ Resistance/ Women's History/ Women's Culture/ Liberation Struggles

0046 King, Deborah Karyn
(1987) "Culture, Black Womanhood, and Womanist Sensibilities." Presented: Luncheon Roundtable Annual Meeting of the American Sociological Association, Chicago, IL.
Women of Color/ African American/ Black Feminism/ Womanism/ Culture/ Womanhood

0047 Kulikoff, Allan
(1977) "The Beginnings of the Afro-American Family in Maryland." in Law, Society and Politics in Early Maryland. Aubry G. Land (ed.). Baltimore: Johns Hopkins University Press. pp. 400.
People of Color/ Maryland/ South/ African Americans/ Culture/ Family/ History

0048 Kyi, Daresha
(1988) "The Thinnest Line." Distributor: Women Make Movies, Inc., 225 Lafayette St., Suite 212, New York, NY 10012. Phone: (212) 925-0606 or Fax: (212) 925-2052.
African American/ Friendships/ Women of Color/ Cultural Identity/ Female Female Relationships/ Female Friendships/ Social Relationships

0049 Larkin, Alile Sharon
(1987) "Miss Fluci Moses." Distributor: Alile Productions/Alile Sharon Larkin, 4843 West 17th St. #7, Los Angeles, CA 90019.
Women of Color/ Culture/ African American/ Life Histories/ Fluci Moses/ Teacher/ Poet/ Literature

0050 Lee See, Letha
(1989) "Tensions between Black Women and White Women: A Study." AFFILIA: Journal of Women and Social Work 4(Summer):2:pp. 31-46.
Women of Color/ Race Relations/ African American/ Social Conflict/ Social Stratification/ Women's Culture

0051 MacKethan, Lucinda H.
(1985) "Mother Wit: Humor in Afro-American Women's Autobiography." Studies in American Humor 4(Fall):pp. 51-62.
African American/ Autobiographies/ Women's Culture/ Women of Color/ Humor/ Literature/ Writing

0052 Malson, Michelene R.
Mudimbe-Boyi, Elisabeth et al. (eds.). (1990) Black Women in America. Chicago: University of Chicago Press. pp. 348.
Women of Color/ Women's Culture/ African American/ Black Feminism/ Experience/ Social Science/ Women's History

0053 Melder, Keith
(1989) "Slaves and Freedmen." Wilson Quarterly 13(January):pp. 77-83.
African Americans/ Slaves/ Plantations/ Freedmen/ People of Color/ Emancipation/ Acculturation

0054 Miller, Randall M.
Smith, John David. (1988) Dictionary of Afro-American Slavery. Westport, CT: Greenwood Press. pp. 880. ISBN 03132381.
People of Color/ Ethnic Studies/ African Americans/ Research Resources/ Social History/ Cultural Heritage/ Slavery/ South

0055 Mosley, Zelma
(1989) "Gender Differences in Black Public Opinion." Presented: National Conference of Black Political Scientists, Baton Rouge, LA.
Women of Color/ Gender Differences/ African American/ Public Opinion/ Women's Culture

0056 Nash, Gary B.
(1989) Forging Freedom: The Formation of Philadelphia's Black Community, 1720-1840. Cambridge, MA: Harvard University Press. pp. 354.
Community/ Racial Stratification/ Pennsylvania/ Support Systems/ African American/ Social Structure/ Freedom/ Ethnic Neighborhoods/ Urban Areas/ Social Stratification

0057 Neel, E. Ann
(1988) "Entangled Lives: Black and White Women in a Midwestern Slaveholding Community." Presented: Annual Meeting of the National Women Studies Association, Minneapolis, MN.
African American/ Race Relations/ European American/ Social Relations/ Midwest/ Relationships/ Slavery/ Socialization/ Social Differences/ Women of Color/ Women's Culture

0058 Nicola-McLaughlin, Andree
(1985) "White Power, Black Despair: Vanessa Williams in Babylon." The Black Scholar (March/April).
Women of Color/ Beauty Queens/ African American/ Beauty Contests/ Discrimination/ Women's Culture/ Oppression/ Exploitation/ Power/ Powerlessness/ Images of Women

0059 Parkerson, Michelle
(1980) ". . . But Then, She's Betty Carter." Distributor: Black Film-maker Foundation, 80 Eighth Ave., Suite 1704, New York, NY 10011. Phone: (212) 924-1198.
Women of Color/ Entertainment/ African American/ Culture/ Betty Carter/ Visual and Performing Arts/ Artistic Ability/ Individual Development/ Singers/ Jazz

0060 Pirsen, William D.
(1988) Black Yankees: The Development of an Afro-American Subculture in Eighteenth Century New England. Amherst, MA: University of Massachusetts Press.
People of Color/ African Americans/ History/ 18th Century/ Culture/ Subculture/ North/ New England/ Socialization

0061 Plant, Deborah G.
(1988) "Zora Neale Hurston's 'Dust Tracks on a Road': Black Autobiography in a Different Voice." Dissertation: University of Nebraska. DAI (April/May), Vol. 49, 1989.
Women of Color/ Zora Neale Hurston/ African American/ Writers/ Authors/ Autobiographies/ Cultural Heritage

0062 Pope, Jacqueline
(1986) "Brooklyn, New York's Black Churches and Disinherited Women in the 1960's: Did the Church Abandon Them?" Research Report Available: Stockton State College, Pomona, NJ 08240.
Women of Color/ Women's Culture/ African American/ Northeast/ New York/ Churches/ Religion/ History

0063 Pope, Jacqueline
(1986) "The Impact of Poverty on Urban African-Americans and Kenyan Women. A Comparative Report: New York and Nairobi in the 1960's." Presented: International Human Rights Symposium and Research Conference Annual Meeting, Columbia University, NY.
Women of Color/ Urban Areas/ African American/ Living Standards/ Poverty/ Basic Human Needs/ Women Living in Poverty/ Crosscultural Studies

0064 Reagon, Bernice Johnson
(1982) "My Black Mothers and Sisters or On Beginning a Cultural Autobiography." Feminist Studies 8:1.
Women of Color/ Cultural Influences/ African American/ Personal Narrative/ Autobiographies/ Women's Culture

0065 Riggs, Marlon
(1987) "Ethnic Notions." Distributor: Film & Video Library, University Library, University of Michigan, 400 Fourth St., Ann Arbor, MI 48103-4816. Phone: (313)764-5360 or 1-800-999-0424.
People of Color/ Discrimination/ African Americans/ Prejudice/ Race Relations/ Culture/ Social History/ Ethnic Studies/ Media Stereotyping

0066 Sears, James T.
(1989) "The Impact of Gender and Race on Lesbians and Gays in the South." NWSA Journal 1(Spring):3:pp. 422-457.
South/ Lesbians/ Race, Class and Gender Studies/ Gender Differences/ African American/ Culture Conflict/ Racial and Ethnic Differences/ Women of Color/ Homosexuality

0067 Sharp, Saundra
(1984) "Back Inside Herself." Distributor: Women Make Movies, Inc., 225 Lafayette, Suite 212, New York, NY 10012. Phone: (212) 925-0606 or Fax: (212) 925-2052.
Women of Color/ Cultural Identity/ African American/ Personal Values/ Self Concept/ Individual Development/ Life Histories

0068 Sherkat, Darren E.
Ellison, Christopher G. (1990) "Religious Mobility among Black Americans." Presented: North Central Sociological Association and Southern Sociological Association Annual Meetings, Louisville, KY.
People of Color/ Religious Reforms/ African Americans/ Religious Traditions/ Religion/ Mobility/ Cultural Influences/ Religious Movements/ Socioeconomic Conditions/ Religious Beliefs

0069 Shockley, Ann Allen
(1984) "The Black Lesbian in American Literature." in Women - Identified Women. Trudy Dorty and Sandra Potter (eds.). Palo Alto, CA: Mayfield.
Women of Color/ Women's Culture/ African American/ Literature/ Lesbian Studies/ Homosexuality/ Women Identified Women

0070 Sigelman, Lee
Welch, Susan. (1984) "Race and Sex Differences in Attitudes toward Blacks and Women as President." Public Opinion Quarterly 48:pp. 467-475.
People of Color/ Racial and Ethnic Differences/ Sex Differences/ Attitudes/ Women in Politics/ African American/ European American

0071 Smith, Eleanor J.
(1983) "Black Women and Culture: A Historical Perspective." Presented: Black Women Caucus Conference, Northwestern Illinois University, Chicago.
Women of Color/ Cultural Influences/ African American/ Culture/ Cultural Identity/ Women's History

0072 Smith, Jacqueline Marie
(1986) "Church Participation and Morale of the Rural, Southern Black Aged: The Effects of Socioeconomic Status, Gender and the Organizational Properties of Churches." Dissertation: DAI (October), Vol. 47(1489-A)4.
Women of Color/ Socioeconomic Status/ African American/ Older Adults/ Religion/ Churches/ Rural Areas/ Women's Culture/ Mental Health/ Social Organizations/ South

0073 Steward, Sue
Garratt, Sheryl. (1984) Signed, Sealed, Delivered: True Life Stories of Women in Pop. Boston: South End Press.
Women of Color/ Employment/ African American/ Popular Culture/ Biographies/ Images of Women/ Music/ Musicians/ Gender Roles/ Sex Discrimination

0074 Sumter, Ellen
(1989) "Savannah." Distributor: Ellen Sumter, 135 Clinton Ave., Brooklyn, NY. Phone: (718) 855-0988.
Women of Color/ Self Concept/ African American/ Communities/ South/ Individual Development/ Rural Living/ Culture/ Social Influences/ Economically Disadvantaged

0075 Thompson, Rose
Beaumont, Charles (eds.). (1982) Hush, Child! Can't You Hear the Music? Athens, GA: University of Georgia Press. pp. 124.
Women of Color/ Music/ African American/ Rural Areas/ Folk Culture/ Oral Tradition/ Oral History/ South

0076 Vermont Folklife Center
(1987) "On My Own: Daisy Turner." Distrubutor: Filmmakers' Library, Inc., 124 East 40th St., Suite 901, New York, NY 10016. Phone: (212) 808-4980.
Women of Color/ Socialization/ African American/ Culture/ Northeast/ Vermont/ Life Histories/ Self Concept/ Independence

0077 Wallace, Michelle
(1990) Invisibility Blues: From Pop Theory towards a Black Feminist Cultural Criticism. New York: Routledge.
Women of Color/ Cultural Feminism/ African American/ Feminist Perspective/ Black Feminism/ Feminist Theory/ Feminist Scholarship

0078 **Wattleton, Faye**
(1989) "The Case for National Action." The Nation 249(July):4:pp. 138-141.
Women of Color/ Cultural Influences/ Television/ African American/ Teenage Pregnancy/ European American/Race, Class and Gender Studies

0079 **Welch, Susan**
Sigelman, Lee. (1989) "A Black Gender Gap?" Social Science Quarterly 10(March):1:pp. 120-133
Women of Color/ Public Opinion/ African American/ Female Male Relationships/ Gender Gap/ Gender Differences/ Attitudes/ Cultural Influences

0080 **Wright, Donald R.**
(1990) African Americans in the Colonial Era: From African Origins through the American Revolution. Arlington Heights, VA: Harlan Davidson.
People of Color/ Cultural Influences/ African Americans/ Race Relations/ Social History/ Revolutionary War/ Colonial Period/ Cultural Heritage

0081 **Yacovone, Donald**
(1988) "The Fruits of Africa: Slavery, Emancipation, and Afro-American Culture." American Quarterly 12(Fall):pp. 127-134.
People of Color/ Cultural Heritage/ African Americans/ Emancipation/ Culture/ Slavery/ Social History/ Plantations

Asian American

0082 **Asian Women United of California**
(1982) "4 Women." Distributor: Asian Women United of CA, University of California at Los Angeles Film & Television Archives, 1438 Melnitz Hall, Los Angeles, CA 90024. Phone: (213) 206-8013.
Women of Color/ Professional Occupations/ Asian American/ Family Histories/ Employment/ History/ Family/ Culture/ Socialization

0083 **Beesley, David**
(1988) "From Chinese to Chinese American: Chinese Women and Families in a Sierra Nevada Town." California History 67(September):pp. 168-179.
Chinese/ Asian/ Families/ Women's History/ California/ West/ Pacific/ Women of Color/ Immigrants/ Acculturation/ Assimilation Patterns

0084 **Boyd, Julia A.**
(1990) "Ethnic and Cultural Diversity: Keys to Power." Women and Therapy 9:1,2:pp. 151-167.
Women of Color/ Feminist Therapy/ Asian American/ Mental Health/ African American/ Crosscultural Studies/ Ethnic Diversity/ Psychotherapy/ Dominant Culture/ Feminist Therapists/ Racial and Ethnic Differences/ Social Psychology

0085 **Chai, Alice Yun**
Janet Sharistanian. (1987) (eds.). Adaptive Strategies of Recent Korean Immigrant Women in Hawaii: Perspectives on Women's Public Lives. New York: Greenwood Press. pp. 65-99.
Women of Color/ Adaptation/ Asian American/ Acculturation/ Korean/ Pacific Islanders/ Hawaii/ Immigration

0086 **Chai, Alice Yun**
(1986) "History of Asian Immigrant Women and Feminist Methodology." Presented:

Asian American Studies Center, University of California, Los Angeles, CA, May 19.
Women of Color/ History/ Asians/ Acculturation/ Immigration/ Immigrants/ Women's Studies / Feminism/ Feminist Methodology

0087 Chai, Alice Yun
(1986) "Life History Method Analysis of Hawaii's Early Picture Brides from Asia." Presented: 9th Annual National Women's Studies Association Conference, University of Illinois at Urbana-Champaign.
Women of Color/ Mail Order Brides/ Asian American/ Marriage/ Hawaii/ Pacific Islanders/ Life Histories/ Research Methods/ Women's Culture

0088 Chai, Alice Yun
(1986) "Sociocultural Factors and Health Care of Korean Immigrant Women." Presented: Asian Women Workshop sponsored by Cicatelli Associates, at the Asia Society, New York, NY, June 17.
Women of Color/ Health Care/ Asian American/ Cultural Influences/ Immigrants/ Korean

0089 Chan, Connie S.
(1988) "Asian American Women: Psychological Responses to Sexual Exploitation and Cultural Stereotypes." in The Psychology of Everyday Racism and Sexism. Lenora Fulani (ed.). New York: Harrington Park Press. pp. 33-38.
Women of Color/ Oppression/ Asian American/ Sexual Exploitation/ Stereotypes/ Assimilation/ Cultural Influences

0090 Chin, Kotin
(1990) Chinese Subculture and Criminality: Non-Traditional Crime Groups in America. Westport, CT: Greenwood Press.
People of Color/ Gangs/ Asians/ Chinese/ Subculture/ Organized Crime

0091 Chow, Esther N.
(1987) "Sex-Role Identity and Socioeconomic and Psychological Well Being of Asian American Women." Psychology of Women Quarterly 11(Winter):1:pp. 69-81.
Women of Color/ Psychological Factors/ Asian American/ Wellness/ Women's Studies/ Social Adjustments/ Cultural Identity/ Sex Roles/ Socioeconomic Conditions

0092 Ding, Loni
(1990) "Frankly Speaking." Distributor: National Asian American Telecommunications Association, Cross Current Media, 346 Ninth St., 2nd Floor, San Francisco, CA 94103.
Women of Color/ Asian American/ Adolescence/ Culture Conflict/ Socialization/ Cultural Influences/ Modesty/ Assimilation Patterns/ Acculturation/ Racial and Ethnic Differences

0093 Films for the Humanities
(1986) "The Asianization of America." Distributor: Films for the Humanities & Social Sciences, P.O. Box 2053, Princeton, NJ 08543. Phone: (609) 452-1128 or 1-800-257-5126.
People of Color/ Culture/ Asian Americans/ Stereotypes/ Economy/ Immigrants

0094 Gardner, Robert W.
Robey, Bryant et al. (1985) "Asian Americans: Growth, Change, and Diversity." Population Bulletin 40(October):pp. 1-44.
Asian Americans/ People of Color/ Demography/ Population Characteristics/ Population Distribution/ Diversity/ Change/ Population Growth/ Cultural Identity

0095 Gee, Deborah

(1987) "Slaying the Dragon." Distributor: National Asian American Telecommunications Association, Cross Current Media, 346 9th St., 2nd Floor, San Francisco, CA 94103. Phone: (415) 552-9550.
Women of Color/ Images of Women/ Asian American/ Women's Culture/ Geishas/ Media Stereotyping

0096 Gilanshah, Farah

(1989) "The Effects of Immigration on Hmong Women in LaCrosse, Wisconsin." Presented: American Sociological Association Annual Meeting, San Francisco, CA.
Women of Color/ Assimilation Patterns/ Asian/ Immigration/ North/ Wisconsin/ Life Styles/ Acculturation/ Hmong/ Vietnamese

0097 Gonzales, Juan L., Jr.

(1986) "The Sikhs Of Northern California: Settlement and Acculturation In Two Communities." Human Mosaic 20:1&2.
Sikhs/ Cultural Identity/ Asian / Communities/ California/ Socialization/ People Of Color/ Pacific/ Acculturation/ Immigration/ Culture/ Middle East

0098 Goodman, Catherine Chase

(1990) "The Caregiving Roles of Asian American Women." Journal of Women and Aging 2(Spring):1.
Women of Color/ Asian American/ Caregivers/ Age/ Aging/ Health Care/ Culture/ Racial and Ethnic Differences/ Health Care Delivery/ Older Adults

0099 Goza, Franklin W.

(1987) Adjustment and Adaption among Southeast Asian Refugees in the United States. Madison, WI: University of Wisconsin.
Refugees/ Asian/ Adjustment/ Acculturation/ Coping Strategies/ Psychological Adjustment/ Social Adjustment/ Emotional Adjustment

0100 Ho, Christine K.

(1990) "An Analysis of Domestic Violence in Asian American Communities: A Multicultural Approach to Counseling." Women and Therapy 9:1-2:pp. 129-150.
Asian American/ Communities/ Domestic Violence/ Violence Against Women/ Counseling/ Women of Color/ Laotian/ Khmer/ Vietnamese/ Chinese/ Subculture/ Value Systems

0101 Hsia, Lisa

(1980) "Made in China, A Search for Roots." Distributor: Filmakers Library, Inc., 124 East 40th St., Suite 901, New York, NY 10016. Phone: (212) 808-4980.
Women of Color/ Family History/ Asian American/ Ethnic Women/ Chinese American/ Ethnic Studies/ Cultural Heritage

0102 Hunt, Linda

(1985) "'I Could Not Figure Out What Was My Village: Gender vs. Ethnicity' in Maxine Hong Kingston's The Woman Warrior." MELUS 12(Fall):3:pp. 5-12.
Women of Color/ Ethnicity/ Asian American/ Writers/ Chinese American/ Literary Criticism/ Literature/ Authors/ Autobiographies/ Gender Identity

0103 Ichioka, Yuji

(1990) The Issei: The World of the First Generation Japanese Immigrants, 1885-1924. New York: The Free Press.
People of Color/ Culture Conflict/ Asian/ Discrimination/ Immigration/ History/ Acculturation/ Japanese

0104 Kibria, Nazli

(1990) "Power, Patriarchy, and Gender Conflict in the Vietnamese Immigrant

Community." Gender & Society 4(March):1:pp. 9-24.
Women of Color/ Gender Differences/ Asian American/ Gender Roles/ Vietnamese/ Cultural Influences/ Immigrants/ Socialization/ Communities/ Power Structure/ Patriarchy/ Roles

0105 Kibria, Nazli
(1990) "Migration and Vietnamese Refugee Women: Women's Status and Women's Traditionalism." Presented: American Sociological Association Annual Meeting, Washington DC.
Women of Color/ Asian American/ Vietnamese/ Status of Women/ Immigration/ Images of Women/ Traditions/ Women's Culture/ Refugees

0106 Kuo, Wen H.
(1989) "Coping with Racial Discrimination: Asian Americans' Strategies." Presented: American Sociological Association Annual Meeting, San Francisco, CA.
Asian Americans/ People of Color/ Coping Strategies/ Racial Discrimination/ Cultural Heritage

0107 McCunn, Ruthanne Lum
(1988) Chinese American Portraits: Personal Histories, 1928-1988. San Francisco: Chronicle Books. pp. 176. ISBN 0877014914.
Chinese/ Life Histories/ Family/ Culture/ Women of Color/ Oral Tradition/ Women's History/ 20th Century/ Asian American

0108 McGoldrick, Monica
Pearce, John K. and Joseph Giordano (eds.). (1982) Ethnicity and Family Therapy. New York: Guilford Press.
Families/ Ethnicity/ Family Therapy/ People of Color/ Ethnic Studies/ Family Life/ Family Structure/ Asian Americans/ Cultural Influences/ Women of Color/ Racial and Ethnic Differences

0109 Minh-ha, Trinh T.
(1989) "Surname Viet, Given Name Nam." Distributor: Women Make Movies, Inc.,225 Lafayette, Suite 212, New York, NY 10012. Phone: (212) 925-0606 or Fax: (212) 925-2052.
People of Color/ Warfare/ Asians/ Poverty/ Vietnamese/ Media Stereotyping/ Culture/ Social Relations/ Roles/ Life Histories

0110 Nakasako, Spencer
(1990) "Talking History." Distributor: National Asian American Telecommunications Association, Cross Current Media, 346 Ninth St., 2nd Floor, San Francisco, CA 94103.
Women of Color/ Asian American/ Women's History/ Oppression/ Racial Discrimination/ Sex Discrimination/ 20th Century/ Poverty/ Women's Culture

0111 Onodera, Midi
(1988) "The Displaced View." Distributor: Women Make Movies, Inc., 225 Lafayette St., Suite 212, New York, NY 10012. Phone: (212) 925-0606 or Fax: (212) 925-2052.
Asian American/ Acculturation/ Japanese American/ Social Identity/ Cultural Identity/ Family History/ Socialization/ Women of Color

0112 Rayson, Ann
(1987) "Beneath the Mask: Autobiographies of Japanese-American Women." MELUS 14(Spring):1:pp. 43-57.
Women of Color/ Literary Criticism/ Asian American/ Incarceration/ Japanese American/ Relocation/ Assimilation Patterns/ Acculturation/ Autobiographies

0113 Soe, Valerie

(1987) "New Year." Distributor: Women Make Movies, Inc., 225 Lafayette St., Suite 212, New York, NY 10012. Phone: (212) 925-0606 or Fax: (212) 925-2052.

Chinese American/ Cultural Identity/ Asian American/ Social Bias/ Family History/ Socialization/ Cultural Heritage/ Discriminatory Practices/ Struggles/ Racial Discrimination/ Prejudice/ Women of Color

0114 Takaki, Ronald

(1989) Strangers from a Different Shore: A History of Asian Americans. Boston: Little, Brown and Company. pp. 570.

People of Color/ History/ Asian Americans/ Immigration/ 19th Century/ Ethnicity/ World War II/ 20th Century/ Employment/ Acculturation/ Refugees

0115 Tien, Juliet

(1986) "Attitudes toward Divorce across Three Cultures." Asian American Psychological Association Journal. pp. 55-58.

People of Color/ Racial and Ethnic Differences/ Asian Americans/ Crosscultural Studies/ Attitudes/ Divorce/ Social Psychology

0116 Tom, Pam

(1989) "Two Lies." Distributor: Women Make Movies, Inc., 225 Lafayette St., Suite 212, New York, NY 10012. Phone: (212) 925-0606 or Fax: (212) 925-2052.

Asian American/ Social Identity/ Chinese/ Family Conflict/ Social Conflict/ Ethnic Studies/ Cultural Identity/ Generation Gap/ Self Concept/ Culture Conflict/ Women of Color

0117 Uehara, Jo Sachiko

et al. (1989) "Managing Intercultural Value Systems: An Asian/Pacific Perspective." The Brown Papers #3, The National Institute for Women of Color.

Women of Color/ Acculturation/ Asian American/ Biculturalism/ Women's Movement/ Social Movements/ Value Systems

0118 Van, Tran Thanh

Byars, Lauretta F. (1987) "Sources of Subjective Well-Being among Vietnamese Women in the United States." Free Inquiry in Creative Sociology 15(November):2:pp. 195-198.

Women of Color/ Acculturation/ Asian American/ Education/ Southwest/ Texas/ Social Support/ Oklahoma/ Social Interaction/ Assimilation Patterns/ Vietnamese

0119 Wang, Veronica

(1985) "Reality and Fantasy: The Chinese American Woman's Quest for Identity." MELUS 12(Fall):3:pp. 23-31.

Women of Color/ Ethnicity/ Asian American/ Cultural Heritage/ Chinese Identity/ Literature/ Images of Women/ Autobiographies/ Gender Identity

0120 Wax, Rosalie H.

(1987) "In and Out of the Tule Lake Segregation Center: Japanese Internment in the West, 1942-1945." Montana (The Journal of Western History) 37(Spring):2:pp. 12-25.

People of Color/ Relocation/ Asian Americans/ Social History/ Japanese/ Internment/ Assimilation Patterns

0121 Wong, Jade Snow

(1989) Fifth Chinese Daughter. Seattle: University of Washington Press. pp. 256.

Women of Color/ Family/ Families/ Asian American/ Acculturation/ Chinese/ Culture/ Daughters/ Life Cycles/ Adolescence

0122 Wong, Sau-Ling Cynthia

(1988) "'Necessity and Extravagance' in Maxine Hong Kingston's The Woman Warrior: Art and the Ethnic Experience." MELUS 15(Spring):1:pp. 3-26.
Women of Color/ Literature/ Asians/ Autobiographies/ Chinese/ Literary Criticism/ Ethnicity

0123 Yamazaki, Hiroko

(1989) "Juxta." Distributor: Women Make Movies, Inc., 225 Lafayette St., Suite 212, New York, NY 10012. Phone: (212) 925-0606 or Fax: (212) 925-2052.
Women of Color/ Social Relations/ Asians/ Culture / Japanese/ Family/ Racial Discrimination/ Interracial Families/ Psychological Factors

0124 Yasui, Lise

Tegnell, Ann. (1988) "Family Gathering." Distributor: New Day Films, 853 Broadway, Suite 1210, New York, NY. Phone: (212) 477-4604.
People of Color/ Cultural Heritage/ Asian Americans/ Cultural Identity/ Images of Women/ World War II/ Family Experiences/ Racial Discrimination/ Internment

0125 Zhang, Ya-jie

(1986) "A Chinese Woman's Response to Maxine Hong Kingston's Woman Warrior." MELUS 13(Fall/Winter):3&4:pp. 103-107.
Women of Color/ Cultural Heritage/ Asian American/ Autobiographies/ Literature/ Chinese American

Latina

0126 Acosta-Belen, Edna

et al. (1988) The Hispanic Experience in the United States: Contemporary Issues and Perspectives. New York: Praeger.
Latinos/ Assimilation Patterns/ Education/ Employment/ Immigration/ People of Color/ Immigrants/ Marital Status

0127 Alarcon, Norma

(1980) Bibliography of Hispanic Women Writers. Bloomington, IN: Chicana-Riqueno Studies.
Women of Color/ Cultural Influences/ Chicana/ Latina/ Writers/ Bibliographies/ Research Resources

0128 Alba, Victoria

(1989) "Perspectives on the Future: Four Hispanics Speak Out." Intercambios Femeniles: A Publication of the National Network of Hispanic Women 3(Winter):3:pp. 6-9.
Women of Color/ Acculturation/ Latina/ Low Income Households/ Educational Patterns/ Family Roles/ Occupational Trends/ Human Rights/ Cultural Heritage/ Health Care/ Assimilation Patterns

0129 Allen, Paula Gunn

(1989) "Where I Come from God Is a Grandmother." Sojourner 13(August):12:pp. 16-18.
Native American/ Economy/ Gender Identity/ Stereotypes/ Cultural Influences/ Chicana/ Latina/ Educational Opportunities/ Women of Color/ Femininity

0130 Angel, Ronald

Worobey, Jacqueline Lowe. (1988) "Acculturation and Maternal Reports of Children's Health: Evidence from Hispanic Health and Nutrition Examination

Survey." Social Science Quarterly 69(September):3:pp. 707-721.
Physical Health/ Economic Factors/ Children/ Acculturation/ Latinos/.People of Color/ Diet

0131 **Bean, Frank D.**
Tienda, Marta. (1988) Hispanic Population in the U.S. New York: Russell Sage Foundation.
People of Color/ Minority Groups/ Latinos/ Subculture

0132 **Benmayor, Rina**
(1988) "Crossing Borders: The Politics of Multiple Identity." Centro Boletin (Spring).
Women of Color/ Immigration/ Latina/ Chicana/ Cultural Heritage/ Cultural Identity/ Assimilation Patterns

0133 **Bose, Christine E.**
(1988) "Gender, Poverty and Ethnicity: The Case of Puerto Rican Women." Presented: Structural Conference on Hispanic Cultures of the U.S., Torredemiborra, Spain. Available: Department of Sociology, State University of New York, Albany, NY.
Women of Color/ Latina/ Chicana/ Gender/ Poverty/ Ethnicity/ Race, Class and Gender Studies

0134 **Bose, Christine E.**
(1989) "Ethnicity, Gender and Poverty: Comparative Analysis of Cuban, Mexican and Puerto Rican Women." Presented: American Sociological Association Annual Meeting, San Francisco, CA.
Latina/ Women of Color/ Ethnicity/ Comparative Studies/ Gender/ Racial and Ethnic Differences/ Cuban/ Mexican/ Puerto Rican/ Poverty/ Race, Class and Gender Studies/ Women Living in Poverty

0135 **Burgos, Nilsa M.**
Perez, Yolanda I. Diaz. (1986) "An Exploration of Human Sexuality in the Puerto Rican Culture." Journal of Social Work and Human Sexuality 5:2.
Women of Color/ Culture/ Puerto Rican/ Life Styles/ Latina/ Cultural Influences/ Sexuality

0136 **Camarillo, Albert**
(1984) Chicanos in California. San Francisco: Boyd and Fraser.
People of Color/ California/ Chicanos/ West Pacific/ Latinos/ Cultural Influences

0137 **Carr, Irene Campos**
(1989) "A Survey of Selected Literature on La Chicana." NWSA Journal 1(Winter):2:pp. 253-273.
Women of Color/ Chicana/ Latina/ Literature Review/ Social Sciences/ Cultural Heritage/ Family Values/ Social History/ Research Resources

0138 **Casaus, L.**
Andrade, Sally. (1983) "A Description of Latinos in the United States: Demographic and Sociocultural Factors of the Past and Future." in Latino Families in the United States. Sally Andrade (ed.). New York: Planned Parenthood Federation.
People of Color/ Cultural Influences/ Latinos/ Demography/ History/ Families

0139 **Cuciti, Peggy**
James, Franklin. (1990) "A Comparison of Black and Hispanic Poverty in Large Cities of the Southwest." Hispanic Journal of Behavioral Sciences

12(February):1:pp. 50-75.
African Americans/ Latinos/ People owest/ Crosscultural Studies

0140 Espin, Oliva L.
(1986) "Cultural and Hispanic Influence on Sexuality in Hispanic/ Latin Women." in All American Women: Lines that Divide, Ties that Bind. Johnnetta B. Cole (ed.). New York: The Free Press.
Women of Color/ Immigration/ Latina/ Oppression/ Sexuality/ Machismo/ Cultural Influences/ Lesbians/ Homosexuality/ Race, Class and Gender Studies/ Language

0141 Film & Video Library
(1985) "Yo Soy." Distributor: Film & Video Library, University Library, University of Michigan, 400 Fourth St., Ann Arbor, MI 48103-4816. Phone: (313) 764-5360 or 1-800-999-0424.
People of Color/ Socialization/ Latinos/ Culture/ Ethnicity/ Ethnic Studies

0142 Forbes, Jack D.
(1983) "Hispano-Mexican Pioneers of the San Francisco Bay Region: An Analysis of Racial Origins." Aztlan 14(Spring):pp. 175-189.
People of Color/ Racial and Ethnic Differences/ Latinos/ Mexican/ California/ West/ Pacific/ Pioneers/ Race

0143 Garcia, Mario T.
(1989) Mexican Americans. New Haven, CT: Yale University Press. pp. 384.
People of Color/ Southwest/ Chicanos/ Latinos/ Ideology/ Social History/ Leadership/ Identity/ Culture

0144 Hazuda, Helen P.
Stern, Michael P. et al. (1988) "Acculturation and Assimilation among Mexican Americans: Scales and Population Based Data." Social Science Quarterly 69(September):3:pp. 687-707.
Acculturation/ Social Movements/ Assimilation Patterns/ Chicanos/ Latinos/ Gender Differences/ Cultural Identity/ People of Color/ Social Adjustment

0145 Herrera-Sobek, Maria
Viramontes, Helena Maria. (1988) Chicana Creativity and Criticism: Charting New Frontiers in American Literature. Houston, TX: Arte Publico Press. pp. 190.
Latina/ Chicana/ Women's Culture/ Literary Criticism/ Literature/ Poetry/ Images of Women/ Women of Color

0146 Kaigler-Walker, Karen
Ericksen, Mary K. (1989) "General Values as Related to Clothing Values of Mexican-American Women." Hispanic Journal of Behavioral Sciences 11(May):2:pp. 156-167.
Women of Color/ Clothing/ Chicana/ Latina/ Values/ Crosscultural Studies/ Cultural Influences

0147 Katsinas, Stephan G.
(1989) "Educational Arrears: Addressing the Underenrollment of Hispanics in Illinois Higher Education." The Urban Review 21(March):1:pp. 35-50.
People of Color/ Public Schools/ High Schools/ Latinos/ Chicanos/ Dropouts/ Labor Force Participation/ Higher Education/ Colleges/ Assimilation Patterns/ Demography/ Enrollment/ Educational Attainment/ Educational Policy/ Manufacturing Industry/ Educational Equity

0148 Keefe, Susan E.
(1979) "Urbanization, Acculturation, and Extended Family Ties: Mexican Americans in Cities." American Ethnologist 6:2:pp. 349-365.
Women of Color/ Family/ Chicana/ Latina/ Urban Areas/ Urbanization/ Support Systems/ Acculturation/ Extended Family

0149 Keefe, Susan E.
(1980) "Acculturation and the Extended Family among Urban Mexican Americans." in Acculturation: Theory, Models and Some New Findings. Amado M. Padilla (ed.). Boulder, CO: Westview Press. pp. 85-110.
Women of Color/ Urban Areas/ Chicana/ Latina/ Acculturation/ Extended Family

0150 Keefe, Susan E.
Padilla, Amado M. (1987) Chicano Ethnicity. Albuquerque, N M: University of New Mexico Press. pp. 248.
Chicano Studies/ People of Color/ Cultural Identity/ Chicanos/ Latinos/ Ethnic Studies/ Assimilation Patterns

0151 Lane, James B.
Escobar, Edward J. (ed.). (1987) Forging a Community: The Latino Experience in Northwest Indiana, 1919-1975. Bloomington, IN: Indiana University Press.
Latinos/ Ethnic Neighborhoods/ North Central/ Indiana/ Culture/ Community Relations/ Support Systems/ Communities/ Subculture/ Social Relations/ Social Structure/ People of Color

0152 Lopez, Adalberto
(1980) The Puerto Ricans: Their History, Culture & Society. Rochester, VT: Schenkman Books, Inc.
People of Color/ Social History/ Latinos/ Puerto Ricans/ Culture/ Society

0153 Lucero, Helen R.
(1986) Hispanic Weavers of North Central New Mexico: Social Historical and Educational Dimensions of a Continuing Artistic Tradition. Albuquerque, NM: University of New Mexico.
Weavers/ Latinos/ Craft Arts/ Traditions/ Artistic Tradition/ Cultural Heritage/ Social Characteristics/ Educational Activities/ People of Color

0154 Mirowsky, John
Ross, Catherine E. (1987) "Support and Control in Mexican and Anglo Cultures." in Health and Behavior: Research Agenda for Hispanics. M. Gaviria and J. D. Arana (eds.). Chicago: Hispanic American Family Center, University of Illinois, Dept. of Psychology.
Women of Color/ Health/ Latina/ Networks/ European American/ Comparative Studies/ Cultural Factors/ Support Systems

0155 Morales, Sylvia
(1979) "Chicana." Distributor: University of California at Los Angeles Instructional Media Laboratory, 46 Powell Library, Los Angeles, CA 90024. Phone: (213) 825-0755.
Chicana/ Latina/ Images of Women/ Traditions/ Social Movements/ Culture/ Exploitation/ Family/ Equality/ Roles/ Socialization

0156 Murguia, Edward
(1982) Chicano Intermarriage. San Antonio, TX: Trinity University Press.
Women of Color/ Cultural Heritage/ Chicana/ Latina/ Ethnic Studies/ Relationships/ Marriage/ Interethnic Families/ Female Male Relationships/ Southwest/ Arizona

0157 Ortiz, Vilma

(1989) "Language Background and Literacy among Hispanic Young Adults." Social Problems 36(April):2:pp. 149-164.

People of Color/ Cultural Influences/ Latinos/ Chicanos/ Literacy/ Education/ Bilingualism/ Cultural Heritage/ Language

0158 Portillo, Lourdes

(1979) "After the Earthquake." Distributor: Women Make Movies, Inc. 225 Lafayette St., Suite 212, New York, NY 10012. Phone: (212) 925-0606 or Fax: (212) 925-2052.

Latina/ Nicaraguan/ Culture/ Immigrants/ Economics/ Identity/ Politics/ Struggles/ Acculturation/ Socialization/ Women of Color/ Natural Disasters

0159 Preciado Martin, Patricia

Louis, Bernal. (1983) Images and Conversations: Mexican-Americans Recall a Southwestern Past. Tuscon, AZ: University of Arizona Press.

Cultural Heritage/ People of Color/ Latinos/ Chicanos/ History/ Southwest

0160 Pulido, Alberto L.

(1989) "Race Relations within the American Catholic Church: An Historical and Sociological Analysis of Mexican American Catholics." Dissertation: University of Notre Dame (Order No. DA8915877).

People of Color/ Race Relations/ Chicanos/ Latinos/ Religion/ Catholicism/ History/ Cultural Identity

0161 Rich, B. Ruby

Lourdes, Arguelles. (1985) "Homosexuality, Homophobia, and Revolution: Notes toward an Understanding of the Cuban Lesbian and Gay Male Experience." SIGNS: Journal of Women in Culture and Society 11(Autumn):1.

Women of Color/ Lesbians/ Latina/ Cuban/ Women's Culture/ Homophobia/ Homosexuality

0162 Rios-Bustamante, Antonio

(1989) Mexican Los Angeles: A Narrative and Pictoral History. Encino, CA: Floricanto Press. pp. 250. ISBN 0915745194.

Mexicans/ Organizational Development/ Chicanos/ Latinos/ Social History/ California/ West/ Culture/ Social Organization/ Political Theory/ Structuralism/ People of Color/ History

0163 Robles, Jennifer Juarez

(1988) "Hispanics Emerging as Nation's Poorest Minority." Chicago Reporter 17(June):6:pp. 1-3.

People of Color/ Economically Disadvantaged/ Latinos/ Cultural Identity/ Poverty/ Minority Experience/ Ethnic Groups/ Disadvantaged

0164 Rochin, Refugio

de la Torre, Adela. (1988) "Strengthening Chicano Studies Programs." La Red/The Net 1:1:pp. 11-30.

Women of Color/ Ethnic Studies/ Latina/ Curriculum Integration/ Education

0165 Rodriguez, Clara E.

(1986) "Profile of Hispanic Women." Presented: Symposium on the Effects of the Feminization of Poverty on the Hispanic Community, Albany, NY.

Women of Color/ Women Living in Poverty/ Chicana/ Latina/ Quality of Life/ Puerto Rican/ Living Conditions/ Ethnicity

0166 Rodriguez, Clara E.
(1986) "Race, Class and Gender: Puerto Ricans in New York." Presented: American Sociological Association Annual Meeting, San Francisco, CA.
Women of Color/ Employment/ Puerto Rican/ Latina/ Wages/ Socioeconomic Status/ Race Stratification/ New York/ Northeast/ Self Concept/ Social Stratification/ Cultural Identity/ Identity/ Race, Class and Gender Studies

0167 Rodriguez, Clara E.
(1989) Puerto Ricans: Born in the USA. Winchester, MA: Unwin Hyman. pp. 256.
People of Color/ Identity/ Puerto Ricans/ Cultural Heritage/ Latinos/ Social Adjustment/ Cultural Identity/ Culture Conflict

0168 Romero, Mary
(1988) "Chicano Discourse about Language Use." Language Problems Language Planning 12:2:pp. 110-129.
People of Color/ Language Skills/ Chicanos/ Latinos/ Language/ Communication/ Culture/ Discourse

0169 Rueschenberg, Erich
Buriel, Raymond. (1989) "Mexican American Family Functioning and Acculturation: A Family Systems Perspective." Hispanic Journal of Behavioral Sciences 11(August):3:pp. 232-244.
People of Color/ Acculturation/ Roles/ Family Life/ Families/ Achievement/ Mothers/ Fathers/ Assimilation Patterns/ Latina/ Chicana

0170 Sanchez, George
(1986) Go after the Woman: Americanization and the Mexican Immigrant Woman. Stanford, CA: Stanford University Press.
Chicana/ Latina/ Socialization/ Women of Color/ Social Policy/ Immigrants/ Cultural Heritage/ Ethnic Studies/ Assimilation Patterns/ Ethnic Groups/ Acculturation/ Southwest

0171 Schlissel, Lillian
Ruiz, Vicki L. and Janice Monk. (1988) Western Women: Their Land, Their Lives. Albuquerque, NM: University of New Mexico Press.
Women of Color/ Women's Culture/ Latina/ West/ Land Use/ Life Styles/ Women's History

0172 Sutton, Constance R.
Chaney, Elsa M. (1987) Caribbean Life in New York City: Sociocultural Dimensions. Center for Migration Studies. New York, NY. pp. 250.
People of Color/ Cultural Heritage/ Caribbean/ Cultural Influences/ Latinos/ New York/ Northeast

0173 Van Harten, Laura L.
(1989) "Mexican-American Migrant Farmworkers' Attitudes toward Breastfeeding." Presented: Southern Anthropological Society Annual Meeting, Memphis, TN.
Chicana/ Latina/ Ethnicity/ Women of Color/ Lower Class/ Farmworkers/ Migrant Workers/ Employment/ Education/ Breastfeeding/ Social Network/ Attitudes/ Maternal and Infant Welfare

0174 Veyna, Angelina F.
(1990) "Women in Early New Mexico: A Preliminary View." in Chicana Voices: Intersections of Class, Race, and Gender. Teresa Cordova et al (eds.) Houston, TX: National Association for Chicano Studies. (available: Felipe Gonzales, Sociology, 1000 Social Science Bldg., U. of NM, Albuquerque, NM 87131.)
Women of Color/ Race, Class and Gender Studies/ Latina/ New Mexico / Southwest/ Women's History/ Women's Culture

0175 Wartenberg, Hannah R.
(1988) "Multiple Identities of Cuban Jewish Women in Miami." Presented: American Sociological Association Annual Meeting, San Francisco, CA.
Women of Color/ Gender Roles/ Latina/ Cuban/ Ethnic Studies/ Jewish/ South/ Florida/ Cultural Identity/ Family Values

0176 Zentella, Ana C.
(1987) "Language and Female Identity in the Puerto Rican Community." in Women and Language in Transition. J. Penfield. Albany, NY: State University of New York Press.
Women of Color/ Women's Culture/ Socialization/ Language/ Puerto Rican/ Identity/ Sex Roles/ Gender Roles

Native American

0177 Ackerman, Lillian A.
(1988) "Sexual Equality on the Colville Indian Reservation in Traditional and Contemporary Contexts." in Women in Pacific Northwest History: An Anthology. Karen J. Blair (ed.). Seattle: University of Washington Press. pp. 152-169.
Women of Color/ Sexual Division of Labor/ Native American/ Sex Discrimination/ Pacific/ Northwest/ Social Change/ Sexual Equality/ Female Male Relationships/ Gender Roles/ Sexual Stratification/ Cultural Heritage

0178 Allen, Paula Gunn
(1981) "Beloved Women: Lesbians in American Indian Cultures." Conditions 7:pp. 67-87.
Women of Color/ Culture/ Native American/ Lesbian Studies/ Lesbians/ Lesbian Relationships/ Bias/ Cultural Influences

0179 Allen, Paula Gunn
(1989) "Where I Come from God Is a Grandmother." Sojourner 13(August):12:pp. 16-18.
Native American/ Economy/ Gender Identity/ Stereotypes/ Cultural Influences/ Chicana/ Latina/ Educational Opportunities/ Women of Color/ Femininity

0180 Allen, Paula Gunn
(1989) Spider Woman's Granddaughters: Traditional Tales and Contemporary Writing by Native American Women. Boston: Beacon Press. pp. 242.
Women of Color/ Cultural Influences/ Native American/ Social Change/ Folk Literature/ Cultural Heritage/ Writers/ Writing/ Literature

0181 Anderson, K.
(1988) "As Gentle as Little Lambs: Images of Huron and Montagnais-Naskapi Women in The Writings of the 17th Century Jesuits." The Canadian Review of Sociology and Anthropology 25(Nov.):pp. 560-576.
Women of Color/ Religious Literature/ Jesuits/ Native American/ Images of Women/ Montagnais/ Naskapi/ Stereotypes / Huron/ 17th Century

0182 Anderson, Owanah P.
(1985) Resource Guide of American Indian and Alaska Native Women. Newton, MA: Women's Educational Equity Act Publishing Center. pp. 250.
Women of Color/ Minority Experience/ Native American/ Guilds/ Research Resources/ Ethnic Women/ Bibliographies/ Pacific/ Alaska

0183 Armitage, Susan H.
(1982) "Everyday Encounters: Indians and White Women in the Palouse." Pacific Northwest Forum 7(Summer/Fall):3-4:pp. 27-30.
Women of Color/ Northwest/ Native American/ Perceptions/ European American/ Attitudes/ Intercultural Relations

0184 Bates, Ann M.
(1987) Affiliation and Differentiation: Intertribal Interactions among the Makah and Ditdaht Indians. Bloomington, IN: Indiana University Press.
People of Color/ Tribal Customs/ Native Americans/ Ethnic Relations/ Makahs/ Ditdahts/ Cultural Heritage/Community

0185 Berryhill, Peggy
(1988) "Weaving Their Dreams: Navajo Women Unite Tradition and Economy." Isis: Women in Action 3:pp. 7-9.
Women of Color/ Tribal Customs/ Native American/ Employment/ Southwest/ Economy/ Navajo/ Tradition/ Craft Arts/ Economic Value of Women's Work/ Culture/ Cultural Heritage

0186 Blackman, Margaret B.
(1982) During My Time: Florence Edenshaw Davidson, a Hadia Woman. Seattle: University of Washington Press. pp. 192.
Women of Color/ Power/ Native American/ Culture/ Northwest/ Childhood

0187 Bowman, Arlene
(1986) "Navajo Talking Picture." Distributor: James W. Mulryan Productions, 1725 The Promenade, Suite 607, Santa Monica, CA 90401. Phone: (213) 394-6883.
Women of Color/ Roles/ Native American/ Social Relations/ Film Producers/ Alienation/ Family/ Families/ Culture

0188 Brant, Beth
(1990) "Grandmothers of a New World." Woman of Power 16(Spring):pp. 40-47.
Women of Color/ Culture Conflict/ Native American/ Virginia/ Images of Women/ Georgia/ Women's History/ Cherokee/ Biographies/ Pocahontas

0189 Buckley, T.
(1982) "Menstruation and the Power of Yurok Women: Methods in Cultural Reconstruction." American Ethnologist 9(February):pp. 47-60.
Native American/ Yurok/ Cultural Heritage/ Menstruation/ Mentrual Cycle/ Change/ Physical Health/ Women of Color/ Power

0190 Carter, Max L.
(1989) "Quaker Relations with Midwestern Indians to 1833." Dissertation: Temple University, Philadelphia, PA. (Order No. DA8920223).
People of Color/ History/ Native Americans/ Religion/ Race Relations/ Midwest/ Quaker/ European Americans/ Cultural Influences

0191 Carver, Kathryn A.
(1986) "The 1985 Minnesota Indian Family Preservation Act: Claiming a Cultural Identity." Law and Inequality 4(July):2.
Native Americans/ Families/ Family/ People of Color/ Cultural Identity/ Adoption/ Racial Discrimination/ Foster Children/ Inequality/ Child Welfare/ Interracial Adoption

0192 Chance, Nancy E.
(1988) "Gender and Culture: North Slope Inupiat Women in Historical Perspective." Dissertation: University of Connecticut. (Order No. DA8913798).
Women of Color/ Sex Roles/ Native American/ Tribal Customs/ Inupiat/ Division of Labor/ Eskimo/ Sexual Stratification/ Alaska / Culture/ Gender Roles/ History

0193 Chatterji, Shoma A.
(1988) The Indian Women's Search for an Identity. New York: Vikas Publishing House. pp. 261.
Native American/ Culture/ Social Identity/ Individual Development/ Self Concept/ Socialization/ Identity Crisis/ Women of Color

0194 Clifton, James A.
(1989) Being and Becoming Indian: Biographical Studies of North American Frontiers. Chicago: Dorsey. pp. 337.
People of Color/ Life Styles/ Native Americans/ Culture/ Socialization/ History/ Biographies/ Tribal Customs

0195 Danielson, Linda L.
(1988) "Storyteller: Grandmother Spider's Web." Journal of the Southwest 30(August):pp. 324-355.
Women of Color/ Folk Literature/ Native American/ Oral Tradition/ Southwest/ New Mexico/ Storytelling/ Pueblo/ Autobiographies/ Literature/ Literary Criticism/ Women's Culture

0196 Danziger, Edmund Jefferson, Jr.
(1990) The Chippewas of Lake Superior. Norman, OK: University of Oklahoma Press. pp. 263.
People of Color/ Tribal Customs/ Native Americans/ Culture/ Chippewas/ Life Styles/ History

0197 DeMallie, Raymond J.
(1983) "Male and Female in Traditional Lakota Culture." in The Hidden Half: Studies of Plains Indian Women. Patricia Albers and Beatrice Medicine. (eds.). Lanham, MD: University Press of America. pp. 238-266.
Women of Color/ Sexual Division of Labor/ Native American/ Sexual Equality/ Sioux/ Sex Discrimination/ History/ Perceptions/ Stereotypes/ Anthropology/ Images of Women/ Gender Roles/ Tradition/ Culture

0198 Deloria, Ella Cara
(1988) Waterlily. Lincoln, NE: University of Nebraska Press.
Women of Color/ Life Styles/ Native American/ Culture/ Sioux/ Cultural Heritage

0199 Emmerich, Lisa E.
(1987) "'To Respect and Love and Seek the Ways of the White Women': Field Matrons, the Office of Indian Affairs and Civilization Policy, 1890-1938." Dissertation: University of Maryland, College Park, MD. DAI Vol. 48, 1988.
Women of Color/ Culture Conflict/ Native American/ Assimilation Patterns/ European American/ Public Policy/ Social Policy/ Social Control/ Women's History/ 20th Century

0200 Evasdaughter, Elizabeth
(1988) "Leslie Marmon Silko's Ceremony: Healing Ethnic Hatred by Mixed-Breed Laughter." MELUS 15(Spring):1:pp. 83-95.
Women of Color/ Interracial Marriage/ Native American/ Racial and Ethnic Differences/ Literature/ Culture Conflict/ Literary Criticism/ Humor/ Southwest

0201 Ferrero, Pat
(1988) "Hopi: Songs of the Fourth World." Distributor: New Day Films, 853 Broadway, Suite 1210, New York, NY 10003. Phone: (212) 477-4604.
Native Americans/ Images of Women/ People of Color/ Religion/ Cultural Heritage/ Economy

0202 Film & Video Library
(1978) "More Than Bows and Arrows." Distributor: Film & Video Library, University Library, University of Michigan, 400 Fourth St., Ann Arbor, MI 48103-4816. Phone: (313) 764-5360 or 1-800-999-0424.
People of Color/ Life Styles/ Native Americans/ Social Roles/ Eskimos/ Aleuts/ Culture/ Technology/ Socialization

0203 Forbes, Jack D.
(1984) "Mulattoes and People of Color in Anglo-North America: Implications for Black-Indian Relations." The Journal of Ethnic Studies 12(Summer):pp. 17-61.
People of Color/ Social Relations/ African Americans/ Interracial Relations/ Native Americans/ Ethnic Studies/ Mulattoes

0204 Forbes, Jack D.
(1988) Black Africans and Native Americans: Color, Race and Caste in the Evolution of Red-Black Peoples. New York: Blackwell. pp. 345.
Women of Color/ Racial Stratification/ History/ 16th Century/ Native American/ Culture Conflict/ African American/ Colonization/ Interracial Relations/ Imperialism/ Race Relations

0205 Grumet, Robert
(1980) "Sunksquaws, Shamans, and Tradeswomen: Middle Atlantic Coastal Algonkian Women during the 17th and 18th Centuries." in Women and Colonization: Anthropological Perspectives. Mona Etienne and Eleanor Leacock (eds.). New York: Praeger. pp. 43-62.
Women of Color/ Folk Healers/ Native American/ Culture Conflict/ Economic Status/ Leadership/ Employment/ Division of Labor/ History/ 17th Century/ Colonization/ 18th Century/ Northeast

0206 Hurtado, Albert L..
(1988) Indian Survival on the California Frontier. New Haven, CT: Yale University Press.
People of Color/ Survival Strategies/ Native Americans/ Culture Conflict/ West Pacific/ California/ History/ 19th Century/ Sexual Exploitation/ Households/ Interracial Relations

0207 Joe, Jennie R.
(1986) "Forced Relocation and Assimilation: Dillon Myer and the Native American." Amerasia Journal 13:2:pp. 161-165.
Women of Color/ Biographies/ Native American/ Relocation/ Writers/ Migration/ Acculturation/ Assimilation Patterns

0208 Kehoe, Alice
(1983) "The Shackles of Tradition." in The Hidden Half: Studies of Plains Indian Women. P. Albers and B. Medicine (eds.). Lanham, MD: University Press of America. pp. 53-76.
Women of Color/ Perceptions/ Native American/ Stereotypes/ Plains/ Anthropology/ Images of Women/ Cultural Heritage

0209 Klein, Laura F.
(1980) "Contending with Colonization: Tlingit Men and Women in Change." in Women and Colonization: Anthropological Perspectives. Mona Etienne and Eleanor Leacock (eds.). New York: Praeger. pp. 88-108.
Women of Color/ Acculturation/ Native American/ Colonization/ Alaska/ Missionaries/ Employment/ Gender Roles/ Division of Labor/ Culture Conflict

0210 Liberty, Margot
(1979) "Plains Indian Women through Time: A Preliminary Overview." in Intermontane and Plains Montana Indians: Lifeways in Honor of J. Verne Dusenberry. Leslie B. Davis (ed.). Bozeman, MT: Montana State University. pp. 137-150.
Women of Color/ Gender Roles/ Native American/ Culture/ Plains/ Montana/ History/ Women's History/ Tribal Customs

0211 Lurie, Nancy Oestreich
(1989) Mountain Wolf Women, Sister of Crashing Thunder: An Autobiography of a Winnebago Indian. Ann Arbor, MI: University of Michigan Press.
Women of Color/ History/ Native American/ Cultural Heritage/ Autobiographies/ Winnebago

0212 Maristuen-Rodakowski, Julie
(1988) "The Turtle Mountain Reservation in North Dakota: Its History as Depicted in Louise Erdrich's 'Love Medicine and Beet Queen'." American Indian Culture and Research Journal 12:3:pp. 33-48.
People of Color/ North Dakota/ Northwest/ Cultural Heritage/ Catholicism/ Social Change/ Literature/ Religion/ History/ Interracial Marriage/ Native Americans

0213 Mavor, James W., Jr.
Dix, Byron E. (1989) Manitou: The Sacred Landscape of New England's Native Civilization. Rochester, VT: Inner Traditions International. pp. 390.
People of Color/ History/ Native Americans/ Manitous/ Northeast/ Religious Beliefs/ Religious Traditions/ Culture

0214 Merrell, James H.
(1989) The Indians' New World: Catawbas and Their Neighbors from European Contact through the Era of Removal. Chapel Hill, NC: University of North Carolina Press.
People of Color/ History/ 18th Century/ Native Americans/ Social Change/ African Americans/ Migration/ European Americans/ Acculturation/ Interracial Relations/ Southeast/ Pioneers/ Culture Conflict

0215 Milloy, John S.
(1988) The Plains Cree: Trade, Diplomacy and War, 1790-1870. Winnipeg: University of Mannitoba Press. pp. 159.
People of Color/ Race Relations/ Native Americans/ History/ 19th Century/ Crees/ Migration/ Trades/ Cultural Influences/ Diplomacy/ Culture Conflict/ War/ Military/ Relocation

0216 Monroe, Suzanne S.
(1988) "Images of Native American Female Protagonists in Children's Literature, 1928-1988." Dissertation: University of Arizona. (Order No. DA8906391).
Women of Color/ Images of Women/ Native American/ Children/ Literature/ 20th Century/ Women's Culture

0217 Mourning Dove
Guie, Hester Dean (eds.). (1990) Coyote Stories. Lincoln, NE: University of Nebraska Press.
Women of Color/ Folk Literature/ Okanogan/ Native American/ Personal Narratives/ Storytelling/ Stories/ Folk Culture/ Life Styles

0218 Namias, June
(1989) "White Captives: Gender and Ethnicity on Successive American Frontiers,

1607-1862." Dissertation: Brandeis University.
Women of Color/ 17th Century/ Native American/ 18th Century/ European American/ 19th Century/ Gender Roles/ Interracial Relations/ Ethnicity/ Culture Conflict/ Survival Strategies/ Women's History

0219 Penn State Audio-Visual
(1980) "Mohawk Basketmaking: A Cultural Profile." Distributor: Penn State Audio-Visual Services, Special Services Building, University Park, PA 16802. Phone: (814) 865-6314 or 1-800-826-0132.
Native American/ Mohawk/ Mary Adams/ Tribal Art/ Cultural Art/ Artists/ History/ Women of Color/ Survival Strategies/ Basketry/ Craft Art

0220 Perdue, Theda
(1979) Slavery and the Evolution of Cherokee Society, 1540-1866. Knoxville, TN: University of Tennessee Press.
People of Color/ Assimilation Patterns/ Native Americans/ Cherokees/ Acculturation/ African Americans/ Social Change/ Interracial Relations/ History/ Culture Conflict/ Slavery/ South East/ Gender Roles

0221 Perdue, Theda
(1989) "Cherokee Women and the Trail of Tears." Journal of Women's History 1(Spring):1:pp. 14-30.
Women of Color/ Beliefs/ Native American/ Relocation/ Cherokee/ Cultural Heritage/ South East/ Social History/ Racial Discrimination/ Customs

0222 Pool, Carolyn Garrett
(1988) "Reservation Policy and the Economic Position of Wichita Women." Great Plains Quarterly 8(Summer):pp. 158-171.
Women of Color/ Social Change/ Native American/ Economic Status/ Plains/ Assimilation Patterns/ Sex Roles/ Women's History/ Division of Labor/ Public Policy

0223 Riley, Glenda
(1984) "Frontiers Women's Changing Views of Indians in the Trans-Mississippi West." Montana (The Journal of Western History) 34(Winter):1:pp. 20-35.
People of Color/ Pioneers/ Native Americans/ Images/ Cultural Influences/ European American/ Perceptions/ Attitudes/ Interracial Relations

0224 Roscoe, Will
(1987) "Living the Tradition: Gay American Indians." in Gay Spirit. Mark Thompson (ed.). New York: St. Martin's Press. pp. 69-77.
People of Color/ Tradition/ Native Americans/ Cultural Influences/ Minority Experience/ Life Styles/ Homosexuality

0225 Roscoe, Will
(1987) "Bibliography of Berdache and Alternative Gender Roles among North American Indians." Journal of Homosexuality 14:3-4: pp. 81-171.
People of Color/ Homosexuality/ Native Americans/ Sexuality/ Bibliographies/ Sex Roles/ Lesbians/ Role Reversal/ Cross Sex Identity/ Women of Color/ Culture

0226 Roscoe, Will
(1990) "'That Is My Road': The Life and Times of a Crow Berdache." Montana (The Journal of Western History) 40(Winter):1:pp. 46-55.
People of Color/ Homosexuality/ Native Americans/ Role Reversal/ Cross-Sex Identity/ History/ Culture/ 19th Century/ Biographies/ Sex Roles / Sexuality

0227 Rothenberg, Diane
(1980) "The Mothers of the Nation: Seneca Resistance to Quaker Intervention." in Women and Colonization: Anthropological Perpectives. Mona Etienne and Eleanor Leacock. New York: Praeger. pp. 63-87.
Culture Conflict/ Native American/ Colonization/ History/ Agriculture/ Missionaries/ Division of Labor/ Resistance/ Matrilineal Kinship/ Iroquois/ Women of Color

0228 Rountree, Helen C.
(1989) The Powhatan Indians of Virginia: Their Traditional Culture. Norman, OK: University of Oklahoma Press. pp. 221.
People of Color/ Interracial Relations/ Native Americans/ Tribal Customs/ South East/ Virginia/ Social History/ History/ 17th Century/ Life Styles/ Ethnography/ Traditions/ Culture/ Gender Roles/ Powhatans

0229 Sharp, Saundra
(1988) "Picking Tribes." Distributor: Women Make Movies, Inc., 225 Lafayette St.,Suite 212, New York, NY 10012. Phone: (212) 925-0606 or Fax: (212) 925-2052.
African American/ Cultural Identity/ Native American/ Family Conflict/ Identity Crisis/ Interethnic Families/ Self Concept/ Women of Color/ Exogamy

0230 Shenandoah Film Productions
(1983) "The Indian Women of the Early Dawn." Distributor: Indian Owned Enterprise, 538 G Street, Arcata, CA 95521. Phone: (707) 822-1030.
Native American/ Female Male Relationships/ Personality Traits/ Personal Relationships/ Cultural Identity/ Women of Color/ Ecofeminism

0231 St. Peter, Christine
(1989) "Woman's Truth and the Native Tradition: Anne Cameron's Daughters of Copper Woman." Feminist Studies 15(Fall):3: pp. 499-523.
Women of Color/ Anne Cameron/ Native American/ Stories/ Mythology/ Pacific/ Northwest/ Anthropology/ Culture/ Women's Roles/ Politics

0232 Swann, Brian
Krupat, Arnold (eds.). (1989) I Tell You Now: Autobiographical Essays by Native American Writers. Lincoln, NE: University of Nebraska Press. pp. 283.
People of Color/ Personal Narratives/ Native Americans/ Authors/ Literature/ Writers/ Autobiographies/ Assimilation Patterns

0233 Swentzell, Rina
(1987) "The Process of Culture - The Indian Perspective." El Palacio 93(Summer/Fall).
Women of Color/ Culture/ Native American/ Cultural Heritage

0234 Tate, Michael L.
(1986) The Indians of Texas: An Annotated Research Bibliography. Metuchen, NJ: Scarecrow Press. pp. 538.
Annotations/ Southwest/ Research Resources/ Oklahoma/ Texas/ Bibliographies/ Native Americans/ Cultural Heritage/ People of Color

0235 Tooker, Elizabeth
(1984) "Women in Iroquois Society." in Extending the Rafters: Interdisciplinary Approaches to Iroquois Studies. M. K. Foster et al. (eds). Albany, NY: State University of New York Press. pp. 109-123.
Women of Color/ Matrilineal Kinship/ Native American/ Culture/ Gender Roles/ Sexual Equality/ Economic Status/ Iroquois

0236 Tsosie, Rebecca

(1988) "Changing Women: The Cross-Currents of American Indian Feminine Identity." American Indian Culture and Research Journal 12:pp. 1-37.
Women of Color/ Feminism/ Native American/ Identity/ Cultural Heritage/ Self Concept

0237 Weist, Katherine

(1983) "Beasts of Burden and Menial Slaves: Nineteenth Century Observations of Northern Plains Indian Women." in The Hidden Half: Studies of Plains Indian Women. P. Albers and B. Medicine (ed.). Lanham, MD: University Press of America. pp. 29-52.
Women of Color/ Images of Women/ Native American/ Gender Roles/ Plains/ Culture Conflict/ Stereotypes/ Perceptions/ 19th Century/ Attitudes/ History/ Oppression

0238 Wong, Hertha D.

(1987) "Pre-Literature Native American Autobiography: Forms of Personal Narrative." MELUS 14(Spring):1:pp. 17-32.
People of Color/ Literary Criticism/ Native Americans/ Personal Narratives/ Sex Roles/ Oral History/ Autobiographies/ Cultural Heritage/ Craft Arts

0239 Young, Mary E.

(1980) "Women, Civilization, and the Indian Question." in Clio was a Woman: Studies in the History of American Women. M. E. Deutrich and V. C. Purdy (eds.). Washington, DC: Howard University Press. pp. 98-110.
Women of Color/ Culture Conflict/ Native American/ Acculturation/ Cherokee/ Assimilation Patterns/ Social Change

0240 Zitkala-Sa

Picotte, Agnes M. (1985) Old Indian Legends. Lincoln, NE: University of Nebraska Press.
People of Color/ Native American/ Culture/ Life Styles/ Legends/ Stories/ Storytelling/ Folk Literature/ Folk Culture

0241 Zitkala-Sa

Fisher, Dexter. (1985) American Indian Stories. Lincoln, NE: University of Nebraska Press.
Women of Color/ Native American/ Personal Narratives/ Life Styles/ Folk Culture/ Stories/ Storytelling/ Folk Literature

Southern

0242 Allured, Janet

(1988) The Women of Arkansas." in Behold, Our Works Were Good: A Handbook of Arkansas Women's History. Elizabeth Jacoway (ed.). Little Rock: Arkansas Women's History Institute in association with August House.
South/ Arkansas/ Status/ 19th Century/ 20th Century/ Social Movements/ Female Male Relationships/ Writers/ Women's History/ Women's Organizations/ Education/ Economy/ Family/ Leadership/ History/ Women's Culture

0243 Bartley, Numan V.

(1988) The Evolution of Southern Culture. Athens, GA: University of Georgia Press. pp. 168.
South/ Slavery/ Slaves/ People of Color/ Religion/ Antebellum/ African Americans/ History/ Agricultural Economics/ Civil War/ Cultural Heritage/ Segregation

0244 Bullard, Robert D.
(1989) In Search of the New South: The Urban Black in the 1970's and 1980's. Tuscaloosa, AL: University of Alabama Press. pp. 232.
People of Color/ Social Change/ African Americans/ Migration/ South/ Culture/ History/ Urban Areas

0245 Burrison, John A.
(ed.). (1989) Storytellers: Folktales and Legends from the South. Athens, GA: University of Georgia Press. pp. 320.
Women of Color/ Rural Areas/ African American/ Folk Literature/ Native American/ Folk Culture/ South/ Oral Tradition/ Oral History

0246 Cantrell, Andrea E.
(1989) Manuscript Resources for Women's Studies. Fayetteville, AR: Special Collection of University of Arkansas Libraries. pp. 37.
South/ Arkansas/ Home Life/ Education/ Women's Culture/ Women's History/ Research Resources/ Women's Groups/ Collections

0247 Carawan, Guy
Carawan, Candie. (1989) Ain't You Got a Right to the Tree of Life?: The People of Johns Island, South Carolina - Their Faces, Their Words, and Their Songs. Athens, GA: University of Georgia Press. pp. 256.
People of Color/ Culture/ African Americans/ History/ South Carolina/ Life Styles/ Music/ Songs

0248 Cody, Cheryll Ann
(1987) "There Was No 'Absalom' on the Ball Plantations: Slave Naming Practices in the South Carolina Low Country, 1720-1865." The American Historical Review 92(June):3:pp. 563-596.
People of Color/ Name Rights/ African Americans/ Slavery/ South/ South Carolina/ History/ 18th Century/ Slave Names/ Cultural Influences/ Plantations

0249 Crake, Mary Claire
(1989) " 'In Unity There is Strength': Women's Clubs in Tampa During the 1930's." Tampa Bay History 11(Fall/Winter):pp. 5-21.
South/ Florida/ Club Women/ Women's History/ Women's Organizations/ Women's Groups/ 1930-1939/ Women's Culture

0250 Cummings, Melbourne S.
(1988) "The Changing Image of the Black Family on Television." Journal of Popular Culture 22(Fall):pp. 75-87.
People of Color/ Communications/ African Americans/ Mass Media/ Image/ Stereotypes/ Popular Culture/ Social Attitudes/ Family

0251 Dillman, Caroline Matheny
(1988) "The Sparsity of Research and Publications on Southern Women." in Southern Women. Caroline Matheny Dillman (ed.). Washington, DC: Hemisphere Publishing Corp.
South/ Images of Women/ Research Resources/ Women's Culture/ Research Bias

0252 Dolensky, Suzanne T.
(1989) "The Daughters of Jefferson Davis: A Study of Contrast." Mississippi 51(November):pp. 313-340.
South/ Women's History/ Civil War/ Economic Value of Women's Work/ Women's Culture

0253 Dongan, Michael B.
(1987) "The Arkansas Married Women's Property Law." Arkansas Historical Quarterly 63(Spring):pp. 19-37.
South/ Women's History/ Property Laws/ Women's Culture/ Arkansas/ Women's Rights/ Marriage and Family Law

0254 Dorgan, Howard
(1989) The Old Regular Baptists of Central Appalachia: Brothers and Sisters in Hope. Knoxville, TN: University of Tennessee Press. pp. 269.
South/ Religion/ Baptist/ Appalachia/ Rural Areas/ Poverty/ Culture

0255 Flynt, J. Wayne
(1989) Poor But Proud: Alabama's Poor Whites. Tuscaloosa, AL: University of Alabama Press. pp. 470.
South/ Alabama/ Rural Areas/ Poverty/ Culture/ Oral History/ Coal Miners/ Employment/ Politics/ Textile Industry/ Farming

0256 Gerster, Patrick
Cords, Nicholas (eds.). (1989) Myth and Southern History Vol I The Old South. Champaign, IL: University of Illinois Press. pp. 224.
South/ History/ Slavery/ Antebellum/ Women's History/ Civil War/ Abolition/ Women's Culture

0257 Gundersen, Joan Rezner
(1982) "The Non-Institutional Church: The Religious Role of Women in Eighteenth Century Virginia." Historical Magazine of the Protestant Episcopal Church (Special Issue) 51(December):4:pp. 347-357.
South/ Virginia/ Religious Practices/ History/ 18th Century/ Sex Roles/ Gender Roles/ Women of Color*/ Women's Roles/ Religion/ Women's Culture

0258 Horton, Laurel
(1989) "19th Century Quiltmaking Traditions in South Carolina." Southern Folklore 46:2:pp. 101-115.
Traditions/ Rural Areas / Quiltmaking/ Cultural Heritage/ South/ South Carolina/ Economics/ Textile Industry/ Networks/ Kinship/ Barter

0259 Inge, Tonette Bond
(1990) Southern Women Writers: The New Generation. Tuscaloosa, AL: University of Alabama Press. pp. 384.
South/ Literary Criticism/ African American/ Biographies/ Writing/ Writers/ Literature/ Essays/ Women's Culture/ Women of Color

0260 Jones-Jackson, Patricia
(1989) When Roots Die: Endangered Traditions on the Sea Islands. Athens, GA: University of Georgia Press. pp. 224.
Women of Color/ Culture/ African American/ Tradition/ South Carolina/ Cultural Heritage/ Georgia/ Life Styles/ South East

0261 Lebsock, Suzanne
(1987) A Share of Honour: Virginia Women, 1600-1945. Richmond, VA: Virginia State Library, Virginia Women's Cultural History Project.
Women's History/ Social History/ Culture Conflict/ Slavery/ European American/ Servants/ South/ Virginia

0262 Lebsock, Suzanne
(1990) "'No Obey': Indian, European, and African Women in Seventeenth Century Virginia." in Women, Families and Communities: Readings in American History,

Vol. I. Nancy A. Hewitt (ed.). Glenview, IL: Scott Foresman. pp. 6-20.
Women of Color/ People of Color/ Interethnic Families/ Native Americans/ Interracial Marriages/ African Americans/ South/ Virginia/ European Americans/ Servants/ Slaves/ Leadership/ Culture Conflict/ History/ 17th Century/ Pocahontas

0263 Lord, Sharon B.
(1985) Appalachian Women. Newton, MA: Women's Educational Equity Act Publishing Center. pp. 184.
South/ Curriculum Integration/ Appalachian/ Rural Areas/ Poetry/ Music/ Minority Experience/ Women's Culture

0264 Lynxwiler, John
Wilson, Michele. (1988) "The Code of the New Southern Belle." in Southern Women. Caroline Matheny Dillman. Washington, DC: Hemisphere Publishing Corp.
South/ Images of Women/ Women of Color*/ Women's Culture

0265 Masson, Ann
Reveley, Bryce. (1988) "When Life's Brief Sun Was Set: Protraits of Southern Women in Mourning - 1830-1860." Southern Quarterly 27(Fall):pp. 33-60.
South/ Mourning/ Death/ Women's History/ Life Histories/ Women's Culture/ 19th Century/ Separate Spheres/ Coverture/ Marriage and Family Law

0266 Mathews, Holly F.
(ed.). (1988) Women in the South: An Anthropological Perspective. Athens, GA: University of Georgia Press. pp. 161.
South/ Anthropology/ Life History/ Life Styles/ Women's Culture/ Women of Color*

0267 May, Robert E.
(1988) "Southern Elite Women, Sectional Extremism, and the Political Sphere: The Case of John A. Quitman's Wife and Female Descendents, 1847-1931." Journal of Mississippi History 50(November):pp. 251-285.
Elites/ South/ Separate Spheres/ Radicalism/ Politics/ Patriarchy/ Women's Culture/ Life Histories/ Women's History/ 19th Century

0268 McKay, Frances Thompson
(1985) Virginia's Voices: An Essay on Virginia Women and Music. Richmond, VA: Virginia State Library, Virginia Women's Cultural History Project.
Virginia/ South Atlantic/ Music/ Musicians/ Essays/ Women's Culture/ Women of Color*

0269 Nash, Jesse
(1989) "Icons of Sensuality and Childishness: Women in New Orleans Advertising." in Women in the South: An Anthropological Perspective. Holly Mathews (ed.). Athens, GA: University of Georgia Press. pp. 18-26.
South/ Women's Culture/ Louisiana/ Media Stereotyping/ Advertising/ Images of Women/ Sensuality

0270 Olds, Madelin J.
(1989) "The Rape Complex in the Postbellum South." Dissertation: Carnegie-Mellon University, Pittsburg, PA. (Order No. DA8918063).
South/ Postbellum/ Racial Discrimination/ Violence Against Women/ Rape/ Rapists/ Cult of True Womanhood/ Fear/ Women's Culture

0271 Palumbo, Kathryn
(1988) "Growing Up Female, White, and Southern in the 1850's and 1860's." in

Southern Women. Caroline Matheny Dillman (ed.). Washington, DC: Hemisphere Publishing Corporation.
South/ 19th Century/ Images of Women/ Separate Spheres/ Antebellum

0272 **Perdue, Theda**
(1984) "Red and Black in Appalachia." Southern Exposure 12(November/December):6: pp. 17-25.
Women of Color/ History/ Native American / Slavery/ African American/ Race Relations/ South/ Cultural Heritage/ Appalachia/ Rural Areas

0273 **Ramsey, Bets**
Waldvogel, Meriday. (1986) The Quilts of Tennessee: Images of Domestic Life Prior to 1930. Nashville, TN: Rutledge Hill Press.
Domesticity/ Craft Arts/ Private Sphere/ Women's Culture/ Images of Women/ Tennessee/ South/ Family Life/ Women of Color*

0274 **Sasna, Morton**
(1987) "Race and Gender in the South: The Case of Georgia's Lillian Smith." Georgia Historical Quarterly 71(Fall):pp. 427-437.
South/ Georgia/ Women's Culture/ Racial Discrimination/ Gender Development/ Race Relations/ Lillian Smith

0275 **Sears, James T.**
(1989) "The Impact of Gender and Race on Lesbians and Gays in the South." NWSA Journal 1(Spring):3:pp. 422-457.
South/ Lesbians/ Race, Class and Gender Studies/ Gender Differences/ African American/ Culture Conflict/ Racial and Ethnic Differences/ Women of Color

0276 **Smith, Jacqueline Marie**
(1986) "Church Participation and Morale of the Rural, Southern Black Aged: The Effects of Socioeconomic Status, Gender and the Organizational Properties of Churches." Dissertation: DAI (October), Vol. 47(1489-A)4.
Women of Color/ Socioeconomic Status/ African American/ Older Adults/ Religion/ Churches/ Rural Areas/ Women's Culture/ Mental Health/ Social Organizations/ South

0277 **Taylor, Alice F.**
(1988) "Mary Noailles Murfree: Southern Women Writer." Dissertation: Emory University. DAI (April/May), Vol. 49, 1989.
South/ Mary Noailles Murfree/ Writers/ Literature/ Authors/ Women's Culture

0278 **Thomas, John K.**
Schiflett, Kathy. (1989) "A Gender Comparison of Former Agricultural Students' Employment Experience." Southern Rural Sociology 6:pp. 80-92.
South/ Scientists/ Male Dominated Employment/ Managers/ Agricultural Industry/ Gender Differences/ Gender Roles/ Educational Attainment

0279 **Weiner, Marli F.**
(1986) "The Intersection of Race and Gender: The Antebellum Plantation Mistress and Her Slaves." Humboldt Journal of Social Relations 13(Fall/Summer):1,2:pp. 374-386.
South/ Agriculture/ Slavery/ Plantations/ Relationships/ Antebellum/ Domestic Services/ Race Differences/ Gender Roles

0280 **Whitehead Scott, Bess**
(1989) You Meet Such Interesting People. College Station, TX: Texas A & M

University Press.
South/ Texas/ Journalists/ Memoirs/ Autobiographies/ Writers/ Authors/ Women's History/ Women's Culture

0281 Williams, Michael Ann
(1990) "Come on Inside: The Role of Gender in Folk Architecture Fieldwork." Southern Folklore 47:1:pp. 45. (Special Issue, Folklore Fieldwork: Sex, Sexuality and Gender).
South / Sex Segregation/ Material Culture/ Folklore/ North Carolina/ Gender/ Architecture/ Oral History/ Women's Roles

0282 Wilson, Charles Reagan
Ferris, William (ed.). (1989) The Encyclopedia of Southern Culture. Chapel Hill, NC: University of North Carolina Press. pp. 1650. Sponsored by the Center for the Study of Southern Culture, University of Mississippi.
South/ Culture/ Research Resources/ Ethnicity/ Agriculture/ Geography/ Industries/ Language/ Politics/ History/ Religion/ Rural Areas/ Social Class/ Urban Areas

0283 Yabsley, Suzanne
(1988) Texas Quilts, Texas Women. College Station, TX: Texas A & M University Press.
Stories/ Women's Culture/ Women's Studies/ Texas/ Southwest/ Craft Arts/ Family Life/ Women of Color*

*Women of Color**

0284 Abel, Emily K.
Pearson, Marjorie L. (eds.). (1989) Across Cultures: The Spectrum of Women's Lives. New York: Gordon and Breach. pp. 156.
Women of Color*/ Religion/ Culture/ Feminism/ Immigrants/ Lesbians/ Working Class/ Health/ Healing/ Employment

0285 Aptheker, Bettina
(1989) Tapestries of Life: Women's Work, Women's Consciousness and the Meaning of Daily Life. Amherst, MA: University of Massachusetts Press.
Women of Color*/ Sisterhood/ Resistance/ Life Styles/ Networks/ Support Systems/ Life Histories/ European American/ Women's Roles/ Comparative Studies/ Women's Culture/ Women's History/ Survival Strategies

0286 Arnold, Regina A.
(1988) "Female Criminality and Female Imprisonment." Presented: John Jay College of Criminal Justice, City University of New York, New York, NY.
Women of Color*/ Imprisonment/ Crime/ Criminal Justice/ Criminals/ Prisoners/ Women's Culture

0287 Baca Zinn, Maxine
(1988) "Sex and Gender Stratification." in In Conflict and Order: Understanding Society. D. Stanley Eitzen and Maxine Baca Zinn. Boston: Allyn and Bacon.
Women of Color*/ Stratification/ Race, Class and Gender Studies/ Sex Discrimination/ Culture Conflict

0288 Beneria, Lourdes
Stimpson, Catharine R. (eds.). (1988) Women, Households, and the Economy. New Brunswick, NJ: Rutgers University Press. pp. 323.
Race, Class and Gender Studies/ Structural Unemployment/ Women of Color*/ Women Living in Poverty/ Ethnicity/ Economy/ Female Headed Households/ Racial Discrimination/ Sex Discrimination/ Balancing Work and Family Life

0289 Carnegie, Mary Elizabeth
Smith, Gloria et al. (1981) Recruitment and Retention of Culturally Different Students in a College of Nursing. Oklahoma City, OK: University of Oklahoma Press.
Women of Color*/ Cultural Identity/ Health Care/ Ethnic Diversity/ Recruitment/ Nursing Education/ Students

0290 Cole, Johnnetta B.
(1986) "Commonalities and Differences." in All American Women: Lines that Divide, Ties that Bind. Johnnetta B. Cole (ed). New York: The Free Press.
Women of Color*/ Racial and Ethnic Differences/ Ethnic Diversity/ Cultural Influences

0291 Cotera, Martha P.
(1985) Multicultural Women's Sourcebook: Materials Guide for Use in Women's Studies and Bilingual Programs. Newton, MA: Women's Educational Equity Act Publishing Center. pp. 162.
Women of Color*/ Research Resources/ Bilingualism/ Women's Studies/ Ethnic Women

0292 Cretser, Gary A.
Leon, Joseph J. (1982) Intermarriage in the United States. Binghamtom, NY: Haworth Press.
People of Color*/ Family/ Families/ Women of Color*/ Interracial Marriage/ Miscegenation/ Racial and Ethnic Differences

0293 Donato, Katharine
(1989) Why So Many Women: Cross-National Variation in Sex Composition of U.S. Immigrants." Presented: American Sociological Annual Meeting, San Francisco, CA.
Women of Color*/ Immigration/ Family/ Racial and Ethnic Differences/ Gender/ Immigrants/ Immigration Laws

0294 Dubofsky, Melvyn
(1989) Women and Minorities during the Great Depression. New York: Garland Publishing. pp. 300.
Women of Color*/ Race/ Gender/ Ethnicity/ Great Depression/ Economic History/ Women's Culture

0295 Dugger, Karen
(1989) "Race Differences in the Belief of Systems of Abortion Proponents and Opponents." Presented: American Sociological Annual Meeting, San Francisco, CA.
Racial and Ethnic Differences/ Freedom of Choice/ People of Color*/ Abortion/ Attitudes/ Reproductive Freedom/ Abortion Rights

0296 Duley, Margot I.
Edwards, Mary I. (1989) The Cross-Cultural Study of Women: A Comprehensive Guide. New York: The Feminist Press. pp. 420.
Women of Color*/ Culture/ Feminism/ Crosscultural Studies/ Research Resources/Ethnic Groups

0297 Elliott, Delbert S.
Morse, Barbara J. (1989) "Delinquency and Drug Use as Risk Factors in Teenage Sexual Activity." Youth and Society 21(September):1:pp. 32-60.
People of Color*/ Class Differences/ Drug Use/ Sexuality/ Alcohol Abuse/ Adolescents/ Substance Abuse/ Delinquent Behavior/ Racial and Ethnic Differences

0298 Ferguson, Ann
(1990) Sexual Democracy: Women, Oppression and Revolution. Boulder, CO: Westview Press. pp. 256.
Women of Color*/ Sexual Revolution/ Racism/ Oppression/ Lesbian Culture/ Sexual Identity

0299 Films for the Humanities
(1988) "Pockets of Hate." Distributor: Films for the Humanities and Social Sciences, P.O. Box 2053 Princeton, NJ 08543. Phone: (609) 452-1128 or 1-800-257-5126.
People of Color*/ Discrimination/ Racial Discrimination/ Subculture/ Crimes/ Criminals/ Attitudes

0300 Garbaccia, Donna
(1989) Immigrant Women in the United States: Selected Annotated Multidisciplinary Bibliographies. Westport, CT: Greenwood Press. pp. 339.
Women of Color*/ Employment/ Immigrants/ Life Styles/ Bibliographies/ Mother Daughter Relationships/ Cultural Heritage/ Migration/ Family/ Families/ Social Movements/ Research Resources

0301 Gentry, Cynthia S.
(1989) "Poverty, Inequality and Race as Predictors of Rape in Metropolitan Communities." Presented: American Sociological Association Annual Meeting, San Francisco, CA.
Poverty/ Urban Areas/ Economically Disadvantaged/ Women of Color*/ Inequality/ Discrimination/ Rape/ Violence/ Sex Crimes/ Women's Culture

0302 Gilliam, Franklin D., Jr.
Whitby, Kenny J. (1989) "Race, Class, and Attitudes toward Social Welfare Spending: An Ethclass Interpretation." Social Science Quarterly 70(March):1:pp. 88-100.
People of Color*/ Social Welfare/ Costs/ Race/ Ethclass/ Attitudes/ Class Differences/ Racial and Ethnic Differences/ Racial Stratification/ Social Stratification

0303 Gonzalez, Rosalinda Mendez
(1987) "Class, and Social Change." in The Women's West. Susan Armitage and Elizabeth Jameson (eds.). Norman, OK: University of Oklahoma Press. pp. 237-251.
Women of Color*/ Household Workers/ West/ Women's History/ Immigrants/ Ethnicity/ Social Change/ Race, Class and Gender Studies/ Diversity

0304 Gundersen, Joan Rezner
(1982) "The Non-Institutional Church: The Religious Role of Women in Eighteenth Century Virginia." Historical Magazine of the Protestant Episcopal Church (Special Issue) 51(December):4:pp. 347-357.
South/ Virginia/ Religious Practices/ History/ 18th Century/ Sex Roles/ Gender Roles/ Women of Color*/ Women's Roles/ Religion/ Women's Culture

0305 Jameson, Elizabeth
(1988) "Toward a Multicultural History of Women in the Western United States." SIGNS: Journal of Women in Culture and Society 13(Summer):4:pp. 761-791.
Women of Color*/ Interracial Relations/ Women's Culture/ Women's History/ Research Resources/ Bibliographies/ West

0306 Jaret, Charles
(1990) "The Changing Characteristics of American Racial and Ethnic Minorities." Presented: North Central Sociological Association and Southern Sociological Association Annual Meetings, Louisville, KY.
People of Color*/ Socialization/ Ethnic Groups/ Social Change/ Ethnicity/ Acculturation/ Labor History/ Socioeconomic Conditions

0307 Kraus, Vered
(1989) "Ethnicity, Gender, and the Process of Status Attainment." Research in Inequality and Social Conflict 1.
Women of Color*/ Inequality/ Ethnicity/ Social Conflict/ Gender/ Mobility/ Status/ Status Attainment

0308 LaGesse, Enid J.
(1989) "Oppressive Technology and Women of Color." Presented: Parallels and Intersections: Racism and Other Forms of Oppression Conference, Iowa City, IA.
Women of Color*/ Oppression/ Technology/ Racial Discrimination/ Impact on Women/ Women's Culture

0309 LeBold, William K.
(1985) Putting It All Together. Newton, MA: Women's Educational Equity Act Pubishing Center.
Model Programs/ Self Concept/ Engineering/ Ethnicity/ Career Counseling/ Women of Color*/ Sexual Equality/ Sex Equity

0310 Levine, Susan
(1986) "Labors in the Field: Reviewing Women's Cultural History." Radical History Review 35(April):pp. 49-56.
Women of Color*/ Economic Trends/ Images of Women/ Feminism/ Women's Movement/ Cultural History/ Female Culture/ Cultural Identity/ Literature Review/ Literary Criticism

0311 Levinson, David
(1989) Family Violence in Cross Cultural Perspective. Newbury Park, CA: Sage Publications, Inc. pp. 152.
Women of Color*/ Family Roles/ Crosscultural Studies/ Child Care/ Family Violence/ Spouse Abuse/ Inequality

0312 Lieberson, Stanley
Waters, Mary C. (1988) From Many Strands: Ethnic and Racial Groups in Contemporary America. New York: Russell Sage Foundation. pp. 304. ISBN 087154525x.
Assimilation Patterns/ European American/ Women of Color*/ Racial Discrimination/ Educational Trends/ Employment Patterns/ Marital Status

0313 Maldonado, Lionel
Moore, Joan. (1985) Urban Ethnicity in the United States. Newbury Park, CA: Sage Publications, Inc.
People of Color*/ Urban Areas/ Ethnicity/ Immigrants/ Minorities/ History/ 20th Century

0314 Mays, Vickie M.
(1988) "The Integration of Gender and Ethnicity in Clinical Training: The UCLA Model." in Teaching Psychology. P. Bronstein and K. Quina (eds.). Washington, DC: American Psychological Association.
Women of Color*/ Education/ Ethnicity/ Clinical Psychology/ Teaching/ Ethnic Groups/ Psychologists

0315 Minh-Ha, Trinh T.
(1989) Woman, Native, Other: Writing Postcoloniality & Feminism. Bloomington, IN: Indiana University Press.
Women of Color*/ Feminist Writings/ Ethnicity/ Feminist Thought/ Cultural Identity/ Storytelling/ Literature

0316 Moeller, Gertrude L.
(1989) "Fear of Criminal Victimization: The Effect of Neighborhood Racial Composition." Sociological Inquiry 59(Spring):2:pp. 208-221.
Stratification/ Ethnic Neighborhoods/ Communities/ Race/ Social Stratification/ Fear/ Victims/ Violence/ Crimes/ Criminals/ Community Problems/ People of Color*

0317 Organization.of American Historians
(1988) Restoring Women to History: Teaching Packets for Integrating Women's History into Courses on Africa, Asia, Latin America, the Caribbean, and the Middle East. Available: Organization of American Historians, 112 N. Bryan St., Bloomington, IN 47403.
Women of Color*/ Curriculum Integration/ Women's History/ Race, Class and Gender Studies/ Crosscultural Studies/ Education/ Third World

0318 Parks, Beverly J.
(1985) Sourcebook of Measures of Women's Educational Equity. Newton, MA: Women's Educational Equity Act Publishing Center.
Women of Color*/ Gender/ Evaluation/ Cultural Identity/ Evaluation Criteria/ Course Evaluation/ Educational Program/ Race/ Curriculum Integration

0319 Pearson, Carol S.
Shavlik, Donna L. et al (eds.). (1989) Educating the Majority: Women Challenge Tradition in Higher Education. New York: MacMillan Publishing Company. pp. 475.
Higher Education/ Women of Color*/ Racial and Ethnic Differences/ Social Stratification/ Ethnic Diversity/ Class Differences/ Racial Diversity

0320 Pearson, Lynn F.
(1988) The Architecture and Social History of Cooperative Living. New York: St. Martin's Press. pp. 284.
Women of Color*/ Cooperatives/ House Design/ Architecture/ Middle Class/ Social History/ Women's Culture

0321 Pedersen, Diana
(1987) "Building Today for the Womanhood of Tomorrow: Businessmen, Boosters, and the YWCA, 1890-1930." Urban History Review 15(February).
Women of Color*/ Womanhood/ YWCA/ Women's Culture/ Voluntary Organizations/ Women's Groups/ Advocacy Groups/ Urban Areas

0322 Pirog-Good, Maureen
Stets, Ian E. (1989) Violence in Dating Relationships: Emerging Social Issues. New York: Praeger Publishers. pp. 302.
Women of Color*/ Ethnic Groups/ Sexual Violence/ Social Problems/ Violence Against Women/ Female Male Relationships/ Sexual Abuse/ Home Life/ Personal Relationships/ Dating/ Anthropology

0323 Rank, Mark R.
(1988) "Racial Differences in Length of Welfare Use." Social Forces 66(June):4:pp. 1080-1101.
Women of Color*/ Racial and Ethnic Differences/ Heads of Households/ Comparative Studies/ Welfare Mothers/ Education/ Employment

0324 Rodriguez, Clara E.
(1986) "Denial as Social Policy: The Deepening Race Contradiction." Presented: Colloquium on Reformed Faith and Economics, Albuquerque, NM.
People of Color*/ Denial/ Race Bias/ Racial Factors/ Racial Equality/ Social Policy/ Ethnicity

0325 Skevington, Suzanne
Baker, Deborah. (1989) The Social Identity of Women. Newbury Park, CA: Sage Publications, Inc. pp. 192.
Women of Color*/ Social Change/ Motherhood/ Careers/ Feminism/ Women's Culture/ Social Identity

0326 Steffensmeier, Darrell
Allan, Emilie and Cathy Streifel. (1989) "Development and Female Crime: Cross-National Test of Alternative Explanations." Social Forces 68(September):1:pp. 262-283.
Women of Color*/ Women's Culture/ Crime/ Gender Equality/ Social Control/ Economic Marginality/ Economic Development

0327 Sweet, James A.
Bumpass, Larry L. (1988) American Families and Households. New York: Russell Sage Foundation. pp. 416.
Women of Color*/ Gender/ European American/ Race/ Ethnicity/ Family/ Families/ Population Trends/ Childbirth/ Crosscultural Studies/ Marriage

0328 Tienda, Marta
(1989) "Race, Ethnicity and the Portrait of Inequality Approaching the 1990's." Sociological Spectrum 9:1:pp. 23-53.
People of Color*/ Racial Inequality/ Ethnic Studies/ Social Trends/ Socioeconomic Status

0329 University of Michigan School of Education
(1989) Equity Coalition: For Race, Gender and National Origin, Vol. 1. Ann Arbor, MI: University of Michigan School of Education.
Women of Color*/ Ethnic Studies/ Education/ Race, Class and Gender Studies/ Educational Equity

0330 Ward, David
(1989) Poverty, Ethnicity, and the American City, 1840-1925: Changing Conceptions of the Slum and the Ghetto. New York: Cambridge University Press. pp. 263.
Poverty/ Urban Areas/ Ethnicity/ Social History/ Slums/ Disadvantaged/ Ghettos/ Women of Color*/ Ethnic Neighborhoods/ Minority Groups

0331 Welch, Susan
Secret, Philip. (1981) "Sex, Race, and Political Participation." Western Political Quarterly 34:pp. 5-16.
People of Color*/ Race/ Sex/ Class Differences/ Gender Differences/ Voting Behavior/ Racial and Ethnic Differences/ Political Participation/ Stratification

EDUCATION

African American

0332 Barnes, Annie S.
(1989) "Single Mothers in Black Households." in Women in the South: An Anthropological Perspective. Holly F. Mathews (ed.). Athens, GA: University of Georgia Press. pp. 47-56.
Women of Color/ Black Colleges/ African American/ Single Mothers/ Women College Students/ Education/ Female Headed Households

0333 Berry, Gordon Lavern
Asamen, Joy Keiko (eds.). (1989) Black Students: Psychosocial Issues and Academic Achievement. Newbury Park, CA: Sage Publications, Inc. pp. 320.
Women of Color/ Peer Influence/ African American/ Self Concept/ Students/ Schools/ Psychological Needs/ Student Motivation/ Social Issues/ Socialization/ Educational Methods/ Curriculum Integration/ Educational Programs/ Education/ Teaching

0334 Brewer, Rose M.
(1989) "Black Women and Feminist Sociology: The Emerging Perspective." The American Sociologist 20(Spring):1:pp. 57-70.
Women of Color/ Interdisciplinary Studies/ African American/ Feminist Theory/ Race Relations/ Sociology/ Race, Class and Gender Studies/ Higher Education

0335 Brooks-Higginbotham, Evelyn
(1989) "Beyond the Sound of Silence: Afro-American Women in History." Gender & History 1(Spring):pp. 50-67.
Women of Color/ History/ African American/ Curriculum Integration/ Invisibility/ Education

0336 Clayton, Constance
(1989) "We Can Educate All Our Children." The Nation Special Issue: Scapegoating the Black Family 249:4:pp. 132-135.
People of Color/ Public Policy/ Public Schools/ Urban Areas/ African Americans/ Family/ Families / Education

0337 Cole, Johnnetta B.
(1988) "She Who Learns, Teaches." New York: Hunter College Occasional Paper #1(Fall).
Women of Color/ Education/ African American/ Liberation Struggles/ Teachers/ Teaching/ Women's Movement

0338 Collins, Patricia Hill
(1989) "The Social Construction of Invisibility: Black Women's Poverty in Social Problems Discourse." in Perspectives on Social Problems, Vol. I. Gale Miller and Jim Holstein (eds.). Greenwich, CT: JAI. pp. 77-93.
Women of Color/ Race, Class and Gender Studies / African American/ Education/ Women Living in Poverty/ Research Bias/ Social Problems/ Social Construction of Reality/ Perceptual Bias

0339 Collins, Patricia Hill
(1989) "Critical Questions: Two Decades of Feminist Scholarship." Presented:

National Women's Studies Association, Towson State University, Baltimore, MD.
Women of Color/ African American/ Black Feminism/ Feminist Scholarship/ Higher Education

0340 Davis, Nathaniel
(1985) Afro-American Reference: An Annotated Bibliography of Selected Resources. Westport, CT: Greenwood Press. pp. 288.
Bibliographies/ People of Color/ Education/ African Americans/ Mass Media/ Annotations/ Families/ Research Resources/ Health/ Sports

0341 Farrell, Charles S.
(1988) "Black Students Seen Facing 'New Racism' on Many Campuses." The Chronicle of Higher Education 27(January):A1:pp. 36-38.
People of Color/ Discrimination/ African Americans/ Relationships/ Students/ Education/ Colleges/ Race Relations

0342 Film & Video Library
(1988) "Racism 101." Distributor: Film & Video Library, University Library, University of Michigan, 400 Fourth St., Ann Arbor, MI 48103-4816. Phone: (313) 764-5360 or 1-800-999-0424.
People of Color/ Campus Security/ African Americans/ Violence/ European Americans/ Colleges/ Race Relations/ Education/ Racial Discrimination

0343 Hayes, Malinda
(1989) "In Affirmation of Black Women." Minority Voices 6(Fall):1:pp. 63-66.
Women of Color/ Sex Stereotypes/ African American/ Professional Status/ Educational Attainment/ Racial Stereotypes

0344 Henry, Charles P.
Foster, Frances Smith. (1982) "Black Women's Studies: Threat or Challenge?" The Western Journal of Black Studies 6:1.
Women of Color/ Black Studies/ African American/ Women's Studies/ Curriculum Integration/ Education

0345 Hill, Ruth Edmonds
(1989) The Black Women's Oral History Collection at the Schlesinger Library, Radcliffe College. (10 Volumes). Westport, CT: Meckler Corp.
Oral History/ Achievement/ Success/ African American/ Racial Discrimination/ Women of Color/ Interviews/ Family Life/ Structural Discrimination/ Childhood/ Education/ Life Histories

0346 Hine, Darlene Clark
Brown, Elsa Barkley et al. (eds.). (1990) Black Women in United States History: From Colonial Times to the Present. (16 Volumes). New York: Carlson Publishing, Inc.
Women of Color/ Slavery/ African American/ History/ Family/ Religion/ Employment/ Exploitation/ Oppression/ Civil Rights Movement/ Women's Movement/ Education

0347 Howard-Vital, Michelle R.
(1989) "African American Women in Higher Education: Struggling to Gain Identity." Journal of Black Studies 20(December):pp. 180-191.
Women of Color/ Identity/ African American/ Higher Education/ Educational Equity/ Equal Educational Opportunity

0348 Hunter, Barbara J.
(1987) The Public Education of Blacks in the City of Pittsburgh, 1920-1950: Actions and Reactions of the Black Community in its Pursuit of Education Equality.

Pittsburgh, PA: University of Pittsburgh Press.
Education/ Pennsylvania/ African Americans/ North/ Educational Equity/ Urban Areas/ Racial Equality/ Communities/ People of Color

0349 Hunter, Lisa K.
(1985) Sources of Strength. Newton, MA: Women's Educational Equity Act Publishing Center.
Women of Color/ Minority Groups/ African American/ Curriculum Integration/ Asian American/ Textbooks/ Economic Power/ Research Resources/ Political Power/ Secondary Schools

0350 Jones-Johnson, Gloria
(1988) "The Victim-Bind Dilemma of Black Female Sociologists in Academe." The American Sociologist 19:pp. 312-322.
African American/ Academia/ Women of Color/ Research Bias/ Racial Discrimination/ Sociology/ Higher Education/ Blaming the Victim

0351 Junne, George
(1988) "Black Women on AFDC and the Struggle for Higher Education." Frontiers: Journal of Women's Studies 10:pp. 39-44.
African American/ Racial Discrimination/ Higher Education/ Welfare/ AFDC/ Women of Color/ Women Living in Poverty

0352 Junne, George
(1988) "Welfare Recipients Against the Odds." Frontiers: Journal of Women's Studies 10:2.
Women of Color/ Higher Education/ African American/ AFDC/ North Central/ Michigan/ Welfare

0353 Kahle, Jane B.
(1985) Lehman, J. D. and C. Carter. "Concept Mapping, Vee Mapping, and Achievement: Results of a Field Study with Black High School Students." Journal of Research in Science Teaching 22:7:pp. 663-673.
Women of Color/ Secondary Education/ African American/ Research Methods/ Academic Achievement

0354 Lewis, Earl
(1990) "Equalizing the Pay of Black Teachers." The University of Michigan Center for Afroamerican and African Studies Newsletter 1:2:pp. 8-13.
Women of Color/ Equal Pay/ African American/ Politics/ History/ Teachers/ Teaching/ Judicial System/ Pay/ Wage Gap/ Segregation/ Racial Discrimination/ Education

0355 Luttrell, Wendy
(1989) "Working-Class Women's Ways of Knowing: Effects of Gender, Race, and Class." Sociology of Education 62(January):pp. 33-46.
African American/ Academic Aspirations/ European American/ Women of Color/ Working Class/ Low Income Households/ Race, Class and Gender Studies/ Educational Opportunities

0356 Luttrell, Wendy
(1989) "Black and White Working Class Women's Schooling: Concepts of Power." Presented: American Sociological Association Annual Meeting, San Francisco, CA.
Working Class/ Autonomy/ African American/ School Attendance/ European American/ Education/ Women of Color/ Woman Power

0357 Mahoney, John S., Jr.
(1990) Merritt, Stephen R. "Educational Aspirations and Disappointments: A Comparison between Black and White High School Seniors in Virginia." Presented:

North Central Sociological Association and Southern Sociological Association Annual Meetings, Louisville, KY.
People of Color/ Academic Aspirations/ African Americans/ Family Influences/ European Americans/ Fear of Failure/ South/ Virginia/ Educational Attainment/ Education/ Educationally Disadvantaged/ High Schools/ Comparative Studies

0358 **Marrett, Cora Bagley**
(1983) "Male-Female Enrollment across Mathematics Tracks in Predominantly Black High Schools." Journal for Research in Mathematics Education 14(March):pp. 113-118.
Women of Color/ Mathematics/ African American/ Adolescents/ Secondary Education/ Educational Patterns/

0359 **Mays, Vickie M.**
(1988) "Even the Rat Was White and Male: Teaching the Psychology of Black Women." in Teaching Psychology. P. Brostein and K. Quina (eds.). Washington, DC: American Psychological Association.
Women of Color/ Psychology/ African American/ Teaching/ Teachers/ Psychologists/ Education/ Curriculum Integration

0360 **McAdoo, Harriette Pipes**
(1985) McAdoo, John L. Black Children: Social, Educational, and Parental Environments. Newbury Park, CA: Sage Publications, Inc. pp. 280.
People of Color/ Social Environment/ African Americans/ Gender Differences/ Children/ Social Influences/ Parent Influence/ Family Environment/ Parent Child Relationships/ Ecological Factors/ Education/ Educational Opportunities

0361 **Moses, Yolanda T.**
(1989) "Black Women in Academe: Issues and Strategies." Available: Project on the Status and Education of Women, Association of American Colleges, 1818 R. Street NW, Washington, DC 20009.
Women of Color/ Black Colleges/ African American/ Universities/ European American/ Academia/ Education/ Students/ Administrators

0362 **Muir, Donal E.**
(1990) "White Fraternity and Sorority Attitudes toward 'Blacks' on a Deep-South Campus." Presented: North Central Sociological Association and Southern Sociological Association Annual Meetings, Louisville, KY.
People of Color/ Fraternities/ African Americans/ Sororities/ European Americans/ Race Relations/ South/ Racial Stereotypes/ Education/ Colleges/ Race Bias/ Social Organizations/ Racial Discrimination

0363 **Muir, Donal E.**
(1990) "A Comparison of 'Black' and 'White' Integration Attitudes on a Deep-South Campus: A Research Note." Sociological Spectrum 10:1:pp. 143-153.
South/ Alabama/ Integration/ People of Color/ Race Relations/ African Americans/ Attitudes/ Students/ European Americans/ Education/ Colleges/ Universities/ Prejudice/ Comparative Studies

0364 **Neill, Donald M.**
(1987) "The Struggles of the Boston Black Community for Equality and Quality in Public Education, 1959-1987." Dissertation: DAI Vol. 58.
People of Color/ History/ 20th Century/ African Americans/ Northeast/ Massachusetts/ Educational Equity/ Public Education/ Educational Reform

0365 Nicola-McLaughlin, Andree
Chandler, Zala. (1988) "Urban Politics in the Higher Education of Black Women: A Case Study." in Women and the Politics of Empowerment. Ann Bookman and Sandra Morgen (eds.). Philadelphia: Temple University Press pp. 180-201.
Women of Color/ Higher Education/ African American/ Educational Equity/ Networks/ Empowerment/ Case Studies/ Public Policy/ Politics/ Urban Areas

0366 Pearson, Willie, Jr.
Bechtel, H. Kenneth. (1989) Blacks, Science and American Education. New Brunswick, NJ: Rutgers University Press.
African Americans/ Science Avoidance/ People of Color/ Educationally Disadvantaged/ Discrimination

0367 Penn State Audio-Visual
(1981) "Success: The Marva Collins Approach." Distributor: Penn State Audio-Visual Services, Special Services Building, University Park, PA 16802. Phone: (814) 865-6314 or 1-800-826-0132.
African American/ Education/ Teachers/ Marva Collins/ Teaching/ Educational Methods/ Student Motivation/ Women of Color

0368 Perlmann, Joel
(1989) Ethnic Differences: Schooling and Social Structure among the Irish, Italians, Jews and Blacks in an American City. New York: Cambridge University Press. pp. 327.
People of Color/ Social Structure/ African Americans/ Youth/ Ethnic Differences/ Northeast/ Rhode Island/ Comparative Studies/ Mobility/ Class/ Education

0369 Schaefer, Richard T.
(1987) "Social Distance of Black College Students at a Predominantly White University." Sociology and Social Research 72:pp. 30-32.
People of Color/ College Students/ African Americans/ Relationships/ European Americans/ Socialization/ Race Relations/ Higher Education/ Colleges

0370 Shapiro, Joan Poliner
(1986) "Afro-American Studies and Women's Studies: Towards a New Definition of Academic Rigor and Excellence in Higher Education." Presented: National Women's Studies Association Meeting, University of Illinois at Urbana-Champaign.
Women of Color/ Education/.African American/ Higher Education/ Academia/ Curriculum Integration

0371 Smith, Eleanor J.
(1983) "Black Studies: Is the University Administration for Real?" Presented: Black Studies Symposium, College of Wooster, Wooster, OH.
People of Color/ Universities/ African Americans/ Colleges/ Higher Education/ Educational Reform/ Black Studies/ Administration/ Administrators/ Curriculum Integration

0372 Smith, Eleanor J.
(1987) "Blacks in Predominantly White Institutions: Strategies for Making it through the System as a Faculty Member." Presented: NAFEO Conference, Washington, DC.
People of Color/ Colleges/ African Americans/ Teachers/ Higher Education/ Promotions/ Faculty/ Occupational Mobility/ Coping Strategies/ Universities/ Job Discrimination/ Upward Mobility

0373 Stanback, Marsha Houston
(1988) "What Makes Scholarship about Black Women and Communication Feminist

Communication Scholarship?" Women's Studies in Communication 10(Spring):pp. 78-85.
Women of Color/ Feminist Theory/ African American/ Communication/ Education

0374 **Stanley, Jeanie R.**
(1986) "Life, Space and Gender Politics in an East Texas Community." Women and Politics 5(Winter):4:pp. 27-49.
Women of Color/ Political Participation/ African American/ Gender Roles/ European American/ Stereotypes/ Southwest/ Texas/ Sexual Politics/ Secondary Education/ Parental Influence/ Socioeconomic Factors

0375 **Turner-Castellano, B.**
Darity, William A. (1987) "Education and Family Planning among Black American Women." International Quarterly of Community Health Education 8:2:pp. 117-127.
Women of Color/ Childbearing/ African American/ Parenting/ Education/ Sex/ Family Planning/ Higher Education

0376 **Wahl, Ana-Maria**
Briggs, Carl M. (1990) "Private Schooling for Southern Blacks: The Determinants of an Alternative System of Education for a Disenfranchised Class." Presented: North Central Sociological Association and Southern Sociological Association Annual Meetings, Louisville, KY.
African Americans/ Alternative Schools/ People of Color/ Institutions/ South/ Organizing/ Education/ Social Change/ Private Schools/ Educational Opportunities/ Educationally Disadvantaged

0377 **Werum, Regina E.**
(1990) "Black Women's Colleges: Racial and Gender Ideologies in the Early 20th Century South." Presented: North Central Sociological Association and Southern Sociological Association Annual Meetings, Louisville, KY.
African American/ Racial Factors/ Women of Color/ Educational Reform/ Colleges/ Educational Opportunities/ Higher Education/ Images of Women

Asian American

0378 **Hunter, Lisa K.**
(1985) Sources of Strength. Newton, MA: Women's Educational Equity Act Publishing Center.
Women of Color/ Minority Groups/ African American/ Curriculum Integration/ Asian American/ Textbooks/ Economic Power/ Research Resources/ Political Power/ Secondary Schools

0379 **Kim, Elaine H.**
Hong, Insook et al. (1987) Education of Koreans in America. Seoul, Korea: Bbori Publishers. (Written in Korean).
Asian Americans/ Immigrants/ People of Color/ Assimilation Patterns/ Education/ Koreans/ Educational Experience/ Educational Opportunities

0380 **Letley, Harriet P.**
Pedersen, Paul B. (eds.). (1986) Cross-Cultural Training for Mental Health Professionals. Springfield, IL: Charles Thomas.
Mental Health/ Asian Americans/ People of Color/ Counselors/ Job Training/ Differences/ Crosscultural Research/ Professional Occupations/ Employment/ Education

0381 **Mau, Rosalind Y.**
(1989) "Barriers to Higher Education for Asian/Pacific American Females."

Presented: American Sociological Association Annual Meeting, San Francisco, CA.
Women of Color/ Science/ Asian American/ Mathematics/ Educational Attainment/ Hawaiian/ Pacific Islander/ Filipino

0382 Tin-Mala
(1986) From the Curriculum to the Mainstream: An Educational Equity Package for Asian American Women. Bethesda, MD: National Network of Asian American Women.
Curriculum Integration/ Racial Equality/ Education/ Sexual Equality/ Asian American/ Women of Color/ Educational Equity

Latina

0383 Arias, M.
(1986) "The Context of Education for Hispanic Students: An Overview." American Journal of Education 95:pp. 26-57.
Latinos/ Chicanos/ Education/ Secondary Education/ Educational Opportunities/ Discrimination/ Low Income Households/ People of Color

0384 Cardona, Luis
(1983) Annotated Bibliography on Puerto Rican Materials. Potomac, MD: Carreta Press.
Women of Color/ Bibliographies/ Latina/ Puerto Rican/ Research Resources/ Education

0385 Chacon, M.
(1982) "Chicanos in Postsecondary Education." Available: Center for Research on Women, Stanford University, CA.
Women of Color/ Diversity/ Latina/ Chicana/ Ethnicity/ Socioeconomic Status/ Higher Education

0386 Garcia, Alma M.
(1990) "Studying Chicanas: Bringing Women into the Frame of Chicano Studies." in Chicana Voices: Intersections of Class, Race, and Gender. Teresa Cordova et al. (eds.). Houston, TX: National Association for Chicano Studies. (Available: Felipe Gonzales, Sociology, 1000 Social Science Bldg., U. of NM, Albuquerque, NM 87131.)
Latina/ Chicana/ Women of Color/ Race/ Minority Groups/ Interdisciplinary Studies/ Chicano Studies/ Curriculum Integration/ Education

0387 Katsinas, Stephan G.
(1989) "Educational Arrears: Addressing the Underenrollment of Hispanics in Illinois Higher Education." The Urban Review 21(March):1:pp. 35-50.
People of Color/ Public Schools/ High Schools/ Latinos/ Chicanos/ Dropouts/ Labor Force Participation/ Higher Education/ Colleges/ Assimilation Patterns/ Demography/ Enrollment/ Educational Attainment/ Educational Policy/ Manufacturing Industry/ Educational Equity

0388 Keller, Gary D.
Magallan, Rafael J. et al. (1989) Curriculum Resources in Chicano Studies. Arizona State Univ., Hispanic Research Ctr., Tempe, AZ: Bilingual Review Press. pp. 346.
Chicanos/ Latinos/ Curriculum Integration/ Chicano Studies/ Education/ Teaching/ Research Resources/ People of Color

0389 Kerr, Louise A.
(1986) "An Administrators View of Chicana/Mexicana History." Presented: Workshop on Chicana/Mexicana History, University of California at Davis.
Women of Color/ Education/ Latina/ Chicana/ Women's History

0390 **Lucero, Helen R.**
(1986) Hispanic Weavers of North Central New Mexico: Social Historical and Educational Dimensions of a Continuing Artistic Tradition. Albuquerque, NM: University of New Mexico Press.
Weavers/ Latinos/ Craft Arts/ Traditions/ Artistic Tradition/ Cultural Heritage/ Social Characteristics/ Educational Activities/ People of Color

0391 **Madrid, Arturo**
(1988) "California Post-Secondary Education for Whom? Changing the Discourse." La Red/The Net 1:1:pp. 3-10.
Women of Color/ Diversity/ Latina/ Post Secondary Education/ West/ California/ Demography

0392 **Moore, Helen A.**
Porter, Natalie K. (1988) "Leadership and Nonverbal Behaviors of Hispanic Females across School Equity Environments." Psychology of Women Quarterly 12(June):2:pp. 147-164.
Women of Color/ School Segregation/ Latina/ Educational Equity/ Leadership/ Nonverbal Behavior/ Primary Education/ Behavioral Research/ Comparative Studies/ Social Status

0393 **Ortiz, Vilma**
(1989) "Language Background and Literacy among Hispanic Young Adults." Social Problems 36(April):2:pp. 149-164.
People of Color/ Cultural Influences/ Latinos/ Chicanos/ Literacy/ Education/ Bilingualism/ Cultural Heritage/ Language

0394 **Rochin, Refugio**
de la Torre, Adela. (1988) "Strengthening Chicano Studies Programs." La Red/The Net 1:1:pp. 11-30.
Women of Color/ Ethnic Studies/ Latina/ Curriculum Integration/ Education

0395 **Rochin, Refugio**
(1988) "Preparing Hispanics for the Workforce of the 21st Century: Challenges for Hispanic Educators." La Red/The Net 1:3,4:pp. 24-30.
Women of Color/ Educational Objectives/ Latina/ Labor Force Participation/ Economy/ Career Education

0396 **Velez, William**
(1989) "High School Attrition among Hispanic and Non-Hispanic White Youths." Sociology of Education 62(April):pp. 119-133.
People of Color/ Discrimination/ European Americans/ Educational Opportunities/ Latinos/ Chicanos/ Teenagers/ Puerto Ricans/ Adolescent/ Ethnic Studies/ Secondary Education

0397 **Veyna, Angelina F.**
(1987) "Integrating Chicana Studies into the Secondary Curriculum." Maestro (March/April).
Women of Color/ Higher Education/ Latina/ Chicana/ Education/ Curriculum Integration/ Secondary Curriculum

0398 **Wiley, Ed III**
(1989) "Stereotypes, Prejudice Hindering Hispanic Women in Academia, Researcher Says." Black Issues in Higher Education 6(March 30):2:pp. 1,8-9.
Women of Color/ Language/ Latina/ Sexism/ Racial Discrimination/ Occupational Mobility/ Stereotypes/ Higher Education/ Employment/ Academia/ Institutional Racism/ Educational Attainment

0399 Zavella, Patricia
(1987) "Integrating Chicana Studies into the Women's Studies Curriculum." Presented: Women's Studies Program, University of Arizona at Tuscon.
Women of Color/ Higher Education/ Chicana/ Latina/ Women's Studies/ Education/ Curriculum Integration

0400 Zavella, Patricia
(1989) "The Problematic Relationship of Feminism and Chicana Studies." Women's Studies 17:1,2:pp. 25-36.
Women of Color/ Education/ Chicana/ Latina/ Feminism/ Chicana Studies/ Feminist Studies/ Social Movements/ Family/ Families

0401 Zavella, Patricia
(1989) "The Problematic Relationship of Feminism and Chicana Studies." in Across Cultures: The Spectrum of Women's Lives. Emily K. Abel and Marjorie L. Pearson (eds.). New York: Gordon and Breach. pp. 25-36.
Women of Color/ Chicana/ Latina/ Feminism/ Social Movements/ Families/ Education/ Family/ Feminist Studies/ Chicana Studies

Native American

0402 Abbott, Devon I.
(1989) "History of the Cherokee Female Seminary, 1851-1910." Dissertation: Texas Christian University. (Order No. DA8919932).
Women of Color/ Women's History/ Native American/ Higher Education/ Cherokee/ Education/ Oklahoma/ Women's Colleges/ 19th Century

0403 Babcock, Barbara A.
(1988) Parezo, Nancy J. Daughters of the Desert: Women Anthropologists and the Native American Southwest, 1880-1980. Albuquerque, NM: University of New Mexico Press. pp. 256.
Women of Color/ Native American/ Southwest/ New Mexico/ Political Activism/ Folk Literature/ Craft Art/ Pueblo/ Research Bias/ Anthropology/ Catalogs

0404 Blackman, Margaret B.
(1989) Sadie Brower Neakok, an Inupiaq Woman. Seattle: University of Washington Press.
Women of Color/ Social Change/ Native American/ Judiciary System/ Alaska/ Eskimo/ Family/ Families/ Anthropology/ Gender Roles/ Education/ Life Cycles/ Sadie Brower Neakok/ Personal Narrative/ Judicial Appointments

0405 Boyer, LaNada
(1987) "Growing Up in E'da How - One Idaho Girlhood." in The Schooling of Native America. Thomas Thompson (ed.). Washington, DC: American Association of Colleges for Teacher Education and Teacher Corps. pp. 28-42.
Women of Color/ Education/ Native American/ Relocation/ Autobiographies/ Activism/ Personal Narratives/ Shoshone/ Idaho/ Mountain

0406 Coleman, Michael C.
(1990) "Motivations of Indian Children at Missionary & U.S. Government Schools, 1860-1918: A Study through Published Reminiscences." Montana (The Journal of Western History) 40(Winter):pp. 30-45.
People of Color/ Native Americans/ Education/ History/ Memoirs/ Student Motivation/ Learning Motivation

0407 **Contemporary American Indian Issues**
(1981) American Indian Issues in Higher Education. Los Angeles: University of California American Indian Studies Center. pp. 206.
People of Color/ Native Americans/ Education/ Higher Education/ Universities/ Colleges/ Educational Policy/ Educationally Disadvantaged

0408 **Haster, Lea**
Schniedemind, Nancy et al. (1988) "Human Rights Education: A Context for Teaching About Women's Lives." Feminist Teacher 3(Fall/Winter):3:pp. 14-18.
Women of Color/ Education/ Native American/ Stereotypes/ Social Movements/ Gender Roles/ Educational Experience/ Women's Studies/ Human Rights/ Educational Opportunities/ Teaching/ Teachers

0409 **Johnston, Basil H.**
(1989) Indian School Days. Norman, OK: University of Oklahoma Press. pp. 250.
People of Color/ Education/ Native Americans

0410 **Kincheloe, Teresa Scott**
Bull, Valda Black. (1982) "The Lakota Sioux and Their Elders: Some Universal Truths." Childhood Education 59(Nov/Dec):2:pp. 114-115.
People of Color/ Personal Narratives/ Native Americans/ Oral History/ Education/ Grandmothers/ Sioux

0411 **LaFromboise, Teresa**
(1989) Circles of Women: Professional Skills Training with American Indian Women. Stanford, CA: Stanford University. pp. 241.
Women of Color/ Career Planning/ Native American/ Financial Management/ Stress/ Financial Planning/ Coping Strategies/ Employment/ Extended Families/ Self Esteem/ Acculturation/ Education

0412 **Lindsey, Donal F.**
(1989) Indian Education at the Hampton Institute, 1877-1923. Kent, OH: Kent State University Press.
People of Color/ Education/ Native Americans/ History

0413 **Miller, Donald E.**
(1987) The Limits of Schooling by Imposition: The Hopi Indians of Arizona." Dissertation: University of Tennessee at Knoxville. DAI Vol. 48.
People of Color/ Southwest/ Native Americans/ Hopi/ Arizona/ Education/ Educational Equity/ Educational Experience/ Educational Opportunities

0414 **Peterson, Susan C.**
(1989) "American Indian Women in Higher Education: A Multicultural Perspective." Minority Voices 6(Fall):1:pp. 47-52.
Women of Color/ Cultural Constraints/ Native American/ Occupational Counseling/ Educational Opportunity/ Career Education/ Sex Discrimination/ Self Image/ Racial Discrimination/ Higher Education/ Health Hazards

0415 **Snipp, C. Matthew**
Sandefur, Gary D. (1988) "Earnings of American Indians and Alaskan Natives: The Effects of Residence and Migration." Social Forces 66(June):4:pp. 994-1008.
People of Color/ Urban Areas/ Native Americans/ Migration/ Education/ Labor Force Participation

0416 **Szasz, Margaret Connell**
(1989) "Listening to the Native Voice: American Indian Schooling in the Twentieth

Century." Montana (The Journal of Western History) 39(Summer):3:pp. 42-53.
People of Color/ Self Determination/ Native Americans/ History/ Education/ 20th Century/ Government Agencies

Southern

0417 Donato, Ruben
(1987) "In Struggle: Mexican Americans in the Pajaro Valley Schools, 1900-1979." Dissertation: Stanford University. DAI Vol. 48, 1988.
People of Color/ Schools/ Chicanos/ Education/ Southwest/ Educational Experience

0418 Gilliland, Hollis Odell, Jr.
(1986) "An Assessment of the Social Studies Achievement of Thirteen Year-Olds in the Rural Schools of North Mississippi." Dissertation: DAI (October), Vol. 47(1276-A)4.
South/ Mississippi/ Racial Differences/ Adolescents/ Rural Areas/ Educational Opportunities/ Schools

0419 Holland, Dorothy
Eisenhart, Margaret A. (1989) "On the Absence of Women's Gangs in Two Southern Universities." in Women in the South: An Anthropological Perspective. Holly F. Mathews. (ed.). Athens, GA: University of Georgia Press. pp. 27-46.
South/ Women of Color/ Education/ African American/ Gender Ideology/ European American/ Alliances/ Universities/ Female Male Relationships

0420 Hooker, Jane Howles
(1988) "A History of the Women's Sports Programs at Memphis State University." Dissertation: University of Mississippi.
Women of Color*/ Colleges/ South/ Tennessee/ Universities/ History/ 20th Century/ Education/ Sports/ Athletics/ Team Playing

0421 Lyson, Thomas A.
(1986) "Race and Sex Differences in Sex Role Attitudes of Southern College Students." Psychology of Women 10(December):4:pp. 421-429.
People of Color*/ College Students/ European Americans/ Education/ South/ Racial Factors/ Sex Differences/ Attitudes/ Sex Roles

0422 Mahoney, John S., Jr.
Merritt, Stephen R. (1990) "Educational Aspirations and Disappointments: A Comparison between Black and White High School Seniors in Virginia." Presented: North Central Sociological Association & Southern Sociological Association Annual Meetings, Louisville, KY.
People of Color/ Academic Aspirations/ African Americans/ Family Influences/ European Americans/ Fear of Failure/ South/ Virginia/ Educational Attainment/ Education/ Educationally Disadvantaged/ High Schools/ Comparative Studies

0423 Muir, Donal E.
(1990) "White Fraternity and Sorority Attitudes toward 'Blacks' on a Deep-South Campus." Presented: North Central Sociological Association and Southern Sociological Association Annual Meetings, Louisville, KY.
People of Color/Fraternities/ African Americans/ Sororities/ European Americans/ Race Relations/ South/ Racial Stereotypes/ Education/ Colleges/ Race Bias/ Social Organizations/ Racial Discrimination

0424 Muir, Donal E.

(1990) "A Comparison of 'Black' and 'White' Integration Attitudes on a Deep-South Campus: A Research Note." Sociological Spectrum 10:1:pp. 143-153.

South/ Alabama/ Integration/ People of Color/ Race Relations/ African Americans/ Attitudes/ Students/ European Americans/ Education/ Colleges/ Universities/ Prejudice/ Comparative Studies

0425 St. Clair, Stephen Issac

(1984) "The Play Day/Sports Day Movement in Selected Colleges in the South." Dissertation: University of North Carolina, Greensboro, NC.

Women of Color*/ Education/ South/ Sports/ Team Playing/ Colleges/ Universities

0426 Usher, Mildred Marie III

(1980) "A History of the Women's Intercollegiate Athletics at Florida State University from 1905-1972." Dissertation: University of Florida.

Women of Color*/ Universities/ South/ Florida/ Team Playing/ Sports/ Competitive Behavior/ Athletics/ Education/ History/ Colleges

0427 Wahl, Ana-Maria

Briggs, Carl M. (1990) "Private Schooling for Southern Blacks: The Determinants of an Alternative System of Education for a Disenfranchised Class." Presented: North Central Sociological Association and Southern Sociological Association Anuall Meetings, Louisville, KY.

African Americans/ Alternative Schools/ People of Color/ Institutions/ South/ Organizing/ Education/ Social Change/ Private Schools/ Educational Opportunities/ Educationally Disadvantaged

0428 Werum, Regina E.

(1990) "Black Women's Colleges: Racial and Gender Ideologies in the Early 20th Century South." Presented: North Central Sociological Association and Southern Sociological Association Annual Meetings, Louisville, KY.

African American/ Racial Factors/ Women of Color/ Educational Reform/ Colleges/ Educational Opportunities/ Higher Education/ Images of Women

*Women of Color**

0429 Andersen, Margaret L.

(1987) "Studying Women and Difference: A Critique of Social Science Method." Presented: Third International Congress on Women, Dublin, Ireland.

Women of Color*/ Social Science Research/ Research Methods/ Scholarship/ Curriculum Integration/ Education

0430 Atcherson, Esther

Muyumba, Francios N. (1988) "Today's Liberal Arts Challenge: Infusing the Experiences of Minorities and Women within Existing College Curricula." Journal of the Association for General and Liberal Studies 18(Fall):3:pp. 40-47.

Higher Education/ Educational Trends/ Curriculum Integration/ Minority Studies/ Women's Studies/ Women of Color*/ Academia

0431 Baca Zinn, Maxine

(1987) "Transforming the Sociology of the Family: New Directions for Teaching and Texts." Available: The Center for Research on Women, Clement Hall, Memphis State University, Memphis, TN 38152.

Women of Color*/ Curriculum Integration/ Social Issues/ Texts/ Family/ Traditional Family/ Education/ Teaching/ Educational Resources/ Educational Methods

0432 Baily, Susan McGee
(1989) The Hidden Discriminator: Sex and Race Bias in Educational Research. Newton, MA: Women's Educational Equity Act Publishing Center.
Women of Color*/ Research Bias/ Sex Discrimination/ Research/ Education/ Racial Discrimination/ Stereotypes/ Gender Bias/ Decision Making/ Race Bias/ Equity

0433 Brooks, Roy L.
(1987) "Anti-Minority Mindset in the Law School Personnel Process: Toward an Understanding of Racial Mindsets." Law and Inequality 5(May):1.
People of Color*/ Cultural Influences/ Social Problems/ Racial Discrimination/ Minority Experience/ Minority Groups/ Laws/ Higher Education/ Law School

0434 Brooks-Higginbotham, Evelyn
(1989) "The Problem of Race in Women's History." in Coming to Terms: Feminism, Theory, Politics. Elizabeth Weed (ed.). New York: Routledge Chapman & Hall.
Women of Color*/ Oppression/ Race, Class and Gender Studies/ Women's History/ Education/ Curriculum Integration

0435 Butler, Johnnella E.
Schmitz, Betty. (1989) "Different Voices: A Model Institute for Integrating Women of Color into Undergraduate American Literature and History Courses." Radical Teacher 37:pp. 4-9.
Women of Color*/ Course Objectives/ Education/ Literature/ Curriculum Integration/ Teaching/ Universities

0436 Butler, Johnnella E.
(1989) "Transforming the Curriculum: Teaching about Women of Color." in Multicultural Education: Issues and Perspectives. James A. Banks and M. Cherry (eds.). Boston: Allyn and Bacon, .
Women of Color*/ Curriculum Integration/ Ethnicity/ Identity/ Education

0437 Campbell, Patricia B.
(1989) The Hidden Discriminator: Sex and Race Bias in Educational Research. Groton, MA: Campbell-Kibler Associates.
Women of Color*/ Research Methods/ Education/ Research Bias/ Sex Discrimination/ Research Problems/ Racial Discrimination

0438 Carnegie, Mary Elizabeth
Smith, Gloria et al. (1981) Recruitment and Retention of Culturally Different Students in a College of Nursing. Oklahoma City, OK: University of Oklahoma Press.
Women of Color*/ Cultural Identity/ Health Care Providers/ Ethnic Diversity/ Recruitment/ Nursing Education/ Students

0439 Chow, Esther N.
(1988) "Studies of Women of Color in the U.S.: Critique and Some Suggestions." Women's Research Bulletin 11(June):pp. 6-8.
Women of Color*/ Women's Studies/ Critique/ Curriculum Integration/ Education

0440 Cole, Phyliss
Lambert, Deborah. (1989) "Gender and Race in American Literature: An Exploration of the Discipline and a Proposal for Two New Courses." Available: Wellesley College, Center for Research on Women, Wellesley , MA. Working Paper #115.
Women of Color*/ Literature/ Curriculum Integration/ Education/ Race, Class and Gender Studies

0441 Eliason, Nancy Carol

(1985) Equity Counseling for Community College Women. Newton, MA: Women's Educational Equity Act Publishing Center. pp. 306.
Counseling/ Women in Transition/ Career Counseling/ Divorce/ Separation/ Coping Strategies/ Widows/ Life Skills/ Higher Education/ Community Colleges/ Women of Color*

0442 Farkas, George

Grobe, Robert P. et al. (1989) "Cognitive and Noncognitive Determinants of School Achievement: Gender, Ethnicity, and Poverty in an Urban School District. Presented: American Sociological Association Annual Meeting, San Francisco, CA.
People of Color*/ Work Habits/ Educational Achievement/ Urban Areas/ Basic Skills/ Poverty/ Stratification/ Absenteeism

0443 Grant, Linda M.

(1988) "Minorities and Education at the Elementary Level: The Shifting Focus of Research." Elementary School Journal 89(May):pp. 482-489.
People of Color*/ Education/ Research/ Elementary Education/ Minority Groups

0444 Haignere, Lois

(1982) "The Admission of Women and Minorities to Medical School: Competition or Coalition?" Available: Center for Women in Government, State University of New York, Albany, NY 12222. Working Paper #8.
Women of Color*/ Competitive Behavior/ Higher Education/ Admissions/ Medical Education

0445 Hall, Elaine J.

Ferree, Myra Marx. (1989) "Images of Society: Gender and Race in Pictures in Sociology Textbooks." Presented: American Sociological Association Annual Meeting, San Francisco, CA.
Women of Color*/ Sexuality/ Textbooks/ Sociology/ Gender/ Photographs/ Racial Equality/ Images of Women/ Stereotypes/ Education/ Media Portrayal

0446 Hall, Eleanor R.

(1983) "Retention of Minority Students in College: Educational vs. Sociological Variables." Presented: Wisconsin Sociological Association, Waukesha, WI.
People of Color*/ Educational Equity/ Students/ Higher Education/ Educational Attainment/ Minority Groups/ Colleges

0447 Higginbotham, Elizabeth

(1989) "It's Time to Talk about Privilege: Developing an Inclusive Curriculum in Sociology." Presented: American Sociological Association Annual Meeting, San Francisco, CA.
Women of Color*/ Racial and Ethnic Differences/ Curriculum Integration/ Education/ Motivation/ Sociology/ Teaching/ Social Stratification/ Course Objectives

0448 Jenkins, Mercilee M.

(1990) "Teaching the New Majority: Guidelines for Cross-Cultural Communication between Students and Faculty." Feminist Teacher 5(Spring):1:pp. 8-14.
People of Color*/ Students/ Teachers/ Education/ Universities/ Communication/ Diversity/ Teacher Student Relationships

0449 Jones, Cleopatra C.

(1986) "Education for Aging in the Urban Community." Presented: Annual Conference of the Urban Affiars Association.
Women of Color*/ Older Adults/ Aging/ Gerontology/ Adult Education/ Urban Areas/ Community/ Life Cycle

0450 Klein, Susan S.
(1989) Handbook for Achieving Sex Equity through Education. Baltimore: Johns Hopkins University Press. pp. 544.
Women of Color*/ Feminism/ Sex Equity/ Sex Differences/ Sex Discrimination in Education/ Sex Role Development/ Sex Stereotypes/ Educational Policy/ Sex Discrimination in Employment/ Coping Strategies/ Economic Factors/ Curriculum Integration

0451 Lewis, Shelby
et al. (1989) "Achieving Sex Equity for Minority Women." in Handbook for Achieving Sex Equity through Education. Susan S. Klein (ed.). Baltimore: Johns Hopkins University Press. pp. 365-390.
Women of Color*/ Double Bind/ Educational Equity/ Bilingualism/ Diversity/ Oppression/ Exploitation/ Educational Attainment/ Images of Women/ Sex Discrimination/ Stereotypes/ Occupational Options

0452 Lyson, Thomas A.
(1986) "Race and Sex Differences in Sex Role Attitudes of Southern College Students." Psychology of Women 10(December):4:pp. 421-429.
People of Color*/ College Students/ European Americans/ Education/ South/ Racial Factors/ Sex Differences/ Attitudes/ Sex Roles

0453 Machung, Anne
(1989) "Talking Career, Thinking Job: Gender Differences in Career and Family Expectations of Berkeley Seniors." Feminist Studies 15(Spring):1:pp. 35-59
Women of Color*/ Economic Patterns/ Higher Education/ Marital Roles/ Career Aspirations/ Gender Differences/ Occupational Trends/ Family Roles/ Employment

0454 Mays, Vickie M.
(1988) "The Integration of Gender and Ethnicity in Clinical Training: The UCLA Model." in Teaching Psychology. P. Bronstein and K. Quina (eds.). Washington, DC: American Psychological Association.
Women of Color*/ Education/ Ethnicity/ Clinical Psychology/ Teaching/ Ethnic Groups/ Psychologists

0455 McIntosh, Peggy
(1987) "Understanding the Correspondence between White Privilege and Male Privilege through Women's Studies Work." Presented: National Women's Studies Association, Spellman College, Atlanta, GA.
Women of Color*/ Patriarchy/ European Americans/ Women's Studies/ Curriculum Integration/ Empowerment/ Education/ Race, Class and Gender Studies/ Socioeconomic Status/ Oppression/ Privilege/ Power

0456 Milner, E. Keith
(1982) "A Status Study of Faculty and Doctoral Students in Health, Physical Education, and Recreation by Ethnic Origin and Sex." Journal of Educational Equity and Leadership 2:2.
Women of Color*/ Racial Discrimination/ Affirmative Action/ Sexual Division of Labor/ Hiring Policy/ Educational Equity/ Employment/ Physical Education/ Sex Discrimination/ College Students/ Faculty/ Higher Education

0457 Minnich, Elizabeth
(1986) "Conceptual Errors across the Curriculum: Towards a Transformation of the Tradition." Available: Center for Research on Women, Memphis State University, Memphis, TN 38152.
Women of Color*/ Race, Class and Gender Studies/ Feminist Scholars/ Education/ Curriculum Integration/ Women's Studies/ Education Programs

0458 Morgen, Sandra
(1986) "To See Ourselves, To See Our Sisters: The Challenge of Re-envisioning Curriculum Change." Available: Center for Research on Women, Memphis State University, Memphis, TN 38152.
Women of Color*/ Feminist Scholars/ Education/ Women's Studies/ Curriculum Integration/ Race, Class and Gender Studies / Educational Programs

0459 National Council for Research on Women
(1990) "Mainstreaming Minority Women's Studies." Available: National Council for Research on Women, 47-49 East 65th St., New York, NY 10021.
Women of Color*/ Curriculum Integration/ Educational Diversity/ Research Grants

0460 Neitz, Mary Jo
(1989) "Sociology and Feminist Scholarship." The American Sociologist 20(Spring):1:pp. 3-13.
Scholarship/ Women of Color*/ Interdisciplinary Studies/ Higher Education/ Feminist Theory/ Black Feminism

0461 O'Malley, Susan
(1989) "The City University of New York: 1988-1989 Faculty Development Seminar on Balancing the Curriculum for Gender, Race, Ethnicity, and Class-A Syllabus: Marie Buncombe and Dorothy Helly, Leaders." Radical Teacher 37:pp. 14-26.
Women of Color*/ Syllabi/ Curriculum Integration/ Course Objectives/ Universities/ Education/ Teaching/ Class Stratification/ Race, Class and Gender Studies

0462 Organization of American Historians
(1988) Restoring Women to History: Teaching Packets for Integrating Women's History into Courses on Africa, Asia, Latin America, the Caribbean, and the Middle East. Available: Organization of American Historians, 112 N. Bryan St., Bloomington, IN 47403.
Women of Color*/ Curriculum Integration/ Women's History/ Race, Class and Gender Studies/ Crosscultural Studies/ Education/ Third World

0463 Parks, Beverly J.
(1985) Sourcebook of Measures of Women's Educational Equity. Newton, MA: Women's Educational Equity Act Publishing Center.
Women of Color*/ Gender/ Cultural Identity/ Evaluation Criteria/ Course Evaluation/ Educational Programs/ Race/ Curriculum Integration

0464 Pearlman, Deborah
(1985) A Common World: Course in Women's Studies for Rural and Urban Communities. Newton, MA: Women's Educational Equity Act Publishing Center.
Curriculum Integration/ Coping Strategies/ Women of Color*/ Survival Strategies/ Women Living in Poverty/ Life Skills/ Education/ Rural Areas/ Urban Areas

0465 Pearlman, Deborah
(1985) Breaking the Silence: Seven Courses in Women's Studies. Newton, MA: Women's Educational Equity Act Publishing Center. pp. 168.
Women of Color*/ Course Objectives/ Curriculum Integration/ Women's History/ Curriculum Guides/ Prisoners/ Women Living in Poverty/ Bibliographies/ Education

0466 Pearson, Carol S.
Shavlik, Donna L. et al (eds.). (1989) Educating the Majority: Women Challenge Tradition in Higher Education. New York: MacMillan Publishing. pp. 475.
Higher Education/ Women of Color*/ Racial and Ethnic Differences/ Social Stratification/ Ethnic Diversity/ Class Differences/ Racial Diversity

0467 Peterson, Barbara Bennett
(1988) "Women in History: Outstanding Women of Hawaii." Women's Studies Quarterly 16(Spring/Summer):1,2.
Women of Color*/ Leadership/ Pacific/ Hawaii/ Research Resources/ Curriculum Integration/ Education/ Women's History

0468 Peterson, Kenneth D.
Deyhle, Donna and William Watkins. (1988) "Evaluation that Accommodates Minority Teacher Contributions." Urban Education 23(July):2:pp. 133-149.
Women of Color*/ Education/ Discrimination/ Course Evaluation/ Educational Facilities/ Job Evaluation/ Teachers/ Diversity/ Employment Practices/ Promotions

0469 Rothenberg, Paula
(1988) "Integrating the Study of Race, Gender, and Class: Some Preliminary Observations." Feminist Teacher 3(Fall-Winter):3.
People of Color*/ Race, Class and Gender Studies/ Feminist Theory/ Lower Class/ Curriculum Integration/ Social Stratification/ Education/ Gender Bias

0470 Sabo, Donald F.
et al. (1989) Minorities in Sports: The Effects of Varsity Sports Participation on the Social, Educational, and Career Mobility of Minority Students. Available: Women's Sports Foundation, 342 Madison Ave., New York, NY. pp. 35.
Women of Color*/ Career Advancement/ Sports/ Career Mobility/ Socialization/ Employment/ Education/ High Schools/ Educational Attainment/ Athletes/ Athletics/ Policy/ Equal Opportunity

0471 Sanders, Beverly
(1985) Women in American History: A Series. Newton, MA: Women's Educational Equity Act Publishing Center.
Women of Color*/ Women's History/ Textbooks/ Curriculum Integration/ Minority Groups/ Education

0472 Simeone, Angela
(1988) Academic Women: Working Towards Equality. Westport, CT: Bergin & Garvey. pp. 176. ISBN 0897891147.
Women of Color*/ Career Opportunities/ Images of Women/ Academia/ Educational Equity/ Sex Discrimination/ Higher Education/ Academic Aspirations

0473 Smith, Barbara
(1980) "Racism and Women's Studies." Frontiers: Journal of Women's Studies 5:1.
Women of Color*/ Education/ Racial Discrimination/ Women's Studies/ Curriculum Integration

0474 Smith, Eleanor J.
(1985) "Before and after Brown: Education Context of Change." in Brown vs. Brown: An Assessment Thirty Years Later. Eleanor J. Smith (ed.). Institute, WV: West Virginia State College and the Mountain State Bar. pp. 130-145.
People of Color*/ Educational Equity/ Desegregation/ Educational Reform/ Segregation/ Educational Opportunities/ Social Change/ Education/ Schools/ Educational Experience

0475 Upchurch, Dawn M.
McCarthy, James. (1990) "Timing of a First Birth and High School Completion." American Sociological Review 55(April):2:pp. 224-234.
Women of Color*/ Birthing/ Childbirth/ Education/ High Schools/ Early Childbearing/ Secondary Education/ Graduation Ceremonies/ Teenage Pregnancy/ Teenage Mothers

0476 Vanfossen, Beth E.

Melnick, Merrill J. et al. (1989) "Social Mobility Opportunities through Sports Participation by Race and Gender." Presented: American Sociological Association Annual Meeting, San Francisco, CA.

Women of Color*/ Comparable Worth/ Social Mobility/ Socioeconomic Status/ Sports/ Educational Attainment/ Academic Performance/ Colleges/ Universities/ Athletes

0477 White, E. Frances

Woodhull-McNeal, Ann. (1986) "Challenging the Scientific Myths of Gender and Race." Radical America 20:4:pp. 25-32

Women of Color*/ Scientific Research/ Race, Class and Gender Studies/ Research Bias/ Education

0478 Wilkinson, Doris

King, Gary. (1987) "Conceptual and Methodological Issues in the Use of Race as a Variable: Policy Implications." Milbank Quarterly 65:pp. 56-71

People of Color*/ Race, Class and Gender Studies/ Methodologies/ Social Science Research/ Education

EMPLOYMENT

African American

0479 Angelou, Maya
(1990) Singin' and Swingin' and Gettin' Merry Like Christmas. New York: Bantam. pp. 192.
Women of Color/ Entertainment/ African American/ Performing Arts/ Autobiographies/ Singers/ Maya Angelou/ Dancers/ Writers/ Employment/ Authors/ Personal Narratives

0480 Archive of American Minority Cultures
(1987) "Working Lives." Distributor: National Federation of Community Broadcasters, 1314 14th St. NW, Washington, DC 20005. Phone: (202) 797-8911.
People of Color/ Culture/ African Americans/ Working Class/ Social History/ South/ Urban Areas/ Minority Studies/ Film

0481 Benjamin, Lois
Stewart, James B. (1989) "The Self-Concept of Black and White Women: The Influence upon its Formation of Welfare Dependency, Work Effort, Family Networks, and Illness." American Journal of Economics and Sociology 48.
African American/ Self Concept/ Comparative Studies/ Welfare/ Women of Color/ Economically Disadvantaged/ Lower Class/ Poverty/ Employment/ Health/ Self Esteem/ Family/ Families

0482 Bergmann, Barbara
(1980) "Occupational Segregation, Wages, and Profits when Employers Discriminate by Race or Sex." in The Economics of Women and Work. Alice H. Amsden (ed.). New York: St. Martin's Press.
Women of Color/ Employment/ African American/ Sex Discrimination/ European American/ Occupational Segregation/ Comparative Studies/ Racial Discrimination/ Wage Gap

0483 Bonacich, Edna
(1989) "Inequality in America: The Failure of the American System for People of Color." Sociological Spectrum 9:1:pp. 77-101.
People of Color/ Employment Patterns/ African Americans/ Discrimination/ Race, Class and Gender Studies/ Racial Inequality/ Capitalism/ Economic Opportunities

0484 Bose, Christine E.
(1984) "Employment of Black and Ethnic Women in 1990." Presented: American Sociological Association Annual Meeting, San Antonio, TX.
Women of Color/ African American/ Employment/ Women's History/ Labor History/ Comparative Studies

0485 Boyd, Robert L.
(1990) "Black and Asian Self-Employment in Large Metropolitan Areas: A Comparative Analysis." Social Problems 37(May):2:pp. 258-272.
People of Color/ Racial and Ethnic Differences/ Asian Americans/ Family Structure/ African Americans/ Minority Experience/ Comparative Studies/ Urban Areas/ Employment/ Business Ownership/ Self Employment/ Family Owned Business

0486 Brand, Dionne
(1987) "Black Women and Work." Fireweed: A Feminist Quarterly 25(Fall):pp. 28-51.
Women of Color/ Employment/ African American

0487 Brimmer, Andrew
(1985) "The Future of Blacks in the Public Sector." Black Enterprise 16:pp. 39-40.
African Americans/ People of Color/ Public Sector/ Future/ Employment/ Government

0488 Carby, Hazel V.
(1989) Reconstructing Womanhood: The Emergence of the Afro-American Woman Novelist. New York: Oxford University Press. pp. 240.
Women of Color/ African American/ Writers/ Literature/ Professional Occupations/ Novelists/ Employment

0489 Carnegie, Mary Elizabeth
(1984) "Black Nurses at the Front." American Journal of Nursing (October).
Women of Color/ Black Studies/ African American/ Health Care Providers/ War/ Military/ Nurses/ Employment

0490 Carnegie, Mary Elizabeth
(1986) The Path We Tread: Blacks in Nursing, 1854-1984. Philadelphia, PA: J.B. Lippincott.
Women of Color/ African American/ History/ Black Studies/ 19th Century/ Discrimination/ 20th Century/ Employment/ Health Care Providers/ Nurses

0491 Carnegie, Mary Elizabeth
(1988) "M. Elizabeth Carnegie." in Making Choices, Taking Chances: Nurse Leaders Tell Their Stories. Thelma M. Schorr and Anne Zimmerman. St. Louis, MO: C.V. Mosby.
Women of Color/ Employment/ African American/ Oral History/ Nurses/ Health Care Providers

0492 Carter, Gregg
(1987) "Local Police Force Size and the Severity of the 1960's Black Rioting." Journal of Conflict Resolution 31(December):4:pp. 601-614.
People of Color/ Police Officers/ African Americans/ Social Control/ Riots/ Protective Service Occupations/ Violence/ Civil Rights Movement/ Protest Actions/ Employment/ History

0493 Clogg, Clifford C.
Sullivan, Teresa A. (1983) "Labor Force Composition and Unemployment Trends, 1969-1980." Social Indicators Research 12:pp. 117-152.
Employment/ African Americans/ Economic Trends/ Labor Force/ Occupational Trends/ Unemployment Rates/ Social Trends/ Labor History/ People of Color

0494 Collins, Gail
Smith, Maxine. (1990) "Their Kingdom Come." New York Woman (March).
Women of Color/ Religion/ African American/ Clergy/ Employment/ Sexual Discrimination

0495 Creighton-Zollar, Ann
(1987) "The Relative Educational Attainment and Occupational Prestige of Black Spouses and Marital Satisfaction." Presented: Southern Sociological Society, Atlanta, GA.
People of Color/ Marital Relationships/ African Americans/ Marriage/ Educational Attainment/ Education/ Occupational Prestige/ Marital Satisfaction

0496 Crew, Spencer R.
(1987) Field to Factory: Afro-American Migration, 1915-1940. Lanham, MD: University of America Press, Inc. pp. 79.
People of Color/ African Americans/ South/ North/ History/ Migration/ Social Change/ Employment

0497 Dahl, Linda
(1989) Stormy Weather: The Music and Lives of a Century of Jazz-Women. New York: Limelight Editions. (Originally published 1984, Pantheon Books).
Women of Color/ African American/ Musicians/ Jazz/ Blues/ Double Discrimination/ Music History/ Occupational Segregation/ Employment

0498 Dungee, Angela B.
(1987) "The Economic Status of Black and White Women in the District of Columbia, 1980: A Class Analysis." Humanity and Sexuality 11(November):4:pp. 498-518.
Women of Color/ Social Class/ African American/ Socioeconomic Status/ European American/ Occupational Options/ Comparative Studies/ South/ Washington, DC

0499 Earley, Charity Adams
(1989) One Woman's Army: A Black Officer Remembers the WAC. College Station, TX: Texas A & M University Press.
Women of Color/ Military Personnel/ African American/ Military Rank/ Armed Forces/ Employment/ Women in the Military

0500 Evans, Mari
(1990) Black Women Writers, 1950-1980. New York: Anchor. pp. 544.
Women of Color/ Essays/ African American/ Literature/ Writers/ Racial Factors/ Authors/ Political Influence/ Life Histories/ History/ Social Change/ Personal Narratives/ Employment

0501 Fields, Jacqueline P.
(1981) "Factors Contributing to Nontraditional Career Choices of Black Female College Graduates." Wellesley College Center for Research on Women, Wellesley College, Wellesley, MA 02181. Working Paper #83.
Women of Color/ Career Opportunities/ African American/ Occupational Options/ Career Choice/ Opportunities/ Career Planning/ Employment

0502 Fink, Leon
Greenberg, Brian. (1989) Upheaval in the Quiet Zone. Champaign, IL: University of Illinois Press. pp. 320.
Women of Color/ Hospitals/ African American/ Employment/ Latina/ Chicana/ Oppression/ Labor Movement/ Unions

0503 First Run Features
(1981) "What Would You Do With A Nickel." Distributor: First Run Features, 153 Waverly Place, New York, NY 10014. Phone: (212) 243-0600.
Women of Color/ Employment/ African American/ Domestic Services/ Household Labor/ Organizing/ Political Activism/ Social Movements/Film

0504 Fosu, Agustin Kwasi
(1987) "Explaining Post-1964 Earnings Gains by Black Women: Race or Sex?" The Review of Black Political Economy 15(Winter):3:pp. 41-55.
Women of Color/ Wage Increases/ African American/ Employment/ Earned Income/ Pay Equity/ Wage Earning Women

0505 Fuke, Richard Paul
(1988) "Planters, Apprenticeship, and Forced Labor: The Black Family Under Pressure in Post-Emancipation Maryland." Agricultural History 62(Fall):pp. 57-74.
People of Color/ Maryland/ African Americans/ Apprenticeships/ Plantations/ Families/ Emancipation/ South Atlantic/ Tenant Farming/ Employment

0506 Gentry, Diane Koos
(1988) Enduring Women. College Station, TX: Texas A & M University Press. pp. 264.
Oral History/ Success/ Life Histories/ Midwives/ Midwifery/ Images of Women/ Household Labor/ African American/ Women of Color/ Women Working Outside the Home

0507 Green, Mildred Denby
(1983) Black Women Composers: A Genesis. Boston: G. K. Hall. pp. 171.
African American/ Margaret Bonds/ Women of Color/ Tulia Perry/ Composers/ Evelyn Pittmen/ Musicians/ Lena Milin/ Biographies/ Employment/ Florence Price/ Entertainment/ Music

0508 Grossman, James R.
(1989) Land of Hope: Chicago, Black Southerners, and the Great Migration. Chicago: University of Chicago Press. pp. 384.
Employment/ African Americans/ Social History/ Migration/ Migration Patterns/ Illinois/ North Central/ People of Color

0509 Ham, Debra Newman
(1986) "The Propaganda and the Truth: Black Women and World War II." Minerva: Quarterly Report on Women in the Military (Winter).
Women of Color/ Images of Women/ African American/ World War II/ Military Personnel/ Employment/ History

0510 Ham, Debra Newman
(1986) "Black Women Workers in the Twentieth Century." SAGE: A Scholarly Journal on Black Women (Spring).
Women of Color/ Workers/ African American/ 20th Century/ Employment

0511 Helmbold, Lois Rita
(1989) "Writing the History of Black and White Working Class Women." in Across Cultures: The Spectrum of Women's Lives. Emily K. Abel and Marjorie Pearson (eds.). New York: Gordon and Breach. pp. 37-48. (Also published in Women Studies Quarterly 17:1,2:pp. 37-48, 1989.)
Women of Color/ African American/ European American/ Working Class/ Women's History/ Household Labor/ Employment/ Wages/ Great Depression/ Urban Areas/ Life Styles

0512 Hine, Darlene Clark
(1989) Black Women in White: Racial Conflict and Cooperation in the Nursing Profession. Bloomington, IN: Indiana University Press. pp. 208.
Women of Color/ African American/ Nursing/ Discrimination/ Employment/ History/ 20th Century/ Female Intensive Occupations/ Health Care Providers/ Caregivers/ Careers/ Professional Status/ Race Relations

0513 Jackson, Muriel
(1985) "The Maids." Distributor: Women Make Movies, Inc., 225 Lafayette, Suite 212, New York, NY 10012. Phone: (212) 925-0606 or Fax: (212) 925-2052.
Women of Color/ Socialization/ African American/ Social Movements/ Employment/ Cultural Influences/ Domestic Services/ Household Workers/ Working Class/ Blue Collar Workers/ Film

0514 Jarrett, Robin L.
(1989) "Gender Roles among Low Income Black Women: The Intersection of Class and Race." Presented: American Sociological Association Annual Meeting, San Francisco, CA.
Women of Color/ Employment/ African American/ Poverty/ Race, Class and Gender Studies/ Gender Roles/ Income/ Low Pay

0515 Jenkins, Edward S.
(1989) "The Remarkable Dr. Jane Cooke Wright." Afro-Americans in New York: Life and History 13(July):pp. 57-64.
Women of Color/ African American/ Jane Cooke Wright/ Physicians/ Professional Occupations/ Health Care Providers

0516 Johnson, Robert J.
Herring, Cedric. (1989) "Labor Market Participation among Young Adults: An Event History Analysis." Youth and Society 21(September):1.
Women of Color/ Young Adults/ African American/ Employment/ Latina/ Disadvantaged/ Labor Force Participation/ Unemployment/ Racial and Ethnic Differences/ Poverty

0517 Kaplan, Elaine Bell
(1984) "I Want Some Kind of Respect: A Black Working Woman Talks about Issues of Equality in Her Life." Feminist Issues 4:1.
Women of Color/ Division of Labor/ African American/ Sex Discrimination/ Double Bind/ Racial Discrimination/ Employment/ Wage Earning Women/ Labor Force Segregation

0518 Kellough, J. Edward
(1990) "Federal Agencies and Affirmative Action for Blacks and Women." Social Science Quarterly 71(March):1:pp. 83-92.
People of Color/ Equal Employment Opportunity/ African Americans/ Evaluation/ Affirmative Action/ Federal Agencies/ Employment

0519 King, Sharon R.
(1988) "At the Crossroads." Black Enterprise (August).
Women of Color/ Employment/ African American/ Business Ownership

0520 Mabee, Carleton
(1990) "Sojourner Truth Fights Dependence on Government: Moves Freed Slaves Off Welfare in Washington to Jobs in Upstate New York." Afro-Americans in New York: Life and History 14(January):pp. 7-26.
Women of Color/ Welfare Programs/ African American/ Independence/ Sojourner Truth/ Employment/ Migration/ Slavery

0521 Makarah, O. Funmilayo
(1989) "Creating a Different Image: Portrait of Alile Sharon Larkin." Distributor: O. F. Makarah, 308 Westwood Plaza, #421, Los Angeles, CA 90024.
Women of Color/ Employment/ African American/ Film/ Alile Sharon Larkin/ Media Occupations/ Visual and Performing Arts

0522 Mann, Karla L.
(1988) "Black Women in Corporate America: Playing the Game to Move Up." SAGE: A Scholarly Journal on Black Women (Student Supplement):pp. 54-55.
African American/ Racial Discrimination/ Stereotypes/ Corporations/ Executives/ Male Dominated Employment/ Women of Color/ Upward Mobility/ Career Opportunities/ Employment/ Power Structure/ Sex Discrimination

0523 Marks, Carole C.
(1987) "The Bone and Sinew of the Race: Black Women, Domestic Work and Labor Migration." Presented: Delaware Women's Seminar, University of Delaware, Newark, Deleware.
Women of Color/ Employment/ African American/ Domestic Services/ Household Labor/ Migration

0524 Mullins, Elizabeth
Sites, Paul. (1990) "The Contribution of Black Women to Black Upper Class Maintenance." Sociological Spectrum 10:2:pp. 187-208.
Women of Color/ Elites/ African American/ Class/ Achievement/ Upper Class/ Economic Value of Women's Work

0525 Neckerman, Kathryn
et al. (1988) "Family Structure, Black Unemployment, and American Social Policy." in The Politics of Social Policy in the United States. Margaret Weir et al (ed.). Princeton, NJ: Princeton University Press.
Women of Color/ Socioeconomic Status/ African American/ Social Policy/ Female Headed Households/ Labor Market/ Unemployment/ Family Structure/ Family/ Families/ Welfare

0526 Nelson, Barbara J.
Ulrich, Rita. (1989) "Founding a New Organization: The Lakeland Black Women's Leadership Conference." Case Study in the Policy Process. Available: Hubert H. Humphrey Institute, University of Minnesota, Minneapolis, MN 55455.
Women of Color/ Social Organizations/ African American/ Organizing/ Leadership Skills/ Employment/ Working Conditions

0527 Nelson, Barbara J.
Kennedy, Lisa. (1989) "Leadership Transformation at the Lucy Prince Community Center." Case Study in the Policy Process. Available: Hubert H. Humphrey Institute, University of Minnesota, Minneapolis, MN 55455.
Women of Color/ Organizing/ African American/ Leadership Skills/ Race Relations/ Public Policy Programs/ Employment/ Empowerment/ Working Conditions/ Social Organizations

0528 Ortiz, Vilma
Fennelly, Katherine. (1988) "Early Childbearing and Employment among Young Mexican Origin, Black, and White Women." Social Science Quarterly 69(December):4:pp. 987-995.
Latina/ Mexican/ Employment Patterns/ African American/ Childcare/ European American/ Pregnancy/ Women of Color/ Low Income Families/ Teenage Pregnancy/ Comparative Studies/ Early Childbearing

0529 Palmer, Phyllis M.
(1989) Domesticity and Dirt: Housewives and Domestic Servants in the United States, 1920-1945. Philadelphia: Temple University Press. pp. 256.
Household Workers/ Women of Color/ African American/ Employment/ Domestic Services/ Socioeconomic Status/ Stratification

0530 Placksin, Sally
(1982) American Women in Jazz. New York: Wideview Books. pp. 332.
Musicians/ Music/ Jazz/ Blues/ African American/ Double Discrimination/ Women of Color/ Racial Discrimination/ Sex Discrimination/ Minority Experience/ Biographies/ Composers/ Employment

0531 Rachleff, Peter
(1989) Black Labor in Richmond, 1865-1890. Champaign, IL: University of Illinois

Press.
Labor Force Participation/ African Americans/ People of Color/ South/ Virginia/ Labor History/ 19th Century/ Minority Experience/ Employment

0532 **Ray, Elaine**
(1988) "Black Female Executives Speak Out On: The Concrete Ceiling." Executive Female (Nov/Dec).
Women of Color/ Sex Discrimination/ African American/ Upward Mobility/ Employment/ Glass Ceiling/ Double Bind/ Occupational Mobility/ Racial Discrimination/ Executives/ Professional Occupations

0533 **Richardson, Herbert N.**
(1987) "Black Workers and Their Responses to Work through the Songs They Sang." Dissertation: Rutgers University, New Brunswick, NJ. DAI Vol. 48, 1988.
People of Color/ Slave Songs/ African Americans/ Vocal Music/ Employment/ Exploitation/ Workers/ Oppression/ Resistance/ Songs

0534 **Riley, Glenda**
(1988) "American Daughters: Black Women in the West." Montana (The Magazine of Western History) 38(Spring):2:pp. 14-27.
Women of Color/ West/ African American/ Women's History/ Employment/ Migration

0535 **Rodgers, Harrell R., Jr.**
(1987) "Black Americans and the Feminization of Poverty - The Intervening Effects of Unemployment." Journal of Black Studies 17(June):4:pp. 402-417.
Women of Color/ African American/ Poverty/ Unemployment

0536 **Rolison, Garry L.**
(1986) The Political Economy of the Urban Underclass: Black Subemployment in Advanced Capitalism. Santa Cruz, CA: University of California.
Economy/ Political Economy/ People of Color/ Employment/ Lower Class/ Underclass/ African Americans/ Urban Areas/ Racial Discrimination/ Employment Opportunities

0537 **Rollins, Judith**
(1986) "Women and Work: Relations between Black and White Women in Historical Perspective." Presented: Women's Theological Center Lecture Series, Boston, MA.
Women of Color/ Relationships/ African American/ Work Experience/ Employment/ Women's History/ European American/ Workers

0538 **Smith, Eleanor J.**
(1987) "Blacks in Predominantly White Institutions: Strategies for Making it through the System as a Faculty Member." Presented: NAFEO Conference, Washington, DC.
People of Color/ Colleges/ African Americans/ Teachers/ Higher Education/ Promotions / Faculty/ Occupational Mobility/ Coping Strategies/ Universities/ Job Discrimination/ Upward Mobility

0539 **Smith, Eleanor J.**
(1984) "Black American Women and Work: Contemporary Strategies of Empowerment." Presented: Second International Interdisciplinary Congress on Women, University of Groningen, Netherland.
Women of Color/ Empowerment/ African American/ Employment/ Power

0540 **Smith, Shelley A.**
(1989) "Sources of Earnings Inequality in the Black and White Female Labor Forces." Presented: American Sociological Association Annual Meeting, San Francisco, CA.
Women of Color/ Economic Equity/ African American/ Comparable Worth/ Employment/ Earnings Gap/ Stratification/ Socioeconomic Status/ European American

0541 **Snapp, Mary Beth**
(1990) "Occupational Stress, Social Support, Depression and Job Dissatisfaction in a Sample of Black and White Professional-Managerial Women." Available: Center for Research on Women, Memphis State University, Memphis, TN 38152. Research paper #12.
African American/ Depression/ Networks/ European American/ Women of Color/ Employment/ Job Satisfaction/ Professional Occupations/ Psychological Stress/ Managerial Occupations/ Racial Factors/ Occupational Stress/ Class Differences

0542 **Sokoloff, Natalie J.**
Price, Barbara Raffel et al. (1989) "A Case Study of Black and White Police-Women in an Urban Police Department: Preliminary Findings." Presented: American Sociological Association Annual Meeting, San Francisco, CA.
Women of Color/ Child Care/ African American/ Employment/ Police Officers/ Racial Discrimination/ Urban Areas/ Gender Discrimination/ Male Dominated Employment/ Occupational Segregation/ European American

0543 **Sokoloff, Natalie J.**
(1988) "The Progress of Black and White Women in the Professions: How Far Have We Come? How Far Must We Go to Reach Equality with White Men?" Presented: American Sociological Association Meeting, Atlanta, GA.
Women of Color/ Employment/ African American/ Progress/ European American/ Comparative Studies/ Professional Occupations/ Equality/ Inequality

0544 **Steward, Sue**
Garratt, Sheryl. (1984) Signed, Sealed, Delivered: True Life Stories of Women in Pop. Boston: South End Press.
Women of Color/ Employment/ African American/ Popular Culture/ Biographies/ Images of Women/ Music/ Musicians/ Gender Roles/ Sex Discrimination

0545 **Tienda, Marta**
(1987) "Industrial Restructuring, Gender Segregation and Sex Differences in Earnings." American Sociological Review 52(April):2:pp. 195-210.
Women of Color/ Sex Segregation/ African American/ Industrial Relations/ Wage Discrimination/ Corporate Policy/ Pay Equity/ Race, Class and Gender Studies/ Male Dominated Occupations

0546 **Tucker, Susan**
(1988) "The Black Domestic in the South: Her Legacy as Mother and Mother Surrogate." in Southern Women. Caroline Matheny Dillman (ed.). Washington, DC: Hemisphere Publishing Corp.
African American/ Family/ Families/ Women of Color/ Relationships/ South/ Mammies/ Mothers/ Domestic Services/ Employment

0547 **Watkins, Mel**
(1986) "Sexism, Racism and Black Women Writers." New York Times Book Review 1(June):pp. 35-37.
Sex Discrimination/ Employment/ Racial Discrimination/ Double Bind/ African American/ Writers/ Authors/ Women of Color

0548 Wilkerson, Margaret B.
(1989) "The Racialization of Poverty." The Nation Special Issue: Scapegoating the Black Family 249:4:pp. 126-132.
People of Color/ Social Problems/ African Americans/ Racial Discrimination/ Job Discrimination/ Structural Discrimination/ Social Policy/ Discrimination/ Poverty/ Employment/ Public Policy/ Wage Discrimination

0549 Woll, Allen
(1989) Black Musical Theater: From Coontown to Dreamgirls. Baton Rouge, LA: Louisiana State University Press.
People of Color/ African Americans/ Performing Arts/ History/ 20th Century/ Theater/ Employment

0550 Woods, Fronza
(1981) "Fannie's Film." Distributor: Black Filmmaker Foundation, 80 Eighth Ave., Suite 1704, New York, NY 10011. Phone: (212) 924-1198.
Women of Color/ Job Evaluation/ African American/ Low Pay/ Employment/ Working Class/ Blue Collar Workers/ Job Satisfaction

0551 Wright, Roosevelt, Jr.
(1987) "Job Satisfaction among Black Female Managers: A Causal Approach." Human Relations 40(August):8:pp. 489-506.
Women of Color/ Occupations/ African American/ Professional Status/ Job Satisfaction/ Managers/ Employment/ Managerial Occupations

0552 Young, Kate Porter
(1989) "Still Sisters after All These Years: Economic Change and Female Solidarity in a Black Sea Island Community." Presented: Southern Anthropological Society Annual Meeting, Memphis, TN.
South/ South Carolina/ Communities/ Women of Color/ African American/ Kinship/ Sisterhood/ Economic Development/ Urbanization/ Industrialization/ Inequality/ Wage Labor/ Wage Gap/ Employment

Asian American

0553 Asian Women United of California
(1982) "4 Women." Distributor: Asian Women United of CA, University of California at Los Angeles Film & Television Archives, 1438 Melnitz Hall, Los Angeles, CA 90024. Phone: (213) 206-8013.
Women of Color/Professional Occupations/ Asian American/ Family Histories/ Employment/ History/ Family/ Culture/ Socialization

0554 Boyd, Robert L.
(1990) "Black and Asian Self-Employment in Large Metropolitan Areas: A Comparative Analysis." Social Problems 37(May):2:pp. 258-272.
People of Color/ Racial and Ethnic Differences/ Asian Americans/ Family Structure/ African Americans/ Minority Experience/ Comparative Studies/ Urban Areas/ Employment/ Business Ownership/ Self Employment/ Family Owned Business

0556 Chai, Alice Yun
(1989) "The State vs. Korean Immigrant Women Vendors in Hawaii: Multi-Level Transformations of Economic, Political, Domestic, and Cultural Oppressions." Presented: Georgetown University Bicentennial Conference on Women in America, Washington, DC.
Women of Color/ Employment/ Asian American/ Vendors/ Hawaii/ Pacific/ Korean/ Immigrants/ Oppression

0557 Chen, May Ying
(1988) "Chinese American Working Women: Out of the Kitchen." Without Ceremony 2:9:pp. 42-46.
Women of Color/ Women Working Outside the Home/ Asian American/ Employment/ Chinese American

0558 Chinen, Joyce N.
(1989) "Filipina Workers in Hawaii's Garment Industry." Presented: Sociologists for Women in Society Annual Meeting, San Francisco, CA.
Women of Color/ Garment Industry/ Asian American/ Hawaii/ Pacific/ Filipina/ Employment

0559 Chow, Esther N.
(1990) "Asian American Women at Work: Survival, Resistance, and Coping." Presented: American Sociological Association Annual Meeting, Washington, DC.
Women of Color/ Asian American/ Wage Earning Women/ Employment/ Women Working Outside the Home/ Coping Strategies/ Survival Strategies/ Resistance

0560 Ding, Loni
(1990) "On New Ground." Distributor: National Asian American Telecommunications Association, Cross Current Media, 346 Ninth St., 2nd Floor, San Francisco, CA 94103.
Women of Color/ Asian American/ Employment/ Family/ Families/ Wage Earning Women/ Balancing Work and Family Life/ Nontraditional Employment/ Industries/ Occupational Options

0561 Kim, Elaine H.
(1986) "Asian American Women at Work." in All American Women: Lines that Divide, Ties that Bind. Johnnetta B. Cole (ed.). New York: The Free Press. pp. 95-100.
Women of Color/ Asian American/ Sisterhood/ Double Bind/ Employment/ Networks/ Triple Jeopardy

0562 Min, Pyong-Gap
(1986) "Filipino and Korean Immigrants in Small Business." Amerasia Journal 13:1:pp. 53-71.
Asian Americans/ Small Business/ Immigrants/ Employment/ Filipinos/ People of Color/ Koreans

0563 Petras, Elizabeth McLean
(1990) "Third World Workers in the U.S.: Asian Women in the Philadelphia Apparel Industry." Presented: American Sociological Association Annual Meeting, Washington, DC.
Women of Color/ Asian/ Textile Industry/ Employment/ Wage Earning Women/ Third World/ Workers/ Laborers/ Factories

0564 Stier, Haya
(1989) "Immigrant Women Go to Work: Analysis of Immigrant Wives' Labor Supply." Presented: American Sociological Association Annual Meeting, San Francisco, CA.
Women of Color/ Immigrants/ Asian/ Socioeconomic Status/ Family Roles/ Gender Roles/ Wives Working Outside the Home/ Employment

0565 Women in the Director's Chair
(1985) "Christine Choy." Distributor: Video Data Bank, Art Institute of Chicago,

Columbus Dr. & Jackson St., Chicago, IL 60603. Phone: (312) 443-3793.
Women of Color/ Professional Occupations/ Asian American/ Employment/ Christine Choy/ Education/ Film Producers/ Film Directors

0566 Yap, Stacy G. H.
(1989) Gather Your Strength, Sisters: The Emerging Role of Chinese Women Community Workers. New York: AMS Press.
Chinese American/ Employment/ Social Workers/ Community Relations/ Occupational Roles/ Asian American/ Women of Color/ Community/ Consciousness Raising

0567 Yu, Stella
(1989) "Occupational Struggles of Chinese-American Women." Minority Voices 6(Fall):1:pp. 27-38.
Asian American/ Social History/ Chinese American/ White Collar Workers/ Education/ Working Class/ Family/ Mental Health/ Employment Opportunities/ Stress

Latina

0568 Borjas, G.
Tienda, M. (eds.). (1985) Hispanics in the U.S. Economy. New York: Academic Press.
Women of Color/ Earnings/ Latina/ Multiple Roles/ Federal Employment/ Fertility/ Economy/ Unemployment/ Wage Discrimination/ Employment

0569 Bose, Christine E.
(1986) "Puerto Rican Women in the U.S.: An Overview." in The Puerto Rican Woman. 2nd edition. Edna Acosta-Belen (ed.). New York: Praeger. pp. 147-169.
Latina/ Puerto Rican/ Women of Color/ Employment/ Gender/ Poverty

0570 Burgos, Nilsa M.
(1986) "Women, Work and Family in Puerto Rico." AFFILIA: Journal of Women and Social Work 1:3:pp. 17-28.
Women of Color/ Balancing Work and Family Life/ Latina/ Family/ Puerto Rican

0571 Burgos, Nilsa M.
(1988) "Work and Family: Women's Dilemma in Puerto Rico." Women's Issues, Poverty and Human Services Organizations. Available: The Ohio State University, College of Social Work, Columbus, OH. pp. 66-80.
Women of Color/ Balancing Work and Family Life/ Latina/ Puerto Rican/ Family/ Employment

0572 Chaney, Elsa M.
Castro, Mary Garcia. (1989) Muchachas No More: Household Workers in Latin America and the Caribbean. Philadelphia: Temple University Press. pp. 498.
Women of Color/ Latina/ Caribbean/ Domestic Services/ Immigrants/ Family Roles/ Gender Roles/ Household Workers/ Employment

0573 Fernandez-Kelly, Maria P.
Garcia, Anna M. (1985) "The Making of an Underground Economy: Hispanic Women, Home Work, and the Advanced Capitalist State." Urban Anthropology 14(Spring/Fall):1,3:pp. 59-90.
Women of Color/ Household Organization/ Latina/ Home Based Work/ Employment/ Cottage Industry/ Economic Opportunities/ Garment Industry/ Labor Market/ Labor Force Participation

0574 Fernandez-Kelly, Maria P.
Garcia, Anna M. (1986) "Advanced Technology, Regional Development and Hispanic Women's Employment in Southern California." in Micro-Electronics in Transition. Richard Gordon (ed.). San Francisco: Westview Press.
Women of Color/ Development/ Latina/ Electronics Industry/ Employment/ Informal Sector/ West/ California/ Economic Value of Women's Work

0575 Fernandez-Kelly, Maria P.
Garcia, Anna M. (1988) "Economic Restructuring in the United States: The Case of Hispanic Women in the Garment and Electronics Industries in Southern California." in Women and Work: An Annual Review. B. A. Gutek et al. (eds.). Newbury Park, CA: Sage Publications, Inc.
Women of Color/ Latina/ Economics/ Employment/ Garment Industry/ West/ California/ Electronics Industry/ Economic Value of Women's Work

0576 Fernandez-Kelly, Maria P.
Garcia, Anna M. (1989) "Hispanic Women and Homework: A Comparison of Mexicans in Los Angeles with Cubans in Miami." in Homework: Historical and Cotemporary Perspectives on Paid Labor at Home. Eileen Boris and Cynthia Daniels. (eds.). Champaign, IL: University of Illinois Press.
Women of Color/ West/ California/ Mexican/ South East/ Florida/ Cuban/ Latina/ Home Based Workers/ Employment/ Comparative Studies/ Home Life/ Industries

0577 Fernandez-Kelly, Maria P.
Garcia, Anna M. (1989) "Informalization at the Core: Hispanic Women, Homework and the State." in The Informal Economy: Comparative Studies in Advanced and Third World Societies. Alejandro Portes et al. (eds.). Baltimore: Johns Hopkins University Press.
Women of Color/ Regulations/ Latina/ Economic Value of Women's Work/ Employment/ Home Based Workers/ Economics/ Piecework Labor Policy/ Politics/ Informal Sector/ Comparative Studies/ Third World

0578 Fink, Leon
Greenberg, Brian. (1989) Upheaval in the Quiet Zone. Champaign, IL: University of Illinois Press. pp. 320.
Women of Color/ Hospitals/ African American/ Employment/ Latina/ Chicana/ Oppression/ Labor Movement/ Unions

0579 Fox, Geoffrey E.
(1979) Working Class Emigres from Cuba. San Francisco: R & E Research Associates.
People of Color/ Working Class/ Latinos/ Chicanos/ Immigration/ Employment

0580 Hewitt, Nancy A.
(1987) "Cuban Women and Work: Tampa, Florida, 1888-1901." Presented: American Historical Association, Washington, DC.
Women of Color/ Employment/ South/ Florida/ Latina/ Cuban/ History/ 19th Century/ Immigrants

0581 Hewitt, Nancy A.
(1987) "Charity or Mutual Aid?: Two Perpectives on Latin Women's Philanthropy." in Working Papers of the Center for the Study of Philanthropy. Available: Graduate Center, City University of New York.
Women of Color/ Support Systems/ Latina/ Networks/ Charitable Work/ Charity/ Philanthropy/ Volunteer Work/ Volunteers

0582 Institute for Puerto Rican Policy

(1985) Selected Data on New York City and State Government Employment of Puerto Ricans and Other Latinos. New York: Institute for Puerto Rican Policy.
Women of Color/ Labor Force/ Northeast/ New York/ Data Sets/ Government Workers/ Public Policy/ Employment/ Puerto Rican/ Latina

0583 Johnson, Robert J.

Herring, Cedric. (1989) "Labor Market Participation among Young Adults: An Event History Analysis." Youth and Society 21(September):1.
Women of Color/ Young Adults/ African American/ Employment/ Latina/ Disadvantaged/ Labor Force Participation/ Unemployment/ Racial and Ethnic Differences/ Poverty

0584 Kingsolver, Barbara

(1989) Holding the Line: Women in the Great Arizona Mine Strike of 1983. Ithaca, NY: ILR Press. pp. 213.
Women of Color/ Labor Movements/ Chicana/ Latina/ Arizona/ Southwest/ Employment/ Labor Unions/ Strike/ Activism

0585 Lamphere, Louise

(1987) From Working Daughters to Working Mothers: Immigrant Women in a New England Industrial Community. Ithaca, NY: Cornell University Press. pp. 390.
Women of Color/ Gender/ Socioeconomic Class/ Ethnicity/ Urban Areas/ Industry/ Immigration/ Women's Work/ Colombian/ Latina/ Extended Family/ Children/ Women Working Outside the Home

0586 Maril, Robert Lee

(1989) The Poorest of Americans: The Mexican-Americans of the Lower Rio Grande Valley of Texas. Notre Dame, IN: University of Notre Dame Press. pp. 173.
Women of Color/ Factories/ Chicana/ Latina/ Employment/ Southwest/ Texas/ Poverty/ Maquiladoras/ Politics/ Economics/ Colonialism

0587 Marin, Patricia

Rodriguez, Cecilia. (1983) "Working on Racism: Centro Obrero." in Of Common Cloth: Women in the Global Textile Industry. Wendy Chapkis and Cynthia Enloe (eds.). Washington, DC: Transnational Institute.
Women of Color/ Employment/ Southwest/ Texas/ Sex Discrimination/ Latina/ Chicana/ Racial Discrimination/ Unions/ Textile Workers/ Strikes/ Factories

0588 McCullough, Barbara

(1980) "Convergence: Interview with Sylvia Morales." Distributor: University of California at Los Angeles Film and Television Archives, 1438 Melnitz Hall, Los Angeles, CA 90024. Phone: (213) 206-8013.
Women of Color/ Socialization/ Latina/ Roles/ Sylvia Morales/ Employment/ Film Producers

0589 Melville, Margarita B.

(1988) Mexicanas at Work: In the United States. Houston, TX: University of Houston. pp. 83. ISBN 093970904x.
Latina/ Women of Color/ Economic Value of Women's Work/ Socialization/ Labor Force Participation/ Stereotypes/ Pay Equity/ Employment/ Wages/ Discrimination/ Career Aspirations

0590 Ortiz, Vilma

Fennelly, Katherine. (1988) "Early Childbearing and Employment among Young Mexican Origin, Black, and White Women." Social Science Quarterly 69(December):4:pp. 987-995.
Latina/ Mexican/ Employment Patterns/ African American/ Childcare/ European American/ Pregnancy/ Women of Color/ Low Income Families/ Teenage Pregnancy/ Comparative Studies/ Early Childbearing

0591 Romero, Gloria J.
Castro, Felipe G. et al. (1988) "Latinas without Work: Family, Occupational, and Economic Stress Following Unemployment." Psychology of Women Quarterly 12(September):3:pp. 281-229.
Women of Color/ Unemployment/ Latina/ Occupational Stress/ Economic Factors/ Domestic Roles/ Family Income/ Family Economics

0592 Romero, Mary
(1988) "Day Work in the Suburbs: The Work Experience of Chicana Private Housekeepers." in The Worth of Women's Work: A Qualitative Synthesis. Anne Statham et al. (eds.). Albany, NY State University of New York Press. pp. 77-92.
Women of Color/ Latina/ Chicana/ Domestic Services/ Immigrants/ Economic Value of Women's Work/ Female Intensive Occupations/ Employment/ Household Workers

0593 Romero, Mary
(1988) "Chicanas Modernize Domestic Service." Qualitative Sociology 11:4:pp. 319-334.
Women of Color/ Household Labor/ Latina/ Chicana/ Employment/ Domestic Services

0594 Ruiz, Vicki L.
(1987) Cannery Women, Cannery Lives, Mexican Women, Unionization, and the California Food Processing Industry, 1939-1950. Albuquerque, NM: University of New Mexico Press.
Women of Color/ Unionization/ Latina/ Chicana/ Pacific/ California/ Employment/ Food Processing Industry/ West/ History/ 1940-1949/ Labor History/ Factory Workers

0595 Ruiz, Vicki L.
(1988) "And Miles to Go: Mexican Women and Work, 1930-1985." in Western Women: Their Land, Their Lives. Lillian Schlissel and Janice Monk. (eds.). Albuquerque, NM: University of New Mexico Press.
Women of Color/ Labor History/ Latina/ Chicana/ Employment/ History/ 20th Century

0596 Segura, Denise A.
(1986) "Chicana and Mexican Immigrant Women at Work: The Impact of Class, Race, and Gender on Occupational Mobility." Gender & Society. 3(March):1: pp. 37-52.
Women of Color/ Assimilation Patterns/Latina/ Chicana/ Acculturation/ Mexican/ Immigration/ Race, Class and Gender Studies/ Occupational Mobility/ Employment Patterns/ Career Aspirations

0597 Valdez, Armando
Camarillo, Albert and Thomas Almaguer. (1983) The State of Chicano Research in Family, Labor and Migration Studies. Stanford, CA: Stanford University Center for Chicano Research.
People of Color/ Migration/ Chicanos/ Latinos/ Research/ Family/ Labor Force Participation/ Employment

0598 Weigle, Marta
(1990) Women of New Mexico: Depression Era Images. Santa Fe, NM: Ancient City Press.
Women of Color/ Employment/ Native American/ The Great Depression/ Latina/ Chicana/ Poverty/ History/ 1930-1939/ Family/ Families/ Photographs/ Women Working Outside the Home/ Family Life/ Women Living in Poverty

0599 Wilcox, Meg
(1988) "Puerto Rican Women Fight Health Hazards." Sojourner 13(August):12:pp.

19-20.
Employment/ Occupational Health/ Puerto Rican/ Latina/ Organizations/ Health Hazards/ Environment/ Industries/ Women of Color/ Blue Collar Workers/ Factories

0600 Zambrana, Ruth E.
Hurst, Marsha. (1984) "The Interactive Effect of Health Status on Work Patterns among Urban Puerto Rican Women." International Journal of Health Services 14:2:pp. 265-277.
Women of Color/ Health/ Employment/ Puerto Rican/ Latina/ Children/ Urban Areas

0601 Zambrana, Ruth E.
(1987) "Latinas in the U.S." in The American Woman, 1987-1988. Sarah E. Rix. (ed.). New York: W.W. Norton. pp. 262-266.
Women of Color/ Occupational Status/ Latina/ Race, Class and Gender Studies/ Academic Achievement/ Socioeconomic Status/ Wage Discrimination/ Female Headed Households/ Single Parent Families

0602 Zambrana, Ruth E.
Erith, Sandra. (1988) "Mexican-American Professional Women: Role Stratification Differences in Single and Multiple Role Application." Special Issue of the Journal of Social Behavior and Personality 3:4:pp. 347-361.
Women of Color/ Socioeconomic Status/ Chicana/ Latina/ Cultural Influences/ Balancing Work and Family Life/ Domestic Roles/ Professional Roles/ Career Stratification/ Occupational Roles/ Comparative Studies/ Role Conflict/ Life Styles

0603 Zavella, Patricia
(1987) "The Impact of 'Sun Belt Industrialization' on Chicanas." in The Women's West. Susan Armitage and Elizabeth Jameson. (eds.). Norman, OK: University of Oklahoma Press. pp. 291-309.
Women of Color/ Balancing Work and Family Life/ Chicana/ Latina/ Cultural Identity/ Women's Work/ Southwest/ History/ 1970-1979/ Employment/ Wages/ Economic Trends

0604 Zavella, Patricia
(1988) "The Politics of Race and Gender: Organizing Chicana Cannery Workers in Northern California." in Women and the Politics of Empowerment: Perspectives from the Workplace and the Community. Ann Bookman and Sandra Morgen. (eds.). Philadelphia: Temple University Press.
Women of Color/ Workplace Organizing/ Chicana/ Latina/ Labor Unions/ California/ Pacific/ Working Conditions/ Race, Class and Gender Studies/ Politics/ Factory Workers/ Minority Employment/ Women and Work

Native American

0605 Albers, Patricia
(1983) "Sioux Women in Transition: A Study of Their Changing Status in Domestic and Capitalist Sectors of Production." in The Hidden Half: Studies of Plains Indian Women. P. Albers and B. Medicine. (eds.). Lanham, MD: University Press of America. pp. 175-234
Women of Color/ History/ Native American/ Anthropology/ Economic Status/ Household Labor/ Sioux/ Social History/ Employment/ Social Change/ Kinship/ Economic Development/ Families

0606 Berryhill, Peggy
(1988) "Weaving Their Dreams: Navajo Women Unite Tradition and Economy."

Isis: Women in Action 3:pp. 7-9.
Women of Color/ Tribal Customs/ Native American/ Employment/ Southwest/ Economy/ Navajo/ Tradition/ Craft Arts/ Economic Value of Women's Work/ Culture/ Cultural Heritage

0607 Cornell, Stephen
(1989) "Land, Labor and Group Formation: Blacks and Indians in the United States." Presented: American Sociological Association Annual Meeting, San Francisco, CA.
People of Color/ Employment/ African Americans/ Organizing/ Native Americans/ Labor/ Group Process/ Land Rights

0608 Gonzales, E. B.
(1982) "An Ethnohistorical Analysis of Micmac Male and Female Economic Roles." Ethnohistory 29:1-4:pp. 117-129.
People of Color/ Native Americans/ Economic Value of Women's Work/ Roles/ Economics/ History/ Micmac/ Social History/ Women of Color

0609 Johnston, Nancy
Creisler, Derek. (1987) "Princess of the Pow-Wow." Distributor: Running Colors Productions, P.O. Box 31821, Seattle, WA 98103.
Women of Color/ Volunteer Occupations/ Native American/ Social Services/ Ella Aquino/ Voluntary Organizations/ Community Organizers/ Community Responsibility/ Film

0610 LaFromboise, Teresa
(1989) Circles of Women: Professional Skills Training with American Indian Women. Stanford, CA: Stanford University Press. pp. 241.
Women of Color/ Career Planning/ Native American/ Financial Management/ Stress/ Financial Planning/ Coping Strategies/ Employment/ Extended Families/ Self Esteem/ Acculturation/ Education

0611 Mahan, James M.
(1982) "Native Americans as Teacher Trainers: Anatomy and Outcomes of a Cultural Immersion Project." Journal of Educational Equity and Leadership 2:2.
Women of Color/ Education/ Cultural Influences/ Employment/ Culture/ Job Training/ Hopi/ Navajo/ Educational Reform/ Native American/ Education Occupations/ Teaching/ Teachers

0612 Peckham, Stewart
(1987) "The Beginnings of a Tradition: Pottery Making Comes to the Southwest." El Palacio 93(Summer/Fall):pp. 20-23.
Women of Color/ History/ Native American/ Culture/ Art/ Southwest/ Craft Arts/ Employment/ Pottery

0613 Schneider, Mary Jane
(1983) "Women's Work: An Examination of Women's Roles in Plains Indian Arts and Crafts." in The Hidden Half: Studies of Plains Indian Women. P. Albers and B. Medicine. (eds.). Lanham, MD: University Press of America. pp. 101-122.
Women of Color/ Craft Arts/ Native American/ Status/ Gender Roles/ Economic Status of Women's Work

0614 Smith, Annick
(1989) "The Two Frontiers of Mary Ronan." Montana (The Journal of Western History) 39(Winter):1:pp. 28-33.
Women of Color/ Biographies/ Native American/ History/ Interracial Relations/ 19th Century/ Government Workers/ Montana/ Mountain/ Pioneers/ Mary Ronan

0615 Trennert, Robert A.

(1988) "Victorian Morality and the Supervision of Indian Women Working in Phoenix, 1906-1930." Journal of Social History 22(Fall):pp. 113-128.

Women of Color/ Public Opinion/ Victorian/ Native American/ Wage Earning Women/ Women's History/ Social History/ Mountain/ Arizona/ Employment/ Morality/ Supervisor Attitudes

0616 Van Kirk, Sylvia

(1980) Many Tender Ties: Women in Fur-Trade Society, 1670-1870. Norman, OK: University of Oklahoma Press.

Native American/ Women of Color/ Trades/ Women's History/ 18th Century/ Minority Experience/ Images of Women/ Male Dominated Employment/ History

0617 Van Kirk, Sylvia

(1984) "The Role of Native Women in the Fur Trade Society of Western Canada." Frontiers: Journal of Women's Studies 7:3.

Women of Color/ Employment/ Native American/ Barter/ Gender Roles/ Interracial Marriages/ Canada

Southern

0618 Anglin, Mary

(1988) "Wage Work, Domestic Labor, and Gender: Women in the Mica Industry in Western North Carolina." NWSA Journal 1:1:pp. 165-166.

South/ North Carolina/ Balancing Work and Family Life/ Wage Labor/ Employment/ Women's History/ Household Labor/ Women Working Outside the Home/ Extractive Industry

0619 Bates, Eric

(1989) "Southern Refugees." Southern Exposure 17(Summer):2:pp. 53-56.

Refugees/ African Americans/ People of Color/ Racial Discrimination/ Employment/ Families/ South

0620 Brown, James S.

(1988) Beech Creek: A Study of a Kentucky Mountain Neighborhood. Berea, KY: College Press. pp. 297.

South/ Rural Areas/ History/ 19th Century/ Kentucky/ Appalachia/ Social Interaction/ Socioeconomic Status/ Social Order/ Kinship/ Networks/ Inequality/ Family/ Families/ Social History/ Employment/ Communities

0621 Bryant, Jan K.

(1988) "Southern Women and Textile Workers: Job Satisfaction." in Southern Women. Caroline Matheny Dillman. (ed.). Washington, DC: Hemisphere Publishing Corp.

South/ Work/ Textile Workers/ Employment/ Work Experience/ Working Conditions/ Job Satisfaction/ Factory Workers/ Women of Color*/ Blue Collar Workers

0622 Campbell, Karen E.

(1988) "Gender Differences in Job Related Networks." Work and Occupations 15(May):2:pp. 179-200.

Images of Women/ Male Dominated Employment/ South/ Old Boy Networks/ Occupational Equality/ Old Girl Networks/ Geographic Mobility/ White Collar Occupations

0623 Ciaramitaro, Bridget

Hyland, Stanley et al. (1988) "The Development of Underdevelopment in the Mid-South: Big Farmers and the Persistance of Rural Poverty." Humanity and Society 12:pp. 347-365.

Underdevelopment/ Female Headed Households/ Poverty/ Agribusiness/ South/ Development/ Rural Areas/ Employment/ African Americans/ People of Color

0624 Cook, Paul W., Jr.

Collins, Thomas W. (1989) "The Plant Is Closed: What Now, Women? A Case Study of the Memphis Furniture Manufacturing Company." in Women in the South: Anthropological Perspective. Holly F. Mathews (ed.). Athens, GA: University of Georgia Press. pp. 71-82.

Women of Color/ Powerlessness/ African American/ Unemployment/ South/ Tennessee/ Furniture Industry/ Unions/ Occupational Segregation/ Economic Structure

0625 Deseran, Forrest A.

(1989) "Part-time Farming and Commuting: Determinants of Distance to Off-Farm Work for Louisiana Farm Couples." Research in Rural Sociology and Development 4.

South/ Louisiana/ Rural Areas/ Dual Career Couples/ Farming/ Employment/ Commuting/ Rural Development

0626 Ellis, Mary Carolyn

Hawks, Joanne V. (1987) "Creating a Different Pattern: Florida's Women Legislators, 1928-1986." Florida Historical Quarterly 66(July):pp. 68-83.

Legislators/ Florida/ South/ South Atlantic/ Social Stratification/ Gender Ideology/ Gender Differences/ Elected Officials/ Employment

0627 Enloe, Cynthia

(1983) "Racism at Work." in Of Common Cloth: Women in the Global Textile Industry. Wendy Chapkis and Cynthia Enloe (eds.). Washington, D.C.: Transnational Institute.

Women of Color*/ Racial Discrimination/ Textile Workers/ Textile Industry/ Employment/ Northeast/ Southwest

0628 Gaventa, John

et al. (1989) Communities in Economic Development. Philadelphia: Temple University Press. pp. 360.

South/ Families/ Mining Industry/ Economic Development/ Office Work/ Employment

0629 Glass, Becky L.

(1988) "A Rational Choice Model of Wives' Employment Decisions." Sociological Spectrum 8:1:pp. 35-48.

Southern/ Images of Women/ Employment Opportunities/ Marital Status/ Occupational Mobility/ Wives Working Outside the Home/ Labor Force Participation/ Employment

0630 Glass, Becky L.

(1988) "Workplace Harassment and the Victimization of Women." Women's Studies International Forum 11:1:pp. 55-67.

Women of Color*/ Occupational Hazards/ Southern/ Victimization/ Employment Patterns/ Sexual Harassment/ Female Male Relationships/ Sex Roles

0631 Hewitt, Nancy A.

(1988) "Southern Women and Work: New Perspectives." Presented: Southern Women's Cultural History from the Civil War to Civil Rights, Consortium of

Southern Humanities Councils Conference, Washington, DC.
Women of Color*/ Textile Workers/ South/ Domestic Services/ Employment/ Factory Workers/ Wage Earning Women

0632 Honey, Michael K.
(1987) "Labor and Civil Rights in the South: The Industrial Labor Movement and Black Workers in Memphis, 1929-1945." Dissertation: Northern Illinois University. DAI (April/May), Vol. 49, 1989.
People of Color/ Labor Movement/ African Americans/ Employment/ South/ Tennessee/ Labor History/ Civil Rights Movement/ Social Movements

0633 Lamphere, Louise
Grenier, G. J. (1988) "Women, Unions, and 'Participative Management': Organizing in the Sunbelt." in Women and the Politics of Empowerment. Ann Bookman and Sandra Morgen (eds.). Philadelphia: Temple University Press. pp. 227-256.
Women of Color/ Ethnicity/ Latina/ Unions/ Employment/ Management/ Practices/ Networks/ Gender/ Labor Activism/ South/ Empowerment

0634 Lohrenz, Mary
(1988) "Two Lives Intertwined on a Tennessee Plantation: Textile Production as Recorded in the Diary of Narcissa L. Erwin Black." Southern Quarterly 27(Fall):pp. 73-94.
Plantations/ Life Histories/ Diaries/ Narcissa L. Erwin Black/ Tennessee/ South/ Textile Making/ Employment/ Textile Industry

0635 Long, Ann
(1989) "Mississippi Still Burning." Southern Exposure 17(Spring):1:pp. 8-11.
South/ Mississippi/ Employment Trends/ Social Policy/ Poverty/ Labor Unions/ Employment

0636 Maggard, Sally Ward
(1989) "Eastern Kentucky Women on Strike: A Study of Gender, Class, and Political Action in the 1970's." Dissertation: University of Kentucky (Order No. DA8914910).
South/ Kentucky/ Labor Disputes/ Employment/ Labor History/ 19th Century/ Factory Workers/ Politics/ Unions/ Political Activism/ Women's History/ Class/ Strikes/ Social Movements/ Gender Studies

0637 Maharidge, Dale
Williamson, Michael. (1989) And Their Children After Them. New York: Pantheon. pp. 262.
South/ Agriculture/ People of Color/ History/ African Americans/ Family/ Families/ European Americans/ Socioeconomic Status/ Poverty/ Racial and Ethnic Differences/ Rural Areas/ Farm Workers

0638 Mann, Susan A.
(1989) "Slavery, Sharecropping, and Sexual Inequality." SIGNS: Journal of Women In Culture and Society 14:4:pp. 774-798.
Women's History/ South/ Race, Class and Gender Studies/ Agriculture/ Racial and Ethnic Differences/ Class Differences/ Gender Differences/ Slavery/ Ethnicity/ Tenant Farming/ Labor/ Employment

0639 Metcalf-Whittaker, Marilyn
(1989) "Women in 'Men's Roles': A Case Study of Female Pastors in the Southern Baptist Convention." Presented: American Sociological Association Annual Meeting, San Francisco, CA.
Southern/ Affirmative Action/ Male Dominated Professions/ Baptists/ Clergywomen/ Ministers/ Religion/ Preaching/ Gender Roles/ Employment

0640 Middleton-Keirn, Susan
Howsden-Eller, J. (1989) "Reconstructing Femininity: The Woman Professional." in Women in the South: An Anthropological Perspective. Holly F. Mathews (ed.). Athens, GA University of Georgia Pres. pp. 57-70.
South/ Femininity/ Professional Status/ Gender Roles/ Employment

0641 Morrissey, Elizabeth S.
(1989) "Determinants of Work Status among Heads of Poor Families in the South." Southern Rural Sociology 6:pp. 64-79.
Southern/ Rural Areas/ Poverty/ Urban Areas/ Heads of Household/ Unemployment/ Families/ Family/ Living Conditions/ Employment/ Welfare

0642 Pfeffer, Max J.
Gilbert, Jess. (1989) "Gender and Class Dimensions of Off-Farm Employment: Response to Farm Crisis in the Cornbelt and Mississippi Delta." Presented: American Sociological Association Annual Meeting, San Francisco, CA.
Southern/ Employment/ Gender Differences/ Agrarian/ Class Differences/ Rural Areas/ Farms/ Wage Earning Women/ Alternative Employment/ Mississippi

0643 Poesch, Jessie
(1984) Newcomb Pottery: An Enterprise for Southern Women, 1895-1940. Exton, PA: Schiffer Publishing, Ltd.
Pottery/ South/ Enterprises/ Employment/ Business/ Labor History/ Organization/ Craft Arts/ Women of Color*

0644 Rachleff, Peter
(1989) Black Labor in Richmond, 1865-1890. Champaign, IL: University of Illinois Press.
Labor Force Participation/ African Americans/ People of Color/ South/ Virginia/ Labor History/ 19th Century/ Minority Experience/ Employment

0645 Roydhouse, Marion W.
(1987) "Big Enough to Tell Weeds from the Beans: The Impact of Industry on the Twentieth Century South." in The South is Another Land. B. Clayton and J. A. Salmond. (eds). New York: Greenwood Press. pp. 85-106.
South/ Employment/ Industry/ Industrialization/ Labor History/ Women's History

0646 Schulman, Michael D.
Reif, Linda et al. (1987) "Supporting Unions: The Case of Southern Textile Workers." Presented: American Sociological Association Annual Meeting, Chicago, IL.
South/ Textile Workers/ Unions/ Employment Strategies/ Blue Collar Workers/ Employment

0647 Schulman, Michael D.
Reif, Linda et al. (1987) "Agrarian Origins, Industrial Experience, and Militancy: An Analysis of Southern Textile Workers." Presented: Rural Sociological Society Annual Meeting, Madison, WI.
South/ Textile Workers/ Employment / Industrial Relations/ Textile Industry/ Work Experience/ Militance

0648 Schulman, Michael D.
Armstrong, Paula S. (1988) "The Farm Crisis: An Analysis of Stress among North Carolina Farm Operators." Presented: Rural Sociological Society Annual Meeting, Athens, GA.
South/ North Carolina/ Social Issues/ Stress/ Farm Workers/ Farming/ Mental Health/ Finances/ Financial Resources

0649 Schulman, Michael D.
Reif, Linda and Michael Belyea. (1988) "The Social Bases of Union Support: An Analysis of Southern Textile Workers." Journal of Political and Military Sociology 16(Spring):pp. 57-75.
South/ Unions/ Textile Industry/ Support Systems/ Social Issues/ Employment

0650 Stamper, Anita
(1988) "One Woman's Work: Clothing the Family in Nineteenth-Century Mississippi." Southern Quarterly 27(Fall):pp. 95-104.
Gender Roles/ Sex Discrimination/ Household Division of Labor/ Gender Bias/ South/ Mississippi/ Inequality/ Sex Roles/ Family Roles/ Clothing/ Seamstress/ Female Intensive Occupations

0651 Timberlake, Michael F.
(1989) "The Development of Underdevelopment and the Persistence of Poverty in the Rural South: The Case of Magnolia County." Presented: Southern Anthropological Society Meeting, Memphis, TN.
South/ Economic Development/ Low Wage/ Women Working Outside the Home/ Poverty/ Racial Discrimination/ Structural Discrimination/ Rural Areas/ Employment/ Underdevelopment/ Mississippi

0652 Timberlake, Michael F.
Dill, Bonnie Thornton et al. (1989) "Race and Poverty in the Rural South: Racial Composition and Economic Development." Presented: American Sociological Association Annual Meeting, San Francisco, CA.
People of Color*/ Employment/ South/ Rural Areas/ Poverty/ Economic Development/ Racial Factors

0653 Tucker, Susan
(1988) "The Black Domestic in the South: Her Legacy as Mother and Mother Surrogate." in Southern Women. Caroline Matheny Dillman (ed.). Washington, DC: Hemisphere Publishing Corp.
African American/ Family/ Families/ Women of Color/ Relationships/ South/ Mammies/ Mothers/ Domestic Services/ Employment

0654 Wise, Leah
Bookser-Feister, John. (1989) Betrayal of Trust: Stories of Working North Carolina. Available: Southerners for Economic Justice, Box 240, Durham, N.C. 27707. pp. 68.
South/ North Carolina/ Sexual Harassment/ Employment/ Interviews/ Racial Discrimination/ Reports/ Work Hazards/ Organizing/ Protest Actions/ Women of Color*

*Women of Color**

0655 Amott, Teresa
Matthaei, Julie. (1990) Race, Gender and Work: A Multi-Cultural Economic History of Women in the United States. Boston: South End Press. pp. 320.
Women of Color*/ Inequality/ Wage Gap/ Domestic Labor/ Economics/ History/ Employment/ Race, Class and Gender Studies/ Oppression/ Feminist Theory

0656 Baca Zinn, Maxine
(1989) "Family, Race, and Poverty in the Eighties." SIGNS: Journal of Women in Culture and Society 14:4:pp. 856-874.
People of Color*/ Employment/ Poverty/ Marriage/ Structural Discrimination/ Demography/ Family/ Double Discrimination/ Family Structure/ Racial Discrimination

0657 **Baron, James N.**
Newman, Andrew E. (1990) "For What It's Worth: Organizations, Occupations, and the Value of Work Done by Women and Non-Whites." American Sociological Review 55(April):2:pp. 155-175.
Women of Color*/ Civil Service/ State Government/ Employment/ Devaluation/ Occupations/ Pay Equity/ Pacific/ California/ Equality/ Inequality/ Economic Value of Women's Work/ Discrimination

0658 **Bell, Laurie**
(1989) Good Girls/Bad Girls: Feminist and Sex Trade Workers Face to Face. Seattle: The Seal Press.
Women of Color*/ Discrimination/ Pornography/ Prostitution/ Working Conditions/ Censorship/ Feminist Theory/ Racial Discrimination

0659 **Bookman, Ann**
(1988) "Unionization in an Electronics Factory: The Interplay of Gender, Ethnicity, and Class." in Women and the Politics of Empowerment. Ann Bookman and Sandra Morgen (eds.). Philadelphia: Temple University Press. pp. 159-179.
Women of Color*/ Labor Movement/ Ethnicity/ Employment/ Social Class/ Race, Class and Gender Studies/ Factory Workers/ Unions

0660 **Bose, Christine E.**
(1984) "Household Resources and U.S. Women's Work: Factors Affecting Gainful Employment at the Turn of the Century." American Sociological Review 49(August):pp. 474-490.
Women of Color*/ Comparative Studies/ Employment/ Economic Value of Women's Work/ Household Labor/ Women's History/ Labor History

0661 **Burstein, Paul**
(1989) "Attacking Sex Discrimination in the Labor Market: A Study in Law and Politics." Social Forces 67(March):3:pp. 641-666.
Women of Color*/ Discrimination Laws/ Women's Studies/ Federal Legislation/ Sex Discrimination/ Employment/ Politics/ Employment Opportunities/ Job Equity

0662 **Carlson, Susan M.**
(1987) Beyond 'Occupational Segregation': Contradictory Labor Market Practices and Their Race/Sex Distributional Consequences in the Post-War United States. Tallahassee, FL: Florida State University Press.
Occupational Segregation/ Inequality/ Markets/ Labor Market/ Employment/ Racial Discrimination/ Sex Discrimination/ Job Discrimination/ People of Color*

0663 **Carroll, Susan J.**
(1989) "The Personal is Political: The Intersection of Private Lives and Public Roles among Women in Elective and Appointive Office." Women and Politics 9:2:pp. 51-68.
Women of Color*/ Public Officials/ Politics/ Employment/ Politicians/ Elected Officials/ Life Styles/ Appointed Officials/ Women in Politics/ Gender Roles/ Men's Roles/ Women's Roles/ Images of Women

0664 **Chinen, Joyce N.**
(1989) "New Patterns in the Garment Industry: State Intervention, Women and Work in Hawaii." Presented: American Sociological Association Annual Meeting, San Francisco, CA.
Women of Color*/ Clothing Workers/ Socioeconomic Status/ State Government/ Employment/ Textile Industry/ Pacific/ Hawaii/ Immigration

0665 Crumbling, Deana
(1989) "Women in Psychology - A Minority Process Model." Minority Voices 6(Fall):1:pp. 39-46.
Women of Color*/ Employment/ Women's Movement/ Male Dominated Occupations/ Discrimination/ Individual Development/ Feminism

0666 Evans, Sara
Nelson, Barbara J. (1989) Wage Justice. Chicago: Universtiy of Chicago Press. pp. 240.
Employment/ Women of Color*/ Wages/ Income/ Pay Equity/ Comparable Worth/ Equal Pay

0667 Farkas, George
Barton, M. and K. Kushner. (1988) "White, Black, and Hispanic Female Youth in Central City Labor Markets." Sociology Quarterly 29(December):pp. 605-622.
Women of Color*/ Urban Areas/ Labor Market/ Youth Employment/ Inner City/ Job Discrimination/ Employment

0668 Films for the Humanities
(1989) "Women Against Women." Distributor: Films for the Humanities and Social Sciences, P.O. Box 2053, Princeton, NJ 08543. Phone: (609) 452-1128 or 1-800-257-5126.
Women of Color*/ Discrimination/ Workplace/ Employment

0669 Frazier, Gloria Rudolf
(1985) How about a Little Strategy. Newton, MA: Women's Educational Equity Act Publishing Center.
Women in Transition/ Balancing Work and Family Life/ Coping Strategies/ Women Living in Poverty/ Women of Color*/ Child Care/ Life Skills/ Financial Aid/ Support Systems/ Survival Strategies

0670 Fuchs, Victor R.
(1988) Women's Quest for Economic Equality. Cambridge, MA: Harvard University Press. pp. 176. ISBN 0674955455.
Women of Color*/ Gender Roles/ Equality/ Economically Disadvantaged/ Labor Force Participation/ Leisure Activities/ Family Roles/ Socioeconomic Status/ Equal Pay for Equal Work

0671 Gindhart, Mary
(1985) New Directions for Rural Women: A Workshop Leader's Manual. Newton, MA: Women's Educational Equity Act Publishing Center.
Women of Color*/ Life Skills/ Rural Areas/ Career Strategies/ Coping Strategies/ Balancing Work and Family Life/ Self Concept

0672 Grant, Don Sherman II
Parcel, Toby L. (1990) "Revisiting Metropolitan Racial Inequality: The Case for a Resource Approach." Social Forces 68(June):4:pp. 1121-1142.
Employment/ Urban Areas/ Women of Color*/ Discrimination/ Labor Force Participation/ Regional Studies/ Wage EarningWomen/ Equality

0673 Haignere, Lois
et al. (1982) "Managerial Promotions in the Public Sector: The Impact of Eligibility Requirements on Women and Minorities." Available: Center for Women in Government, State University of New York-Albany, Albany, NY.
Women of Color*/ Institutionalized Discrimination/ Managers/ Professional Status/ Promotions/ Employment/ Racial Discrimination/ Sex Discrimination

0674 Haraway, Donna
(1989) Primate Visions: Gender, Race, and Nature in the World of the Modern Science. New York: Routledge Chapman & Hall. pp. 544.
Feminist Theory/ Careers/ Multiple Roles/ Balancing Work and Family Life/ Scientists/ Family/ Heterosexuality/ Gender/ Race/ People of Color*

0675 Hartman, Heidi
Hoytt, Eleanor et al. (1989) "The Wage Gap and Women of Color." Presented: First Annual Women's Policy Research Conference, Washington, DC.
Women of Color*/ Wage Discrimination/ Wage Gap/ Pay Equity/ Inequality/ Employment/ Racial Discrimination/ Doubly Disadvantaged

0676 Hossfield, Karen J.
(1989) "Small Foreign and Female: Immigrant Workers and Racial Hiring Dynamics in Silicon Valley." Presented: American Sociological Association Annual Meeting, San Francisco, CA.
Women of Color*/ Employment Practices/ Immigrants/ Electronics Industry/ Pacific/ Racial Discrimination/ West/ California

0677 Hughey, A. M.
(1990) "The Incomes of Recent Female Immigrants to the United States." Social Science Quarterly 72(June):1:pp. 383-390.
Women of Color*/ English/ Language Skills/ 20th Century/ Educational Attainment/ Employment/ Income/ Economic Factors/ Immigrants/ Language Development/ Labor Force Participation/ Verbal Ability

0678 Jones, Jo Ann
Rosenfield, Rachel A. (1989) "Women's Occupations and Local Labor Markets: 1950-1980." Social Forces 67(March):3:pp. 666-693.
Women of Color*/ Employment/ Labor History/ Labor Force Participation/ Women's History/ Occupational Patterns

0679 Kessler-Harris, Alice
(1989) A Women's Wage. Lexington, KY: University of Kentucky Press. pp. 216.
Women of Color*/ Wage Discrimination/ Equal Pay for Equal Work/ Women's Roles/ Employment/ Wages/ Income

0680 Michael, Robert T.
Hartman, Heidi I. et al. (1989) Pay Equity: Empirical Inquiries. Washington, DC: National Academy Press.
Women of Color*/ Employment/ Occupational Segregation/ Wage Gap/ Pay Equity

0681 Morales, Rebecca
Ong, P. et al. (1989) "The Employment of Immigrant Women in the Restructured Economy: A View from Los Angeles." Presented: International Symposium "Women in International Migration: Social, Cultural and Occupational Issues--With Special Attention to the Second Generation." Berlin, West Germany.
Women of Color*/ Poverty/ Immigrants/ Labor Force/ Employment/ Socioeconomic Status/ Upward Mobility/ California/ West/ Pacific

0682 National Committee on Pay Equity
(1989) "The Wage Gap." Briefing Paper #1, National Committee on Pay Equity. Available: 1201 Sixteenth Street NW, Suite 420, Washington, DC 20036.
Women of Color*/ Low Pay/ Wage Gap/ Occupational Segregation/ Wage Discrimination/ Wages/ Employment/ Earnings

0683 Peterson, Kenneth D.
Deyhle, Donna and William Watkins. (1988) "Evaluation that Accommodates Minority Teacher Contributions." Urban Education 23(July):2:pp. 133-149.
Women of Color*/ Education/ Discrimination/ Course Evaluation/ Educational Facilities/ Job Evaluation/ Teachers/ Diversity/ Employment Practices/ Promotions

0684 Phelps, Edmund S.
(1980) "The Statistical Theory of Racism and Sexism." in The Economics of Women and Work. Alice H. Amsden (ed.). New York: St. Martin's Press.
Women of Color*/ Employment/ Sexual Discrimination/ Racial Discrimination/ Career Opportunities/ Hiring Practices

0685 Rakow, Lana F.
Kramarae, Cheris. (1990) The Revolution in Words: Righting Women, 1868-1871. New York: Routledge. pp. 304.
Women of Color*/ Suffrage/ Women's History/ Racial Discrimination/ Inequality/ Child Care/ Maternity Rights/ Legal System/ Legislation/ Male Dominated Employment/ Language/ Politics/ Religion

0686 Riccucci, Norma M.
(1986) "Female and Minority Employment in City Government: The Role of Unions." Policy Studies Journal 15(September):1:pp. 3-17.
People of Color*/ Unions/ Minority Employment/ Minority Groups/ Employment/ Labor Policy/ City Government/ Urban Areas

0687 Riccucci, Norma M.
(1989) Women, Minorities, and Unions in the Public Sector. Westport, CT: Greenwood Press. ISBN 0313260435.
Women of Color*/ Employment/ Organizations/ Unions/ Minority Employment/ Public Sector/ Labor Movement

0688 Rix, Sara E.
(1990) The American Woman, 1990-1991. New York: W. W. Norton. pp. 446.
Women of Color*/ Equality/ Family/ Families/ Gender/ Child Care/ Poverty/ Employment/ Female Headed Households/ Housing/ Household

0689 Romero, G. L.
Garza, R.T. (1986) "Attributions for the Occupational Success/ Failure of Ethnic Minority and Nonminority Women." Sex Roles 14:pp. 445-452.
Women of Color*/ Employment/ Racial and Ethnic Differences/ Job Satisfaction/ Success/ Failure

0690 Romero, Mary
(1987) "Being One of the Family: Contemporary Experiences of Women of Color Employed by White Employers." Presented: ALLUCL Conference on the Comparative Study of Race, Ethnicity, Gender and Class, Davis, CA.
Women of Color*/ Race, Class and Gender Studies/ Employment/ Ethnicity/ Interracial Relationships/ Household Workers/ European American/ Domestic Services/ Quality of Work Life

0691 Romero, Mary
(1988) "Sisterhood and Domestic Service: Race, Class, and Gender in the Mistress-Maid Relationship." Humanity and Society 12:4:pp. 318-346.
Women of Color*/ Quality of Work Life/ Race, Class and Gender Studies/ Household Labor/ Relationships/ Sisterhood/ Domestic Services/ Employment

0692 Russell, Diana E. H.
(1989) Sexual Exploitation. Newbury Park, CA: Sage Publications, Inc. pp. 320.
Women of Color*/ Sexual Exploitation/ Sexual Abuse/ Harassment/ Employment

0693 Sacks, Karen Brodkin
(1989) "Toward a Unified Theory of Class, Race, and Gender." American Ethnologist 16:3:pp. 534-550.
Women of Color*/ Domestic Labor/ Race, Class and Gender Studies/ Patriarchy/ Feminist Theory/ Women's History/ Feminism/ Employment/ Oppression

0694 Simon, Barbara Levy
(1988) "Social Work Responds to the Women's Movement." AFFILIA: Journal of Women and Social Work 3(Winter):4:pp. 60-68.
Social Work/ Women of Color*/ Welfare/ Women's Movement/ Feminist Movement/ Female Intensive Occupations/ Consciousness Raising

0695 Smith, Barbara
(1989) "A Press of Our Own. Kitchen Table: Women of Color Press." Frontiers: Journal of Women's Studies 10:3.
Women of Color*/ Print Media/ Publishing Industry/ Feminist Publications/ Writing/ Small Business/ Entrepreneurs/ Business Ownership/ Employment/ Women Owned Business

0696 Smith, Eleanor J.
(1983) "Upward Mobility of Women and Black Faculty and Staff." Presented: First Ohio Conference on Issues Facing Women, Black Faculty and Administrators in Higher Education, Miami University, Oxford, OH.
Women of Color*/ Universities/ Faculty/ Education/ Higher Education/ Colleges/ Teachers/ Upward Mobility/ Occupational Mobility/ African American

0697 Stafford, Walter
(1985) Closed Labor Markets: Underrepresentation of Blacks, Hispanics, and Women in New York City's Core Industries and Jobs. New York: Community Service Society.
Women of Color*/ Labor Turnover/ Employment/ Labor Force/ Northeast/ New York/ Labor Market/ Racial Discrimination/ Industries/ Job Discrimination

0698 Stein, Eileen
(1988) "Perseverance, Growth Cornerstones of Pay Equality Movement in 1988." Newsnotes 9(December):2.
Women of Color*/ Employment/ Pay Equity/ Sexual Equality/ Earnings/ Wages/ Social Movements

0699 Stichter, Sharon B.
Parpart, Jane L. (1988) Patriarchy and Class. Boulder, CO: Westview Press. pp. 233.
Women of Color*/ Race, Class and Gender Studies/ Power/ Patriarchy/ Labor Force/ Employment

0700 Task Force on Women, Minorities, and the Handicapped
(1988) "Changing America: The New Face of Science and Engineering." Interim Report of Task Force on Women, Minorities, and the Handicapped in Science and Technology, Washington, DC.
Women of Color*/ Science/ Engineering/ Male Dominated Professions/ Scientific & Technical Occupations/ Division of Labor/ Employment/ Disabled

0701 Thompson, Donna E.

DiTomaso, Nancy. (1988) Ensuring Minority Success in Corporate Management. New York: Plenum Publishing Co. pp. 414.

People of Color*/ Minority Employment/ Labor History/ Minority Groups/ Employment/ Disadvantaged Groups/ Professional Occupations/ Managerial Occupations/ Corporate Policy

0702 Walby, Sylvia

(1988) Gender Segregation at Work. New York: Taylor & Francis International Publishers. pp. 224.

Images of Women/ Occupational Discrimination/ Sex Discrimination/ Racial Discrimination/ Women of Color*/ Economic Disadvantage/ Employment Patterns/ Labor Force Participation/ Occupational Segregation

0703 Wilson, Marie C.

(1985) Minority Women's Survival Kit: Personal and Professional Development for Minority Women. Newton, MA: Women's Educational Equity Act Publishing Center. pp. 74.

Women of Color*/ Human Rights/ Survival Strategies/ Employment Opportunities/ Coping Strategies/ Communication/ Stress/ Life Skills/ Discrimination/ Job Hunting

0704 Women's Educational Equity Act

(1987) "Career Planning for Minority Women." Available: Women's Educational Equity Act Publishing Center, Newton, MA.

Women of Color*/ Research Methods/ Career Planning/ Employment/ Career Strategies/ Career Counseling/ Career Awarness/ Teacher Education

0705 Women's Educational Equity Act

(1987) "Management Basics for Minority Women." Available: Women's Educational Equity Act Publishing Center, Newton, MA.

Women of Color*/ Verbal Communication/ Management/ Employment/ Management Techniques/ Aspirations/ Education/ Research Methods/ Business

FAMILY

African American

0706 **Alladi, Uma**

(1988) Woman and Her Family in Indian and Afro-American Literature. New York: Envoy Press

Families/ Family/ African American/ Women's Culture/ Women of Color/ Family Roles/ Family Relationships/ Literature

0707 **Angelou, Maya**

(1990) Gather Together in My Name. New York: Bantam. pp. 192.

Women of Color/ Life Histories/ History/ African American/ Mothers/ Autobiographies/ Mother Son Relationships/ Writers/ Authors/ Teenage Mothers/ Self Help/ Family/ Maya Angelou

0708 **Armstead, Myra B.**

(1987) The History of Blacks in Resort Towns: Newport, Rhode Island and Saratoga Springs, New York, 1870-1930. Chicago: University of Chicago Press.

African Americans/ History/ People of Color/ Vacations/ Home Life/ Rhode Island/ New York/ Middle Atlantic/ New England

0709 **Baca Zinn, Maxine**

(1987) "Minority Families in Crisis: The Public Discussion." Available: The Center for Research on Women, Clement Hall, Memphis State University, Memphis, TN 38152.

People of Color/ Family Structure/ African Americans/ Economy/ Black Studies/ Feminist Scholarship/ Families/ Economically Disadvantaged/ Poverty

0710 **Ball, Richard E.**

(1990) "Children and Marital Happiness of Black Americans." Presented: North Central Sociological Association and Southern Sociological Association Annual Meeting, Louisville, KY.

African Americans/ Families/ People of Color/ Child Rearing Practices/ Marriage/ Children/ Married Couples/ Marital Satisfaction/ Family Relationships/ Family Roles

0711 **Beck, Rubye W.**

Beck, Scott, H. (1989) "The Incidence of Extended Households among Middle-Aged Black and White Women: Estimates from a 15-Year Panel Study." Journal of Family Issues 10(June):2:pp. 147-167.

Women of Color/ Single Parent Families/ European American/ Extended Families/ African American/ Middle Age/ Households/ Caregivers/ Family Structure

0712 **Beckley, Gemma Douglas**

(1987) "Internal Supports in Rural Black Families around the Event of Childbirth." DAI (January), Vol. 47(2736-A)7.

Women of Color/ Family Roles/ African American/ Low Income Households/ South/ Mississippi/ Childbearing/ Support Systems/ Rural Areas

0713 Benjamin, Lois

Stewart, James B. (1989) "The Self-Concept of Black and White Women: The Influence upon its Formation of Welfare Dependency, Work Effort, Family Networks, and Illness." American Journal of Economics and Sociology 48.

African American/ Self Concept/ Comparative Studies/ Welfare/ Women of Color/ Economically Disadvantaged/ Lower Class/ Poverty/ Employment/ Health/ Self Esteem/ Family/ Families

0714 Bennet, Lerone, Jr.

(1986) "The Ten Biggest Myths about the Black Family." Ebony 41(August):10.

Women of Color/ Stereotypes/ African American/ Myths/ Families

0715 Bennett, Neil G.

(1989) "The Divergence of Black and White Marriage Patterns." American Journal of Sociology 95(November):pp. 692-722.

Women of Color/ Marriage/ People of Color/ Family Planning/ African Americans/ Marriage Customs/ European Americans/ Marriage Rates/ Family/ Families/ Racial and Ethnic Differences/ Comparative Studies

0716 Berkeley, Kathleen C.

(1989) "Days of Jubilo and Sorrow: Black Women's Quest for Freedom in the Post Civil War South." Presented: Southern Anthropological Society Meeting, Memphis, TN.

Minority Experience/ Women's History/ Freedom/ Agriculture/ Families/ Violence/ Economic Value of Women's Work/ Communities/ Wives/ African American/ Mothers/ Women of Color

0717 Berlin, Ira

(1988) "Afro-American Families in the Transition from Slavery to Freedom." Radical History Review 42(Fall):pp. 89-121.

African Americans/ Families/ Slavery/ Freedom/ People of Color/ Social Change/ Reconstruction

0718 Billingsley, Andrew

(1987) "Black Families in Changing Society." in The State of the Black American. Janet Dewart (ed.). New York: National Urban League. pp. 97-111.

People of Color/ Social Change/ African Americans/ Families

0719 Billops, Camille

Hatch, J. (1982) "Suzanne, Suzanne." Distrubutor: Third World Newsreel, 335 West 38th St., 5th Floor, New York, NY 10018.

Women of Color/ Alcohol Abuse/ African American/ Substance Abuse/ Mother Daughter Relationships/ Middle Class/ Family/ Health/ Domestic Violence/ Drug Abuse

0720 Brown, Diane Robinson

Momeni, Jamshid. (1986) "How Well Housed are Black Female Headed Households: An Analysis of 1970 and 1980 Census Data." Availble: Institute for Urban Affairs and Research, Washington, DC.

Women of Color/ Housing/ African American/ Female Headed Households/ Living Conditions/ Family/ Families

0721 Browne, Dorothy C. Howze

(1989) "Incarcerated Mothers and Parenting." Journal of Family Violence 4(June):2:pp. 211-221.

Women of Color/ Self Esteem/ African American/ Parenting/ European American/ Parent Child Relationships/ Child Abuse/ Child Rearing Practices/ Prevention

0722 Burnham, Margaret A.
(1987) "An Impossible Marriage: Slave Law and Family Law." Law and Inequality 5(July):2:pp. 187-227.
African American/ Women of Color/ Marriage and Family Law/ Civil Rights/ Women's History/ Plantations/ Slaves/ South/ Power/ Exploitation/ Patriarchy/ Inequality

0723 Butts, June Dobbs
(1981) "Is Homosexuality a Threat to the Black Family?" Ebony (April).
People of Color/ African Americans/ Homosexuality/ Tolerance/ Family Structure

0724 Carnegie Foundation
(1988) "Black Churches: Can They Strengthen the Black Family?" Carnegie Quarterly 33:1.
Women of Color/ Churches/ African American/ Support Systems/ Religion/ Networks/ Socialization/ Families

0725 Chisholm, Cheryl
(1987) "On Becoming a Woman: Mothers and Daughters Talking Together." Distributor: Women Make Movies, Inc., 225 Lafayette, Suite 212, New York, NY 10012. Phone: (212) 925-0606 or Fax: (212) 925-2052.
Women of Color/ Teenage Pregnancy/ African American/ Sexual Relationships/ Families/ Birth Control/ Health/ Mother Daughter Relationships/ Sexuality/ Menstruation

0726 Collins, Sharon M.
(1983) "The Making of the Black Middle Class." Social Problems 30:pp. 369-382.
African Americans/ Wealth Distribution/ People of Color/ Class Formation/ Social Stratification/ Middle Class/ Families/ Social Class

0727 Collins, Patricia Hill
(1988) "Black Motherhood under White Partiarchy." Presented: Penn Mid-Atlantic Seminar for the Study of Women in Society, University of Pennsylvania.
African American/ Women of Color/ Motherhood/ Parent Child Relationships/ Families/ Patriarchy

0728 Collins, Patricia Hill
(1989) "A Comparison of Two Works on Black Family Life." SIGNS: Journal of Women in Culture and Society 14(Summer):4. pp. 875-884.
Women of Color/ Race, Class and Gender Studies/ African American/ Unemployment/ Family/ Families/ Socioeconomic Status/ Perceptual Bias/ Deviant Behavior/ Discrimination/ Inequality

0729 Davis, Robert
(1980) "Black Suicide and the Relational System: Theoretical and Empirical Implications of Communal and Familial Ties." Research in Race and Ethnic Relations 2.
People of Color/ Support Systems/ African Americans/ Communities/ Family/ Suicide/ Mental Health

0730 Dressler, William W.
(1985) "Extended Family Relationships, Social Support, and Mental Health in a Southern Black Community." Journal of Health and Social Behavior 26(March):1:pp. 39-48.
Women of Color/ Depression/ African American/ Extended Families/ South/ Family Roles/ Relationships/ Support Systems/ Mental Health

0731 Featherston, Elena
(1989) "Visions of the Spirit." Distributor: Women Make Movies, Inc., 225 Lafayette, Suite 212, New York, NY 10012. Phone: (212)925-0606 or Fax: (212)925-2052.
Women of Color/ Family/ African American/ Social Relations/ Alice Walker/ Life Histories/ Writers/ Activism/ Literature

0732 Film & Video Library
(1986) "Vanishing Family: Crisis in Black America." Distributor: Film & Video Library, University Library, University of Michigan, 400 Fourth St., Ann Arbor, MI 48103-4896. Phone: (313) 764-5360 or 1-800-999-0424.
Women of Color/ Family History/ African American/ Families/ Family/ Liberation Struggles/ Family Conflict/ Family Structure

0733 Film & Video Library
(1984) "Strengths of Black Families." Distributor: Film & Video Library, University Library, University of Michigan, 400 Fourth St., Ann Arbor, MI 48103-4816. Phone: (313) 764-5360 or 1-800-999-0424.
People of Color/ Family Structure/ African Americans/ Families/ Family/ Liberation Struggles/ Family History/ Support Systems

0734 Finkelman, Paul
(1988) Articles on American Slavery, Volume 9: Women and the Family in a Slave Society. Binghampton, NY: State University of New York. pp. 472. ISBN 0824067894.
African American/ Mothers/ Women of Color/ Culture/ Women's History/ Family History/ Child Rearing Practices/ Slavery/ Emancipation

0735 Flynn, Clifton P.
(1990) "Sex Roles and Women's Response to Courtship Violence." Journal of Family Violence 5(March):1:pp. 83-94.
Women of Color/ Sexual Behavior/ African American/ Female Male Relationships/ Home Life/ Attitudes/ Sex Roles/ Violence Against Women

0736 Gaudin, James M., Jr.
Davis, Katheryn B. (1985) "Social Networks of Black and White Rural Families: A Research Report." Journal of Marriage and the Family 47(November):4:pp. 1015-1021.
Women of Color/ Family Roles/ African American/ Family Support/ European American/ Support Systems/ Socialization/ Rural Areas/ Networks

0737 Greshman, Jewell Handy
(1989) "The Politics of Family in America." The Nation Special Issue: Scapegoating the Black Family 249(July):4:pp. 116-124.
African Americans/ Family/ People of Color/ Politics/ Racial Discrimination/ Structural Discrimination

0738 Hamilton, Sylvia
Preito, C. (1989) "Black Mother, Black Daughter." Distributor: National Film Board of Canada, 16th Floor, 1251 Avenue of the Americas, New York, NY 10020. Phone: (212) 586-5131.
Women of Color/ History/ African American/ Traditions/ Mother Daughter Relationships/ Families/ Film

0739 Hampton, Robert L.
(1987) Violence in the Black Family: Correlates and Consequences. Lexington, MA:

Lexington Books. pp. 288. ISBN 066914584X.
People of Color/ Female Male Relationships/ African American/ Child Rearing/ Racial Stereotypes/ Child Abuse/ Spouse Abuse/ Family Violence/ Family Life/ Domestic Violence

0740 **Height, Dorothy**
(1989) "Self-Help: A Black Tradition." The Nation Special Issue: Scapegoating the Black Family 249(July):4:pp. 136-141.
African Americans/ People of Color/ Lower Class/ Self Sufficiency/ Self Help/ Neighborhoods/ Communities/ Extended Families/ Advocacy Groups

0741 **Hine, Darlene Clark**
(1989) "Rape and the Inner Lives of Black Women in the Middle West." SIGNS: Journal of Women in Culture and Society 14(Summer):4:pp. 912-920.
Women of Color/ African American/ Urban Areas/ Rape/ Violence/ West/ Sex Discrimination/ Domestic Violence/ Home Life

0742 **Hobbs, Richard S.**
(1989) The Cayton Legacy: Two Generations of a Black Family, 1859-1976. Seattle: University of Washington.
Home Life/ History/ Women of Color/ Families/ African American/ Support Systems

0743 **Hudgins, John L.**
(1989) "The Strengths of Black Families Revisited." Presented: Southern Sociological Society Annual Meeting, Norfolk, VA.
People of Color/ Employment Patterns/ African Americans/ Support Systems/ Family Roles/ Economic Patterns/ Family Relationships

0744 **Jewell, Karen Sue**
(1988) Survival of the Black Family: The Institutional Impact of American Social Policy. Westport, CT: Praeger Publishers. pp. 207. ISBN 027592985X.
People of Color/ Economic Status/ African Americans/ Support Systems/ Families/ Socioeconomic Status/ Social Policy/ Family Structure

0745 **Kaplan, Elaine Bell**
(1988) "Where Does a Black Teenage Mother Turn?" Feminist Issues 8(Spring):1:pp. 51-83.
Women of Color/ Race, Class and Gender Studies/ African American/ Maternal and Infant Welfare/ Teenage Mothers/ Welfare Mothers/ Unwanted Pregnancy/ Family/ Contraception/ Sex Education

0746 **Kiecolt, K. Jill**
Acock, Alan C. (1990) "Childhood Family Structure and Adult Psychological Well-Being of Black Americans." Sociological Spectrum 10:2:pp. 169-186.
People of Color/ Psychological Adjustment/ African Americans/ Child Development/ Families/ Home Life/ Family Structure/ Childhood/ Adults

0747 **Kissman, Kris**
(1989) "Social Support, Parental Belief Systems, and Well Being." Youth and Society 21(September):1:pp. 120-130.
Women of Color/ Belief Systems/ African American/ Stress/ Support Systems/ Depression/ Teenage Mothers/ Family/ Teenage Pregnancy/ Teenagers/ Parental Attitudes

0748 **Lewis, Mary H.**
(1988) Herstory: Black Female Rites of Passage. Available: African American Images, 9204 Commercial, Suite 308, Chicago, IL 60617. pp. 138.
Women of Color/ Rites of Passage/ African American/ Life Cycle/ Pregnancy/ Parental Attitudes/ Teenage Mothers/ Female Male Relationships/ Parent Child Relationships

0749 Maharidge, Dale
Williamson, Michael. (1989) And Their Children After Them. New York: Pantheon. pp. 262.
South/ Agriculture/ People of Color/ History/ African Americans/ Family/ Families/ European Americans/ Socioeconomic Status/ Poverty/ Racial and Ethnic Differences/ Rural Areas/ Farm Workers

0750 Mahoney, John S., Jr.
(1990) Merritt, Stephen R. "Educational Aspirations and Disappointments: A Comparison between Black and White High School Seniors in Virginia." Presented: North Central Sociological Association & Southern Sociological Association Annual Meetings, Louisville, KY.
People of Color/ Academic Aspirations/ African Americans/ Family Influences/ European Americans/ Fear of Failure/ South/ Virginia/ Educational Attainment/ Education/ Educationally Disadvantaged/ High Schools/ Comparative Studies

0751 Malone, Ann Patton
(1987) "Searching for the Family and Household Structure of Rural Louisiana Slaves, 1810-1864." Louisiana History 28(Fall).
People of Color/ Family Structure/ African Americans/ Culture/ Slavery/ Home Life/ South/ Louisiana/ Households

0752 Malson, Michelene R.
(1983) "Black Families and Childrearing Support Networks." Research in the Interweave of Social Roles 3.
Women of Color/ Support Systems/ African American/ Families/ Children/ Child Rearing Practices/ Networks

0753 McAdoo, Harriette Pipes
(1986) "Societal Stress: The Black Family." in All American Women: Lines that Divide, Ties that Bind. Johnnetta B. Cole (ed.). New York: The Free Press.
Women of Color/ Economy/ Income/ African American/ Socioeconomic Status/ Stress/ Coping Skills/ Families/ Support Networks/ Social Environment/ Roles/ Discrimination

0754 McFalls, Joseph A.
Masnick, George S. (1981) "Birth Control and the Fertility of the U.S. Black Population, 1880-1980." Journal of Family History 6:pp. 89-106.
Women of Color/ 19th Century/ African American/ Fertility/ Families/ Contraception/ History/ 20th Century/ Birth Control/Reproductive Health

0755 Parks, Sheri
(1989) "The Black Mother and American Mythology." Presented: Women in America: Legacies of Race and Ethnicity Conference, Georgetown University, Washington, DC.
Women of Color/ Literature/ African American/ Television/ South/ Mammies/ Roles/ Images of Women/ Motherhood/ Matriarchy/ Stereotypes/ Families/ Films/ History

0756 Payne, Essie K.
(1989) Mama and the Hills of My Youth." Daughters of Sara 15(March/April):2:pp. 3-5.
Women of Color/ Families/ African American/ Vocal Music/ Mothers/ Children/ Rural Areas/ Poverty

0757 Pearce, Diana M.
(1989) "The Feminization of Poverty -- A Second Look." Presented: Women's Policy Research Conference, Washington, DC.
Women of Color/ Public Policy/ African American/ Poverty/ Women Living in Poverty/ Economically Disadvantaged/ Female Headed Households/ Families

0758 **Richie, Beth**
(1985) "Battered Black Women: A Challenge for the Black Community." The Black Scholar (March/April).
Women of Color/ Home Life/ African American/ Violence Against Women/ Battered Women/ Physical Abuse/ Families

0759 **Ricketts, Erol**
(1989) "The Origin of Black Female-Headed Families." Focus 12(Spring/Summer):1:pp. 32-36.
Women of Color/ Family Structure/ African American/ Socioeconomic Conditions/ Female Headed Households

0760 **Sites, Paul**
Mullins, Elizabeth I. (1985) "The American Black Elite." Phylon 46(September):pp. 269-80.
People of Color/ African Americans/ Elites/ Social Class/ Families

0761 **St. John, Craig**
(1990) Rowe, David. "Adolescent Background and Fertility Norms: Implications for Racial Differences in Early Childbearing." Social Science Quarterly 71(March):1:pp. 152-162.
Women of Color/ Education/ College/ African American/ Family Influence/ European American/ Premarital Relations/ Childbearing/ Childbirth/ Early Childbearing/ Family Structure/ Fertility/ Pregnancy/ Adolescents/ Adolescence/ Race/ Family History

0762 **Staples, Robert**
(1987) "Social Structure and Black Family Life: An Analysis of Current Trends." Journal of Black Studies 17(March):pp. 267-286.
People of Color/ Family Life/ Social Structure/ Home Life/ African Americans/ Families

0763 **Tolnay, Stewart E.**
(1985) "Black American Fertility Transition, 1800-1940." Sociology and Social Research 70:pp. 2-7.
Women of Color/ Families/ African American/ Fertility/ 19th Century/ History/ 20th Century

0764 **Tolnay, Stewart E.**
(1986) "Family Economy and the Black American Fertility Transition." Journal of Family History 11:pp. 267-283.
Women of Color/ Families/ African Americans/ Fertility/ Income/ Family Economics/ Socioeconomic Status

0765 **Tolnay, Stewart E.**
(1987) "The Decline of Black Marital Fertility in the Rural South: 1910-1940." American Sociological Review 52:2:pp. 211-217.
Women of Color/ Rural Areas/ African American/ Marriage/ South/ Fertility Rates/ Family Size/ History/ 20th Century/ Maternal and Infant Welfare

0766 **Wilson, M. N.**
(1987) "Raising the Awareness of Wife Battering in Rural Black Areas of Central Virginia." in Violence and the Black Family. R. L. Hampton (ed.). Lexington, MA: Lexington Books.
Women of Color/ South/ Virginia/ African American/ Rural Areas/ Wife Abuse/ Battered Women/ Family Environment/ Domestic Violence/ Violence Against Women

0767 Wilson, William J.

Neckerman, Kathryn. (1987) "Poverty and Family Structure: The Widening Gap Between Evidence and Public Policy Issues." in The Truly Disadvantaged. William J. Wilson. Chicago: University of Chicago Press. pp. 63-92.

Women of Color/ Family Structure/ African American/ Labor Force Participation/ Unemployment/ Female Headed Households/ Public Policy/ Financial Resources/ Disadvantaged Groups/ Social Structure/ Poverty/ Economic Structure

0768 Wineberg, Howard

(1990) "The Timing of International Fertility." Social Science Quarterly 71(March):1:pp. 175-183.

Women of Color/ Birthing/ African American/ Racial Factors/ European American/ Fertility/ Marriage/ Divorce/ Childbirth/ Childbearing

0769 Wyatt, Gail Elizabeth

(1985) "The Sexual Abuse of Afro-American and White American Women in Childhood." Child Abuse Neglect 9:pp. 507-519.

African American/ Home Life/ European American/ Sexual Abuse/ Women of Color/ Early Experience/ Child Abuse/ Family Violence/ Violence Against Women

0770 Wyatt, Gail Elizabeth

(1990) "The Aftermath of Child Sexual Abuse of African American and White Women: The Victim's Experience." Journal of Family Violence 5(March):1:pp. 61-81.

Women of Color/ Early Experience/ African American/ Victimization/ European American/ Disadvantaged Groups/ Comparative Studies/ Child Abuse/ Sexual Abuse/ Family Violence

Asian American

0771 Burns, Maryviolet C.

(1986) The Speaking Profits Us: Violence in the Lives of Women of Color. Seattle: Center for the Prevention of Sexual and Domestic Violence.

Asian American/ Women of Color/ Domestic Violence/ Violence Against Women/ Coping Strategies/ Racial Factors/ Social Problems/ Families/ Family

0772 Caplan, Nathan

Whitmore, John K. and Marcella H. Choy. (1989) The Boat People and Achievement in America: A Study of Family Life, Hard Work, and Cultural Values. Ann Arbor, MI: University of Michigan Press. pp. 248.

Women of Color / Asian American/ Family/ Families/ Educational Attainment/ Cultural Influences/ Employment/ Socioeconomic Status/ Oral History/ Refugees/ Job Training/ Poverty/ Labor Force Participation

0773 Chai, Alice Yun

Kawakami, Barbara F. (1988) "Picture Brides: Feminist Analysis of Life Histories of Hawaii's Early Immigrant Women from Japan, Okinawa, and Korea." Available: Women's Studies Program, University of Hawaii, Porteus 722, 2424 Maile Way, Honolulu, HI 96822.

Women of Color/ Family/ Hawaii/ Pacific/ Stereotypes/ Asian/ Marriage/ Women's History/ Oppression/ 20th Century/ Immigrants/ Family History/ Wives

0774 Gonzales, Juan L., Jr.

(1988) "Exogamous Marriage Patterns among Sikhs of California: 1904-1945." International Journal of Contemporary Sociology 25(Jan/April):1,2. International

Journal of Sociology of theFamily 17(Autumn, 1987):2.
Asian American/ Pacific/ California/ Sikhs/ Home Life/ Marriage/ Female Male Relationships/ History/ 20th Century/ Exogamy/ Women of Color

0775 Hsia, Lisa
(1980) "Made in China, A Search for Roots." Distributor: Filmakers Library, Inc., 124 East 40th St., Suite 901, New York, NY 10016. Phone: (212) 808-4980.
Women of Color/ Family History/ Asian American/ Ethnic Women/ Chinese/ Ethnic Studies/ Cultural Heritage

0776 Lee, Mary Paik
(1990) Quiet Odyssey: A Pioneer Korean Woman in America. Seattle: University of Washington. pp. 264.
Women of Color/ Asian/ Korean/.Families/ Poverty/ Storytellers/ Pioneers

0777 McGoldrick, Monica
Pearce, John K. and Joseph Giordano (eds.). (1982) Ethnicity and Family Therapy. New York: Guilford Press.
Families/ Ethnicity/ Family Therapy/ People of Color/ Ethnic Studies/ Asian American Studies / Family Life/ Family Structure / Asian Americans/ Cultural Influences/ Women of Color/ Racial and Ethnic Differences

Latina

0778 Alvarez, David
Bean, Frank D. and Dorie Williams. (1988) "The Mexican American Family." in Ethnic Families in America: Patterns and Variations (3rd edition). Charles H. Mindel and Robert W. Hobenstein (eds.). New York: Elsevier. pp. 269-292.
Family History/ Ethnic Studies/ Family Relationships/ Family Roles/ Chicanos/ Latinos/ People of Color/ Relationships

0779 Andrade, Sally J.
(1982) "Family Roles of Hispanic Women: Stereotypes, Empirical Findings and Implications for Research." in Work, Family and Health: Latino Women in Transition. Ruth Zambrana (ed.). New York: Hispanic Research Center.
Women of Color/ Health/ Latina/ Stereotypes/ Employment/ Family Roles

0780 Anzaldua, Gloria
(1987) Borderlands/La Frontera: The New Mestiza. San Francisco: Spinsters/Aunt Lute.
Race, Class and Gender Studies/ Family/ Essays/ Poems/ Chicana/ Latina/ Racial Discrimination/ Women of Color

0781 Burgos, Nilsa M.
(1986) "Women, Work and Family in Puerto Rico." AFFILIA: Journal of Women and Social Work 1:3:pp. 17-28.
Women of Color/ Balancing Work and Family Life/ Latina/ Family/ Puerto Rican

0782 Burgos, Nilsa M.
(1988) "Work and Family: Women's Dilemma in Puerto Rico." in Women's Issues, Poverty and Human Services Organizations. Available: The Ohio State University, College of Social Work. pp. 66-80.
Women of Color/ Balancing Work and Family Life/ Latina/ Puerto Rico/ Family/ Employment

0783 Griswold del Castillo, Richard
(1984) La Familia: The Mexican-American Family in the Urban Southwest. Notre Dame, IN: University of Notre Dame.
People of Color/ Urban Areas/ Latinos/ Chicanos/ Family/ Southwest

0784 Gutierrez, Ramon
(1986) Sex, Marriage, and the Family in Colonial New Mexico. Stanford, CA: Stanford University Press.
People of Color/ Latinos/ Sex/ Marriage/ Family/ Southwest/ New Mexico/ History/ Colonial Period

0785 Herbstein, Judith F.
(1985) "Middle Class Hispanic Women in the U.S.: One Migrant's Story." Working Paper #100, Office of Women in International Development, 202 International Center, East Lansing, MI 48824-1035.
Women of Color/ Middle Class/ Chicana/ Latina/ Home Life/ Immigrants/ Immigration/ Race, Class and Gender Studies

0786 Keefe, Susan E.
(1979) "Urbanization, Acculturation, and Extended Family Ties: Mexican Americans in Cities." American Ethnologist 6:2:pp. 349-365.
Women of Color/ Family/ Chicana/ Latina/ Urban Areas/ Urbanization/ Support Systems/ Acculturation/ Extended Family

0787 Keefe, Susan E.
(1980) "Acculturation and the Extended Family among Urban Mexican Americans." in Acculturation: Theory, Models and Some New Findings. A. M. Padilla (ed.). Boulder, CO: Westview Press. pp. 85-110.
Women of Color/ Urban Areas/ Chicana/ Latina/ Acculturation/ Extended Family

0788 Maldonado, Alfred C.
(1988) "Sources of Support and Parental Performances: A Descriptive Study of Mexican-American Female Single Parents." Dissertation: DAI (February), Vol. 48(2169-A)8.
Women of Color/ Support Systems/ Latina/ Family Support/ Female Headed Households/ Single Parents/ Parent Child Relationships

0789 Moore, Joan W.
(1989) "Is There A Hispanic Underclass?" Social Science Quarterly 70(June):2:pp. 265-284.
Women of Color/ Teenage Pregnancy/ Families/ Socioeconomic Status/ Female Headed Households/ Latina/ Race, Class and Gender Studies

0790 Moore, Joan W.
Devitt, Mary. (1989) "The Paradox of Deviance in Addicted Mexican American Mothers." Gender & Society 3(March):1:pp. 53-70.
Chicana/ Latina/ Traditional Values/ Drug Addiction/ Gender Roles/ Mothering/ Low Income Households/ Parent Child Relationships/ Women of Color/ Deviant Behavior/ Role Models

0791 Murguia, Edward
(1982) Chicano Intermarriage. San Antonio, TX: Trinity University Press.
Women of Color/ Cultural Heritage/ Chicana/ Latina/ Ethnic Studies/ Relationships/ Marriage/ Interethnic Families/ Female Male Relationships/ Southwest/ Arizona

0792 **Oral History Review**
(1988) "Oral History and Puerto Rican Women." Oral History Review 16:2.
Women of Color/ Sexual Violence/ Latina/ Puerto Rican/ Politics/ Research Methods/ Religion/ Oral History/ Families/ Consciousness Raising/ Identity

0793 **Sanchez-Ayendez, Melba**
(1986) "Puerto Rican Elderly Women: Shared Meanings and Informal Supportive Networks." in All American Women: Lines that Divide, Ties that Bind. Johnnetta B. Cole (ed.). New York: The Free Press.
Women of Color/ Support Systems/ Puerto Rican/ Community/ Latina/ Families/ Poverty/ Aging/ Gender Roles/ Older Adults/ Networks/ Value Systems

0794 **Schumm, Walter R.**
et al. (1988) "Differences Between Anglo and Mexican American Family Members on Satisfaction with Family Life." Psychology of Women Quarterly 10(March):1:pp. 39-54.
Women of Color/ Urban Areas/ Latina/ Chicana/ Educational Attainment/ European American/ Family Income/ Comparative Studies/ Family Life/ Family Influence/ Family Environment/ Family Relationships

0795 **Terkel, Studs**
(1986) "Jesusita Navarro." in All American Women: Lines that Divide, Ties that Bind. Johnnetta B. Cole. (ed.). New York: The Free Press.
Women of Color/ Female Headed Households/ Latina/ Chicana/ Personal Narratives/ Employment/ Midwives/ Poverty/ Midwifery/ Feminization of Poverty/ Childbirth/ Family/ Families/ Childbearing

0796 **Torres, Aida**
Singh, S. (1986) "Contraceptive Practices among Hispanic Adolescents." Family Planning Practices 18:pp. 193-194.
Women of Color/ Pregnancy Prevention/ Contraception/ Sexual Behavior/ Adolescents/ Latina/ Family Planning

0797 **Williams, Norma**
(1990) The Mexican American Family: Tradition and Change. Dix Hills, NY: General Hall, Inc. pp. 170.
People of Color/ Rituals/ Latinos/ Chicanos/ Working Class/ Life Styles/ Decision Making/ Families/ Family/ Middle Class/ Southwest/ Texas

0798 **Zambrano, Myrna**
(1988) Mejor Sola Que Mal Acompanada: For the Latina in an Abusive Relationship/ Para La Mujer Golpeada. Seattle: Seal Press. pp. 352. ISBN 0931188377. (Book is in bilingual format).
Latina/ Emotional Abuse/ Women of Color/ Female Male Relationships/ Wife Abuse/ Home Life/ Battered Women/ Abusive Relationships/ Cultural Influences

Native American

0799 **Adams, W. Y.**
(1983) "Once More to the Fray: Further Reflections on Navajo Kinship and Residence." Journal of Anthropological Research 39(Winter):pp. 393-414.
People of Color/ Families/ Native Americans/ Kinship/ Navajos/ Home Life/ Family Structure

0800 Babcock, Barbara A.
(1990) Pueblo Mothers and Children: Essays by Elsie Clews Parsons, 1915-1924. Santa Fe, NM: Ancient City Press.
Women of Color/ Southwest/ Roles/ Gender Identity/ Pueblo/ Sexuality/ Identity/ Cultural Heritage/ Anthropology/ History/ Child Rearing Practices/ Midwifery

0801 Bachtold, L. M.
(1982) "Children's Social Interaction and Parental Attitudes among Hupa Indians and Anglo-Americans." Journal of Social Psychology 116(February):pp. 9-17.
People of Color/ Family Influence/ European American/ Children's Relationships/ Native American/ Hupa/ Parental Attitudes/ Socialization/ Social Relations

0802 Gilman, Carolyn
Schneider, Mary Jane. (1987) The Way to Independence: Memories of a Hidatsa Indian Family, 1840-1920. St. Paul, MN: Minnesota Historical Society Press. pp. 371.
Families/ Native Americans/ Hidatsa/ Social History/ People of Color/ Independence

0803 Maxwell, Eleanor Krassen
Maxwell, Robert J. (1990) "Housing for Plains Indians Elderly: A Pattern of Seasonal Use." Presented: North Central Sociological Association and Southern Sociological Association Annual Meetings, Louisville, KY.
Native Americans/ Older Adults/ Plains/ Housing/ Communes/ Temporary Housing/ People of Color/ Home Life

0804 Peterson, Jacqueline
(1981) "The People in Between: Indian-White Marriage and the Genesis of a Metis Society and Culture in the Great Lakes Region, 1680-1830." Dissertation: University of Illinois at Chicago Circle.
Native Americans/ 17th Century/ People of Color/ 18th Century/ Families/ 19th Century/ Social History/ North/ Interracial Marriage/ Great Lakes

0805 Peterson, Jacqueline
(1988) Women Dreaming: The Religio - Psychololgy of Indian-White Marriage in the Western Great Lakes Fur Trade." in Western Women: Their Lands, Their Lives. Lillian Schlissel et al (eds.). Albuquerque, NM: University of New Mexico.
Women of Color/ Religion/ Native American/ Psychology/ Family/ Interracial Marriage/ History/ 18th Century

0806 Schneider, Mary Jane
(1979) "Woman's Work: An Examination of Women's Roles in Plains Arts and Crafts." Plainswoman 2(May/June):pp. 8-11.
Women of Color/ Anthropology/ Native American/ Traditions/ Sex Roles/ Women's Roles/ Home Life/ Craft Art/ Division of Labor

Southern

0807 Alexander, Pamela C.
Lupfer, Shirley L. (1987) "Family Characteristics and Long-Term Consequences Associated with Sexual Abuse." Archives of Sexual Behavior 16(June):3:pp. 235-245.
Women of Color*/ Incest/ South/ Child Development/ Sexual Abuse/ Family Roles/ Parent Child Relationships/ Traditionalism

0808 Badger, Lee W.

Green, Nicholas A. et al. (1988) Child Abuse in the Deep South: Geographical Modifiers of Abuse Characteristics. Tuscaloosa, AL: University of Alabama Press. pp. 168.

South/ Alabama/ Family Conflict/ Child Abuse/ Cultural Factors/ Child Welfare/ Violence/ Family Problems

0809 Bardaglio, Peter W.

(1987) "Families, Sex and the Law: The Legal Transformation of the Nineteenth-Century Southern Household." Dissertation: Stanford University, Stanford, CA. DAI Vol. 48, 1988.

19th Century/ Households/ South/ Home Life/ Laws/ Legal Issues/ Marriage and Family Law/ Family Structure

0810 Burnley, Cynthia S.

(1987) "Caregiving: The Impact on Emotional Support for Single Women." Journal of Aging Studies 1(Fall):3:pp. 253-264.

South/ Tennessee/ Personal Relationships/ Images of Women/ Support Systems/ Caregivers/ Emotions/ Health Care Providers/ Family Roles/ Single Women

0811 Crissman, James

(1989) "Family Type and Familism in Contemporary Appalachia." Southern Rural Sociology 6:pp. 29-45.

Southern/ Employment/ Appalachia/ Church Attendance/ Families/ Family Roles/ Family Structure/ Family Influence/ Gender/ Family Problems/ Race/ Family Policy

0812 Dillman, Caroline Matheny

(1989) "Southern Women: In Continuity or Change?" in Women in the South: An Anthropological Perspective. Holly F. Mathews (ed.). Athens, GA: University of Georgia.

South/ Family Influence/ Gender Identity/ Traditions/ Social Identity/ Femininity/ Social Attitudes/ Female Male Relationships/ Personal Values/ Gender Roles/ Self Concept

0813 Fishel, Anne H.

(1987) "Children's Adjustment in Divorced Families." Youth and Society 19(December):2:pp. 173-196.

South/ North Carolina/ Family Change/ Parent Child Relationships/ Emotional Adjustment/ Divorce/ Social Welfare/ Family Roles

0814 Gundersen, Joan Rezner

Gampel, Gwen Victor. (1982) "Married Women's Legal Status in Eighteenth Century New York and Virginia." The William and Mary Quarterly 39(January):pp. 114-134.

South/ Virginia/ Status/ Women's History/ Northeast/ New York/ Legal Issues/ 18th Century/ Marriage and Family Law/ Marital Status/ Legal Status/ Women's Studies

0815 Kilgore, Meg

(1988) "Bethel May - An Oral History." in Behold, Our Works Were Good: A Handbook of Arkansas Women's History. Elizabeth Jacoway (ed.). Little Rock, AR: Arkansas Women's History Institute in association with August House.

South/ Arkansas/ Motherhood/ Women's History/ Childcare/ Oral History/ 20th Century/ Quality of Life/ Life Styles/ Women's Organizations/ Household Division of Labor/ Biographies/ Bethel May Stockburger Jones

0816 Lebsock, Suzanne

(1990) "'No Obey': Indian, European, and African Women in Seventeenth Century Virginia." in Women, Families and Communities: Readings in American History, Vol. I. Nancy A. Hewitt (ed.). Glenview, IL: Scott Foresman. pp. 6-20.
Women of Color/ People of Color/ Interethnic Families/ Native Americans/ Interracial Marriages/ African Americans/ South/ Virginia/ European Americans/ Servants/ Slaves/ Leadership/ Culture Conflict/ History/ 17th Century/ Pocahontas

0817 Lems, Bonnie Yegidis

(1987) "Psychosocial Factors Related to Wife Abuse." Journal of Family Violence 2(March):1:pp. 1-10.
Women of Color*/ Socialization/ South/ Florida/ Families/ Comparative Studies/ Wife Abuse/ Violence

0818 Malone, Ann Patton

(1987) "Searching for the Family and Household Structure of Rural Louisiana Slaves, 1810-1864." Louisiana History 28(Fall).
People of Color/ Family Structure/ African Americans/ Culture/ Slavery/ Home Life/ South/ Louisiana/ Household

0819 Marks, Paula Mitchell

(1989) Turn Your Eyes toward Texas: Pioneers Sam and Mary Maverick. College Station, TX: Texas A & M University . pp. 323.
Southwest/ Texas/ Families/ History/ 19th Century/ Politics/ Married Couples/ Secession/ Pioneers/ Biographies

0820 McCarty, Loretta M.

(1986) "Mother - Child Incest: Characteristics of the Offender." Child Welfare 65(September/October):5:pp. 447-458.
Southwest/ Texas/ Victims/ Parent Child Relationships/ Offenders/ Mothers/ Parenting/ Incest/ Sexual Abuse/ Child Welfare

0821 Shoffner, Sarah M.

(1986) "Child Care in Rural Areas: Needs, Attitudes and Preferences." American Journal of Community Psychology 14(October):5:pp. 521-539.
South/ Parental Roles/ Rural Areas/ Family/ Child Care/ Social Welfare/ Public Policy/ North Carolina/ South Carolina

0822 Tickamyer, Ann R.

Tickamyer, Cecil H. (1988) "Gender and Poverty in Central Appalachia." Social Science Quarterly 69(December):4:pp. 874-892.
Rural Areas/ Gender Studies/ Poverty/ Economy/ Low Income Households/ Women Living in Poverty/ Female Headed Households/ South/ Appalachia/ Social Problems/ Family

*Women of Color**

0823 Bauer-Maglin, Nan

Schniedewind, Nancy. (1989) Women and Stepfamilies: Voices of Anger and Love. Philadelphia: Temple University Press.
Women of Color*/ Blended Families/ Family Roles/ Family Trends/ Stepfamilies/ Parenting/ Race, Class and Gender Studies

0824 Blau, P. M.

Blum, T. C. and J. E. Schwartz. (1982) "Heterogeneity and Intermarriage." American Sociological Review 47:pp. 45-62.
Women of Color*/ Family/ Marriage/ Exogamy/ Intermarriage

0825 Boyd, Herb

(1989) "The Crisis in Affordable Housing." The Crisis 96(May):5:pp. 11. Available: Crisis Publishing Co., 4805 Mt. Hope Dr., Baltimore, MD 21215.
Public Housing/ Racial Discrimination/ People of Color*/ Homeless/ Urban Areas/ Economically Disadvantaged/ Reagan Administration/ Low Income Families/ Poverty/ Middle Class Families/ Neighborhoods

0826 Boyd, Robert L.

(1989) "Minority Status and Childlessness." Sociological Inquiry 59(Summer):3:pp. 331-342.
Women of Color*/ Marriage Forms/ Childlessness/ Educational Attainment/ Income/ Comparative Studies/ Childless Couples/ Fertility/ Racial and Ethnic Differences/ Career Choices/ Socioeconomic Status

0827 Browne, Irene

(1989) "Class Advantage, Kinship and Race: The Process Determining Financial Assistance to Women Heading Families from Their Kin." Presented: American Sociological Association Annual Meeting, San Francisco, CA.
Kinship/ Families/ Women of Color*/ Support Systems/ Support Groups/ Financial Aid/ Female Headed Households

0828 Cole, Johnnetta B.

(1986) "Families." in All American Women: Lines the Divide, Ties that Bind. Johnnetta B. Cole. New York: The Free Press.
Women of Color*/ Family/ Families/ Balancing Work and Family Life/ Female Headed Households/ Nuclear Family/ Single Parents

0829 Coleman, James C.

(1984) Intimate Relationships, Marriages, and Families. Mountain View, CA: Mayfield Publishing Company. pp. 624. ISBN 0672615398.
People of Color*/ Family/ Class Differences/ Ethnicity/ Relationships/ Employment

0830 Cook, C. C.

(1984) "Factors Influencing the Residential Location of Female Householders." Urban Affairs Quarterly 20(September):pp. 78-86.
Women of Color*/ Disadvantaged Groups/ Family/ Householders/ Single Mothers/ Female Headed Households/ Housing/ Inequality

0831 Cooksey, Elizabeth C.

(1989) "The Influence of Family Background on Resolution of Adolescent First Premarital Pregnancies in the United States." Presented: American Sociological Association Annual Meeting, San Francisco, CA.
Women of Color*/ Family Influence/ Diversity/ Parent Influence/ Abortion/ Premarital Pregnancy/ Adoption/ Single Mothers/ Race/ Teenage Pregnancy

0832 Dressel, Paula

(1987) "Patriarchy and Social Welfare Work." Social Problems 34(June):pp. 294-309.
Women of Color*/ Family/ Patriarchy/ Social Welfare/ Welfare System/ Poverty/ Women Living in Poverty/ Female Headed Households

0833 Ellwood, David T.

(1987) "Divide & Conquer: Responsible Security for America's Poor." Occasional Paper: Ford Foundation Project on Social Welfare and American Future, New York, NY. pp. 58.
Women of Color*/ Poverty/ Welfare System/ Social Welfare/ Welfare Programs/ Human Needs/ Welfare Mothers/ Family/ Families/ Responsibility/ Heads of Households/ Women Living in Poverty

0834 Ferando, Annette

Newbert, David. (1985) Single Mother's Resource Handbook. Newton, MA: Women's Educational Equity Act Publishing Center.

Single Mothers/ Women Living in Poverty/ Women of Color*/ Female Headed Households/ Coping Strategies/ Behavior Change/ Life Skills/ Family Problems/ Counseling/ Problem Solving/ Self Concept

0835 ord Foundation

(1985) "Women, Children and Poverty in America." Available: Ford Foundation Working Paper, New York, New York.

Women of Color*/ Female Headed Households/ Family/ Families/ Women Living in Poverty/ Employment/ Children/ Poverty/ Paporization of Poverty/ Race, Class and Gender Studies

0836 Garfinkel, Irwin

McLanahan, Sara S. (1986) Single Mothers and Their Children: A New American Dilemma. Washington, DC: Urban Institute Press.

Parenting/ Mothers/ Welfare/ Parent Child Relationships/ Employment Opportunities/ Female Headed Households/ Economically Disadvantaged/ Public Policy/ Poverty/ Women of Color*/ Family Roles

0837 Gove, Walter R.

Shin, Hef-Choon. (1989) "The Psychological Well-Being of Divorced and Widowed Men and Women: An Empirical Analysis." Journal of Family Issues 10(March):1:pp. 102-122.

People of Color*/ Comparative Studies/ Divorce/ Self Esteem/ Widows/ Satisfaction/ Adjustment/ Women in Transition/ Stress/ Home Life/ Social Psychology

0838 Helburn, Suzanne

(1989) "Welfare Reform and the Adequacy of Poverty Budgets." Presented: Women's Policy Research Conference, Washington, DC.

Women of Color*/ Budgets/ Family Life/ Impact on Women/ Welfare Reforms/ Women Living in Poverty/ Social Policy/ Public Policy

0839 Humphrey, John A.

Palmer, Stuart. (1987) "Race, Sex, and Criminal Homicide Offender-Victim Relationships." Journal of Black Studies 18(September):1:pp. 45-57.

Women of Color*/ Crimes/ Victims/ Violence/ Relationships/ Murder/ Home Life

0840 Kane, Emily Wright

(1989) "Race and Ideological Consensus in Gender Relations." Presented: American Sociological Association Annual Meeting, San Francisco, CA.

Women of Color*/ Female Male Relationships/ Race/ Ideology/ Gender Relations/ Attitudes/ Gender

0841 Kitson, Gay C.

(1989) Bahri, Karen Benson et al. "Adjustment to Widowhood and Divorce: A Review." Journal of Family Issues 10(March):1:pp. 5-32.

Women of Color*/ Support Groups/ Home Life/ Stress/ Race, Class and Gender Studies/ Divorce/ Widows/ Women in Transition/ Adjustment

0842 Mayfield-Brown, Lorraine P.

(1989) "Family Status of Low Income Adolescent Mothers." Journal of Adolescent Research 4(April):2:pp. 202-213.

Women of Color*/ Status/ Low Income/ Family Structure/ Adolescence/ Support Systems/ Teenage Mothers/ Sexual Behavior/ Age/ Marriage/ Early Childbearing

0843 Morgan, Leslie A.
(1989) "Economic Well-Being Following Marital Termination: A Comparison of Widowed and Divorced Women." Journal of Family Issues 10(March):1:pp. 86-101.
Women of Color*/ Women Living in Poverty/ Women in Transition/ Economic Status/ Economically Disadvantaged/ Widows/ Divorce/ Home Life/ Comparative Studies

0844 Nelson, Barbara J.
(1988) "The Gender, Race and Class of Early Welfare Policy of the U.S. Welfare State: A Comparison of Workman's Compensation and Mother's Aid." in Women, Change, and Politics. Tilly Gurin and Patricia Gurin (eds.). New York: Russell Sage Foundation.
Women of Color*/ AFDC/ Welfare Programs/ Race, Class and Gender Studies/ Compensation Packages/ Public Policy/ Welfare Mothers/ Families/ Family

0845 Ramey, C.
Dorval, D. et al. (1981) "Group Day Care and Socially Disadvantaged Families: Effects on the Child and the Family." in Advances in Early Education and Day Care, Vol. 3. S. Kilmer (ed.). Greenwich, CT: JAI Press Inc.. pp. 69-106.
Women of Color*/ Families/ Child Care/ Race, Class and Gender Studies/ Wage Earning Women/ Socioeconomic Status/ Poverty/ Child Day Care Centers/ Socially Disadvantaged

0846 Riley, Norman
(1989) "Public Low Income Housing." The Crisis 96(May):5:pp. 17. Available: Crisis Publishing Co., 4085 Mt. Hope Dr., Baltimore, MD 21215.
People of Color*/ Urban Areas/ Racial Segregation/ Middle Class Families/ Economically Disadvantaged/ Employment/ Public Housing/ Community/ Neighborhoods/ Support Systems/ Low Income Families

0847 Shinagawa, Larry H.
Pany, Gin. (1989) "Racial Stratification and Household Structure." Presented: American Sociological Association Annual Meeting, San Francisco, CA.
Racial Stratification/ Racial Discrimination/ Households/ Family Structure/ People of Color*/ Home Life

0848 Simon, Rita J.
Altstein, Howard. (1987) Transracial Adoptees and Their Families: A Study of Identity and Commitment. New York: Praeger Publishers.
People of Color*/ Adoption/ Race Relations/ Parent Child Relationships/ Interracial Adoption/ Identity/ Racial Identity/ Adoptive Parents/ Self Esteem/ Family Life/ Qualitative Analysis/ Interviews

0849 VanVliet, W.
et al. (1985) Housing Needs and Policy Approaches. Durham, NC: Duke University Press.
Women of Color*/ Women Living in Poverty/ Low Income Households/ Public Policy/ Female Headed Households/ Single Mothers/ Mobility/ Family/ Housing/ Disadvantaged Groups/ Policy Making

0850 Zopf, Paul E., Jr.
(1989) American Women in Poverty. Westport, CT: Greenwood Press. pp. 226. ISBN 0313259801.
Poverty/ Low Pay/ Women Living in Poverty/ Lower Class/ Class Discrimination/ Families/ Family/ Structural Discrimination/ Female Headed Households/ Economically Disadvantaged/ Women of Color*/ Living Standards

HEALTH

African American

0851 Ahmed, Fred
(1989) "Smoking among Urban Black Women in Reproductive Ages." Presented: American Public Health Association Annual Meeting, Chicago, IL.
Women of Color/ Maternal and Infant Welfare/ African American/ Urban Areas/ Smoking/ Reproductive Health

0852 Amaro, Hortensia D.
Beckman, L. J. et al. (1987) "A Comparison of Black and White Women Entering Alcoholism Treatment." Journal of the Studies of Alcohol 48:3:pp. 220-228.
Women of Color/ Comparative Studies/ African American/ Alcoholism/ Health/ Rehabilitation/ Alcohol Abuse/ European American/ Treatment

0853 Benjamin, Lois
Stewart, James B. (1989) "The Self-Concept of Black and White Women: The Influence upon its Formation of Welfare Dependency, Work Effort, Family Networks, and Illness." American Journal of Economics and Sociology 48.
African American/ Self Concept/ Comparative Studies/ Welfare/ Women of Color/ Economically Disadvantaged/ Lower Class/ Poverty/ Employment/ Health/ Self Esteem/ Family/ Families

0854 Boone, Margaret S.
(1989) Capital Crime: Black Infant Mortality in America. Newbury Park, CA: Sage Publications, Inc. pp. 256.
Women of Color/ African American/ Infant Mortality/ Family/ Families/ Female Headed Households/ Health Care/ Teenage Mothers/ Reproduction/ Fertility/ Maternal and Infant Welfare

0855 Boone, Margaret S.
(1982) "A Socio-Medical Study of Infant Mortality among Disadvantaged Blacks." Human Organization 41(Fall):3:pp. 227-236.
Women of Color/ Social Support/ African American/ Family Support/ Economically Disadvantaged/ Networks/ Prenatal Care/ Infant Mortality/ Maternal and Infant Welfare/ Health/ Stress

0856 Boyd-Franklin, Nancy
(1987) "Group Therapy for Black Women - A Therapeutic Support Model." Journal of American Orthopsychiatry 57(July):3:pp. 394-401.
Women of Color/ Networks/ African American/ Group Therapy/ Mental Health/ Support Groups/ Women's Groups/ Support Systems

0857 Bright, Doris V.
(1990) "Urban Black Folk Religion, African Traditional Religion and Black Female Natural Helpers in Urban Black Mental Health Services: The Contribution of Female Natural Helpers." Presented: North Central Sociology Association and Southern Sociological Society, Louisville, KY.
African American/ Health Care/ Religion/ Mental Health Treatment/ Health Care Providers/ Urban Areas/ Healing/ Folk Healers/ Community/ Folk Medicine/ Women of Color

0858 Campbell, Marie

(1989) Folks Do Get Born. New York: Garland Publishing. pp. 260.
Women of Color/ African American/ South/ Georgia/ Midwifery/ Childbirth/ Public Health/ Nurses/ Rural Areas/ Health Care Providers

0859 Cannon, Lynn Weber

Higginbotham, Elizabeth and Rebecca F. Guy. (1989) "Depression among Women: Exploring the Effects of Race, Class, and Gender." Available: Center for Research on Women, Memphis State University, Memphis, TN 38152.
Women of Color/ Inequalities/ African American/ Employment Status/ Race, Class and Gender Studies/ Mental Health/ Socioeconomic Status/ Depression/ Comparative Studies

0860 Crawley, Brenda

(1988) "The Social Service Needs of Elderly Black Women." AFFILIA: Journal of Women and Social Work 3:2.
Women of Color/ Support Systems/ African American / Elderly Care/ Older Adults/ Social Services/ Health/ Housing/ Social Services

0861 Ekert, D.

Stengle, W. et al. (1989) "Preliminary Results of the Use of Black Nurses as Reinforcers of Mammography Referral for Women 40+ Years of Age in Five Inner-City Health Settings in Detroit, Michigan." Presented: American Public Health Association Meeting, Chicago, IL.
Women of Color/ Mammography/ African American/ Health Care Providers/ Nurses/ Relationships/ Health Care/ Urban Areas/ North/ Michigan

0862 Geronimus, Arline

Anderen, H. Frank et al. (1989) "Differences in Hypertension Prevalence among U.S. Black and White Women of Childbearing Age." Presented: American Public Health Association Annual Meeting, Chicago, IL.
Women of Color/ African Americans/ European Americans/ Health/ Comparative Studies/ Childbearing/ Pregnancy

0863 Gussow, Zachary

(1989) Leprosy, Racism, and Public Health: Social Policy in Chronic Disease Control. Boulder, CO: Westview Press.
Diseases/ Stereotyping/ Public Health/ African Americans/ At Risk Population/ People of Color/ Illness/ Wellness/ Social Policy/ Race Bias/ Prevention/ Health Care Policy/ Racial Discrimination

0864 Herd, Denise

(1988) "Drinking by Black and White Women: Results from a National Survey." Social Problems 35(December):5:pp. 493-505.
Women of Color/ Health/ African American/ Marital Status/ European American/ Socioeconomic Status/ Age/ Employment Status/ Drinking

0865 Holahan, Charles J.

Betak, John F. et al. (1983) "Social Interaction and Mental Health in a Bi-Racial Community." American Journal of Community Psychology 11(June):3:pp. 301-311.
People of Color/ Social Interaction/ African Americans/ Social Support/ European Americans/ Networks/ Southwest/ Texas/ Social Relations/ Mental Health/ Community Relations

0866 Husaini, Baqur A.

Linn, J. G. (1989) "Six-Month Prevalence of Psychiatric Disorders among Southern

Urban Blacks." Presented: American Sociological Association Annual Meeting, San Francisco, CA.
Women of Color/ Depression/ African American/ Psychiatric Illness/ South/ Urban Areas/ Phobias/ Mental Health

0867 Kessler, Ronald C.
Neighbors, Harold W. (1986) "A New Perspective on the Relationships among Race, Social Class, and Psychological Distress." Journal of Health and Social Behavior 27(June):pp. 107-115.
People of Color/ Mental Disorders/ African Americans/ Social Class/ Mental Health/ Socioeconomic Status/ Racial Factors/ Social Behavior

0868 Rice, Mitchell
Jones, Woodrow, Jr. (1990) Health of Black Americans from Post Reconstruction to Integration, 1871-1960: An Annotated Bibliography of Contemporary Sources. Westport, CT: Greenwood Press. pp. 256.
People of Color/ History/ African Americans/ Health Care Services/ Bibliographies/Inequality/ Reference Resources/ Health Seeking Behavior/ Health Care Practices

0869 Russo, Ann
(1989) "Exploring AIDS in the Black Community." Sojourner: The Women's Forum (September):1:pp. 38-39.
People of Color/ Health/ African Americans/ Acquired Immune Deficiency Syndrome/ Family/ Community/ Disease

0870 St. John, Craig
(1990) Rowe, David. "Adolescent Background and Fertility Norms: Implications for Racial Differences in Early Childbearing." Social Science Quarterly 71(March):1:pp. 152-162.
Women of Color/ Education/ African American/ Family Influence/ European American/ Premarital Relations/ Childbirth/ Early Childbearing/ Family Structure/ Fertility/ Pregnancy/ Adolescence/ Race/ Family History

0871 Thomas, Veronica G.
Milburn, Norweeta G. et al. (1988) "Social Support and Depressive Symptoms among Blacks." The Journal of Black Psychology 14(February):2:pp. 35-45.
People of Color/ Coping Strategies/ Women of Color/ Support Systems/ African Americans/ Mental Health/ Depression

0872 Vaughn, D. C.
(1986) "Stress and the American Black Woman: Analysis of Research." International Journal for the Advancement of Counseling 9:4:pp. 341.
Women of Color/ Stress/ African American/ Mental Health/ Counseling

0873 Weston, Guy
(1986) "At Risk: AIDS in the Black Community." Blackout 1(Fall):2.
Women of Color/ Health/ African American/ Risk Taking Behavior/ Acquired Immune Deficiency Syndrome

0874 White, Evelyn C.
(1990) The Black Women's Health Book: Speaking for Ourselves. Seattle: Seal Press.
Women of Color/ Health Care Providers/ African American/ Midwives/ Doctors/ Health Care/ Teenage Pregnancy/ Health Care Utilization/ Reproductive Rights/ Healing/ Acquired Immune Deficiency Syndrome/ Folk Healers/ Folk Medicine

Asian American

0875 Endo, Russell

Sue, Stanley et al (eds.). (1980) Asian Americans: Social and Psychological Perspectives, Vol. II. Palo Alto, CA: Science and Behavior Books.

Asian Americans/ Social Psychology/ People of Color/ Mental Health/ Behavior/ Images of Women

0876 Rumbaut, Ruben

Weeks, John R. (1989) "Infant Health among Indochinese Refugees: Patterns of Infant Mortality, Birthweight and Prenatal Care in Comparative Perspective." Research in the Sociology of Health Care 8.

Women of Color/ Infant Mortality/ Asian/ Prenatal Care/ Birthweight/ Refugees/ Health/ Infant Health/ Maternal and Infant Welfare/ Indochinese

0877 Sue, Stanley

Morishima, James K. (1982) The Mental Health of Asian Americans. San Francisco: Jossey Bass.

Asian Americans/ Mental Health/ Therapy/ Psychology

0878 Thomas, Phillip

(1990) "The State of Health of Asian Americans in the United States." Presented: North Central Sociological Association and Southern Sociological Association Annual Meetings, Louisville, KY.

Asian Americans/ Health Care Policy/ People of Color/ Health Care Services/ Medical Education/ Older Adults/ Medical Care/ Mental Health/ Physical Health

0879 Yu, Elena S. H.

Cypress, Beulah. (1982) "Visits to Physicians by Asian/Pacific Americans." Medical Care 20(August):8:pp. 809-820.

Women of Color/ Patient Doctor Relationships/ Asian American/ Health/ Pacific Islander/ Health Seeking Behavior

Latina

0880 Acuna-Lillo, Eugenia

(1988) "The Reproductive Health of Latinas in New York City: Making a Difference at the Individual Level." Centro Bulletin (Fall)pp. 28-38.

Women of Color/ Northeast/ New York/ Latina/ Health Care Services/ Cultural Influences/ Reproductive Health/ Socialization

0881 Amaro, Hortensia D.

(1988) "Considerations for Prevention of HIV Infection among Hispanic Women." Psychology of Women Quarterly 12(December):pp. 429-443.

Women of Color/ Cultural Influences/ Latina/ Health Behavior/ Acquired Immune Deficiency Syndrome/ Health Education/ Health Care Services/ Prevention/ Communicable Diseases/ Sexual Behavior/ Wellness/ Illness

0882 Aneshensel, Carol S.

Fielder, Eve P. et al. (1989) "Fertility and Fertility-Related Behavior among Mexican American and Non-Hispanic White Female Adolescents." Journal of Health and Social Behavior 30(March):1:pp. 56-77.

Women of Color/ Comparative Studies/ European American/ Contraception/ Latina/ Chicana/ Fertility Rates/ Adolescents/ Teenage Pregnancy/ Reproductive Health/ Sexual Behavior

0883 Angel, Ronald
Worobey, Jacqueline Lowe. (1988) "Acculturation and Maternal Reports of Children's Health: Evidence from Hispanic Health and Nutrition Examination Survey." Social Science Quarterly 69(September):3:pp. 707-721.
Physical Health/ Economic Factors/ Children/ Acculturation/ Latinos/ Health

0884 Boddy, P.
Samaniego, L. et al. (1989) "Concepts of Health and AIDS in a Latino Community." Available: Logan Heights Family Health Center, 1809 National Avenue, San Diego, CA 29113.
People of Color/ Health Care Utilization/ Latinos/ Family/ Comparative Studies/ Health/ Acquired Immune Deficiency Syndrome/ Gender Roles

0885 Comas-Diaz, Lillian
(1981) "Effects of Cognitive and Behavioral Group Treatment on the Depressive Symptomatology of Puerto Rican Women." Journal of Consulting and Clinical Psychology 49:5:pp. 627-632.
Women of Color/ Psychotherapy/ Latina/ Chicana/ Psychology/ Puerto Rican/ Mental Health Treatment/ Mental Disorders/ Depression

0886 Comas-Diaz, Lillian
(1988) "Feminist Therapy with Hispanic/Latina Women: Myth or Reality." in The Psychology of Everyday Racism and Sexism. Lenora Fulani (ed.). New York: Harrington Park Press. pp. 39-61.
Women of Color/ Oppression/ Latina/ Power/ Feminist Theory/ Feminist Therapy/ Social Issues/ Mental Health Treatment/ Acculturation

0887 Engle, Patricia L.
Zambrana, Ruth et al. (1989) "Prenatal and Postnatal Anxiety in Women of Mexican Origin and Descent Giving Birth in L.A." Available: Department of Psychology and Human Development, California Poly-Technic State University, San Luis Obispo, CA 93407.
Mexican/ Latina/ Anxiety/ Health/ Childbirth/ California/ West/ Pacific/ Maternal and Infant Welfare/ Women of Color/ Reproductive Health

0888 Golding, Jacqueline M.
Karno, Marvin. (1988) "Gender Differences in Depressive Symptoms among Mexican Americans and Non-Hispanic Whites." Hispanic Journal of Behavioral Sciences 10(March):1:pp. 1-20.
Women of Color/ Comparative Studies/ Men/ European American/ Mental Health/ Latina/ Chicana/ Depression/ Race, Class and Gender Studies

0889 Mirowsky, John
Ross, Catherine E. (1987) "Support and Control in Mexican and Anglo Cultures." in Health and Behavior: Research Agenda for Hispanics. M. Gaviria and J. D. Arana (eds.). Chicago: Hispanic American Family Center, University of Illinois, Dept. of Psychology.
Women of Color/ Health/ Latina/ Networks/ European American/ Comparative Studies/ Cultural Factors/ Support Systems

0890 Newell, Guy R.
Mills, Paul K. (1986) "Low Cancer Rates in Hispanic Women Related to Social and Economic Factors." Women and Health 11(Fall/Winter):3,4:pp. 23-39.
Women of Color/ Illness/ Cancer/ Latina/ Statistics/ European American/ Health Care Issues/ Socioeconomic Factors/ Life Styles

0891 Nyamathi, Adeline
Vasquez, Rose. (1989) "Impact of Poverty, Homelessness and Drugs on Hispanic Women at Risk for HIV Infection." Hispanic Journal of Behavioral Sciences 11(November):4:pp. 299-314.
Women of Color/ Health/ Latina/ Housing/ Poverty/ Disadvantaged/ Drugs/ Risk Taking Behavior/ Acquired Immune Deficiency Syndrome/ Homeless

0892 Peleato, Jaime
Villabos, Gloria. (1989) "Patterns of Access to Health Care Delivery Services within the Hispanic Population of the Atlanta Area." Presented: Southern Anthropological Society Annual Meeting, Memphis, TN.
Health Care/ Economically Disadvantaged/ Urban Areas/ South/ Georgia/ People of Color/ Latinos/ Health Care Delivery/ Health Seeking Behavior/ Illness/ Wellness/ Hospitals

0893 Perrone, Bobette
Stockel, Henrietta and Victoria Krueger. (1989) Medicine Women, Curanderas and Women Doctors. Norman, OK: University of Oklahoma Press.
Women of Color/ Folk Healers/ Native American/ Health Care Providers/ Medical Procedures/ Latina/ Chicana/ Interviews/ Witchcraft/ Cherokee/ Navajo/ Midwives/ Medical Care/ Apache/ Women's Health Movement/ New Mexico/ Personal Narratives/ Health Care Delivery

0894 Powell-Griner, Eve
(1988) "Differences in Infant Mortality among Texas Anglos, Hispanics, and Blacks." Social Science Quarterly 69(June):2:pp. 452-468.
Women of Color/ Racial Factors/ Latina/ Comparative Studies/ African American/ Infant Mortality/ European American/ Childbearing/ Southwest/ Reproductive Health/ Texas/ Marital Status/ Maternal and Infant Welfare

0895 Rosenberg, Terry J.
(1989) "The Risk of Low Birthweight among Hispanic Women in New York City: How Important Is Descent?." Presented: American Sociological Association Annual Meeting, San Francisco, CA.
Women of Color/ Puerto Rican/ New York/ Heredity/ Latina/ Pregnancy/ Maternal and Infant Welfare/ Birthweight/ Health/ Mothers

0896 Salgado de Snyder, V. Nelly
Padilla, A. M. (1987) "Social Support Networks: Their Availability and Effectiveness." in Health and Behavior: Research for Hispanics. M. Gaviria and J. D. Araua (eds.). Chicago: University of Chicago Press.
Women of Color/ Mental Health/ Health Seeking Behavior/ Latina/ Support Systems/ Coping Strategies/ Networks/ Stress/ Risk Taking

0897 Sullivan, Oona
(1990) "Partners in the Desert." The Ford Foundation Letter 21 (Spring):1:pp. 12-13.
Women of Color/ Families/ Latina/ Chicana/ Basic Human Needs/ Rural Areas/ Water Pollution/ Southwest/ Water Utilities/ Water Resources/ Environmental Health

0898 Tajalli, Irene Queiro
(1989) "Hispanic Women's Perceptions and Use of Prenatal Health Care Services." AFFILIA: Journal of Women and Social Work 4:2.
Women of Color/ Health Care Services/ Latina/ Maternal and Infant Welfare/ Health/ Health Care Delivery/ Health Seeking Behavior/ Prenatal Care/ Pregnancy

0899 Wilcox, Meg
(1988) "Puerto Rican Women Fight Health Hazards." Sojourner 13(August):12:pp. 19-20.
Employment/ Occupational Health/ Puerto Rican/ Latina/ Organizations/ Health Hazards/ Environment/ Industries/ Women of Color/ Blue Collar Workers/ Factory/ Factories

0900 Zambrana, Ruth E.
Hurst, Marsha. (1984) "The Interactive Effect of Health Status on Work Patterns among Urban Puerto Rican Women." International Journal of Health Services 14:2:pp. 265-277.
Women of Color/ Health/ Employment/ Puerto Rican/ Latina/ Children/ Urban Areas

0901 Zambrana, Ruth E.
Silva-Palacios, Victor. (1989) "Gender Differences In Stress among Mexican Immigrant Adolescents in Los Angeles." Available: University of California at Los Angeles, School of Social Welfare, 405 Highland Ave., Dodd Hall 247E, Los Angeles, CA 90024-1452.
Gender/ Mental Health/ Stress/ Adolescents/ Mexican/ Latina/ Immigrants/ California/ Women of Color/ Comparative Studies/ West/ Pacific

Native American

0902 Buckley, T.
(1982) "Menstruation and the Power of Yurok Women: Methods in Cultural Reconstruction." American Ethnologist 9(February):pp. 47-60.
Native American/ Yurok/ Cultural Heritage/ Menstruation/ Mentrual Cycle/ Change/ Physical Health/ Women of Color/ Power

0903 Howard, James H.
(1990) Oklahoma Seminoles: Medicines, Magic, and Religion. Norman, OK: University of Oklahoma. pp. 279.
People of Color/ Religious Traditions/ Native Americans/ Religious Beliefs/ Seminoles/ Magic/ Oklahoma/ Folk Medicine/ Health Care/ Medicine/ Religion/ Tribal Customs

0904 May, P. A.
Hymbaugh, K. J. (1989) "A Macro-Level Fetal Alcohol Syndrome Prevention Program for Native Americans and Alaska Natives: Description and Evaluation." Journal of Studies on Alcohol 50(November):pp. 508-518.
Native American/ Eskimo/ Pregnancy/ Fetuses/ Fetal Alcohol Syndrome/ Health Care/ Disease Prevention/ Alcohol Abuse/ Prenatal Care

0905 Owsley, D. W.
Bradtmiller, B. (1983) "Mortality of Pregnant Females in Arikara Villages: Osteological Evidence." American Journal of Physical Anthropology 61(July):pp. 331-336.
Native American/ Arikara/ Mothers/ Women of Color/ Maternal Mortality/ At Risk Populations/ Pregnancy/ Health/ Mortality Rates

0906 Perrone, Bobette
Stockel, Henrietta and Victoria Krueger. (1989) Medicine Women, Curanderas and Women Doctors. Norman, OK: University of Oklahoma Press.
Women of Color/ Folk Healers/ Native American/ Health Care Providers/ Medical Procedures/ Latina/ Chicana/ Interviews/ Witchcraft/ Cherokee/ Navajo/ Midwives/ Medical Care/ Apache/ Women's Health Movement/ New Mexico/ Personal Narratives/ Health Care Delivery

0907 Tanner, Helen Hornbeck
(1979) "Coocoochee, Mohawk Medicine Woman." American Indian Culture and Research 3:3:pp. 23-42.
Women of Color/ Medical Care/ Native American/ Medical Procedures/ Iroquois/ Biographies/ Folk Healers/ Health/ Health Care Providers/ Medicine Woman

0908 **Temkin-Greener, H.**
et al. (1981) "Surgical Fertility Regulation among Women on the Navajo Indian Reservation, 1972-1978." American Journal of Public Health 71(April):pp. 403-407.
Women of Color/ Contraception/ Fertility/ Native American/ 20th Century/ Navajo/ Reproductive Health/ Sterilization/ Reproductive Technologies

0909 **Weigle, Marta**
(1987) "Creation and Procreation, Cosmogony and Childbirth: Reflections on Ex Nihilo, Earth Diver, and Emergence Mythology." Journal of American Folklore 100(Oct/Dec).
Women of Color/ Folk Medicine/ Native American/ Spiritualism/ Reproduction/ Fertility/ Childbirth/ Reproductive Health

0910 **Young, M. Jane**
(1987) "Women, Reproduction, and Religion in Western Puebloan Society." Journal of American Folklore 100(Oct/Dec).
Women of Color/ Folk Healers/ Native American/ Health/ Pueblo/ Folk Medicine/ Reproduction/ Religion/ Fertility/ Sex Roles

Southern

0911 **Bertoli, F.**
et al. (1984) "Infant Mortality by Socioeconomic Status for Blacks Indians, and Whites: A Longitudinal Analysis of North Carolina, 1968-1977." Sociology and Social Research 68(April):pp. 364-377.
African American/ Native American/ European American/ Comparative Studies/ South Atlantic/ North Carolina/ Infant Mortality/ Health/ Socioeconomic Status/ Class Differences/ Economic Factors/ Women of Color

0912 **Bigbee, Jeri L.**
(1988) "Rurality, Stress and Illness among Women: A Pilot Study." Health Care for Women International 9:1:pp. 43-61.
South/ Texas/ Illness/ Wellness/ Rural Areas/ Stress/ Urban Areas/ Health Care

0913 **Holmes, Linda Janet**
(1986) "African American Midwives in the South." in The American Way of Birth. Pamela S. Eakins (ed.). Philadelphia: Temple University Press.
Women of Color/ Families/ African American/ Maternal and Infant Welfare/ South/ Reproductive Health/ Health Care Providers/ Midwives/ Childbirth

0914 **Hurtado, Aida**
(1987) "A View from Within: Midwife Practices in South Texas." International Quarterly of Community Health Education 8:4:pp. 317-339.
Southwest/ Texas/ Health Care Providers/ Maternal and Infant Welfare/ Midwifery/ Physical Health/ Folk Medicine

0915 **Landry, Evelyn**
(1986) Bertrand, Jane T. et al. "Teen Pregnancy in New Orleans: Factors that Differentiate Teens Who Deliver, Abort and Successfully Contracept." Journal of Youth and Adolescence 15(June):3:pp. 259-274.
Educational Aspirations/ Socioeconomic Factors/ Contraception/ Childbirth/ Abortion/ Maternal and Infant Welfare/ Teenage Pregnancy/ Education/ Sexual Behavior/ South/ Louisiana/ Reproductive Health

0916 Logan, Onnie Lee
(1989) Motherwit: An Alabama Midwife's Story. New York: E. P. Dulton.
Women of Color/ Health Care Providers/ African American/ South/ Alabama/ Rural Areas/ History/ 20th Century/ Midwives/ Health

0917 Martin, S. Michelle
(1989) Battles, Lisa L. "Screening for HIV in the Lesbian Community: Is It Necessary?" Presented: American Public Health Association Conference, Chicago, IL.
South/ Communicable Diseases/ Texas/ Blood Tests/ Lesbians/ Research Methods/ Health Education/ Bisexuality/ Acquired Immune Deficiency Syndrome/ Drug Use/ Sexual Behavior

0918 Savitt, Todd L.
Young, James Harvey. (1989) Disease and Distinctiveness in the American South. Knoxville, TN: University of Tennessee Press. pp. 232. ISBN 0870495720.
South/ Plantations/ Illness/ Wellness/ Diseases/ Health/ Health Care Services/ Educational Opportunities

0919 Walton, Marsha D.
Sachs, Diane et al. (1988) "Physical Stigma and the Pregnancy Role: Receiving Help from Strangers." Sex Roles 18(March):5,6:pp. 323-331.
South/ Tennessee/ Pregnancy/ Childbearing/ Helping Behavior/ Physical Health/ Stigmas/ Handicapped/ Disabled

0920 Wiley, Richard W.
(1986) "Keeping Infants from Becoming Statistics: The Southern States are Making Important Strides." Public Welfare 44(Fall):4:pp. 23-29.
Medical Care/ South/ Nutrition/ Infant Mortality/ Public Health Care/ Childbearing/ Health Care Delivery/ Parenting/ Mothers/ Maternal and Infant Welfare/ Prenatal Care

*Women of Color**

0921 Bakeman, Roger
(1986) "AIDS Risk-Group Profiles in Whites and Members of Minority Groups." The New England Journal of Medicine 313(July):4.
Women of Color*/ Risk Taking Behavior/ European American/ Health/ Acquired Immune Deficiency Syndrome

0922 Bauman, Raquel
(1988) "Effects of Racism in the Technolgy and Science of Human Reproduction Control." Feminists in Science and Technology 1:2:pp. 8-11.
Racial Discrimination/ Abortion/ Reproduction/ Population Control/ Reproductive Technologies/ Women in Science/ Women of Color*/ Medical Procedures/ Health

0923 Cochran, S. D.
Mays, Vickie M. et al. (1988) "Ethnic Minorities and AIDS." in Nursing Care of Patients with AIDS/ARC. A. Lewis (ed.). Rockville, MD: Aspen Publishers.
People of Color*/ Sexually Transmitted Diseases/ Ethnic Groups/ Illness/ Health/ Health Care/ Acquired Immune Deficiency Syndrome/ Health Care Providers/ Diseases/ Nursing/ Sexual Behavior

0924 Evans, Karen Muth
(1987) "The Female AIDS Patient." Health Care for Women International 8:1:pp. 1-7.
Women of Color*/ Images of Women/ Acquired Immune Deficiency Syndrome/ Health Care Issues/ Family Support/ Health Care Providers

0925 Farrell, Stephen W.

Kohl, Harold W. et al. (1987) "The Independent Effect of Ethnicity on Cardiovascular Fitness." Human Biology 59(August):4:pp. 657-666.

People of Color*/ Exercise/ Fitness/ Southwest/ Texas/ Health Care/ Illness/ Wellness/ Cultural Influences/ Comparative Studies/ Cardiovascular Diseases/ Ethnicity

0926 Fulani, Lenora

(1988) "Poor Women of Color Do Great Therapy." in The Psychology of Everyday Racism and Sexism. Lenora Fulani (ed.). New York: Harrington Park Press. pp. 39-120.

Women of Color*/ Discrimination/ Mental Health Treatment/ Therapy/ Poverty

0927 Fulani, Lenora

(1989) The Politics of Race and Gender in Therapy. Binghamton, NY: Haworth Press, Inc. ISBN 0866567232.

Women of Color*/ Self Concept/ Mental Health/ Psychotherapy/ Ethnicity/ Feminist Therapy/ Psychology/ Psychiatry/ Race, Class and Gender Studies

0928 Lopez, Iris

(1988) "Barriers to the Timely Use of Prenatal Care among Poor Non-White Women in New York City." Center-Bulletin (Fall):pp.73-77.

Women of Color*/ Prenatal Care/ Low Income Household/ Cultural Influences/ Maternal Health Science/ Health Care Delivery/ Maternal and Infant Welfare/ Poverty/ Health

0929 Maracle, Marilyn

(1989) "Beyond Abstinence: A Case Study of Recovery among Women in Alcoholics Anonymous." Dissertation: Washington University, St. Louis, MO.

Women of Color*/ Abstinence/ Alcohol Abuse/ Mental Health/ Treatment/ Coping Strategies/ Health/ Therapy/ Self Help/ Support Groups

0930 Mays, Vickie M.

Comas-Diaz, L.(1989) "Feminist Therapy with Ethnic Minority Populations: A Closer Look at Blacks and Hispanics." in Feminist Psychotherapies: Integration of Therapeutic and Feminist Systems. M. A. Douglas et al. Norwood, NJ: Ablex Publishers.

Women of Color*/ Feminist Theory/ Feminism/ Feminist Perspective/ Ethnic Groups/ Therapy/ Psychotherapy/ Psychology/ Mental Health

0931 National AIDS Outreach Project

(1989) "High Risk Behaviors among IV Drug Users Linked to HIV/AIDS and Other Infectious Diseases." ADAMHA News on Alcohol, Drug Abuse and Mental Health 15(August):6:pp. 3-5.

Women of Color*/ Sexually Transmitted Disease/ Drugs/ Sexual Activity/ Addiction/ Acquired Immune Deficiency Syndrome/ Disease/ Infections/ Health Behavior/ Risk Taking Behavior

0932 Nsiah-Jefferson, Laurie

(1989) "Reproductive Laws, Women of Color, and Low-Income Women." in Reproductive Laws for the 1990s. Sherrill Cohen and Nadine Taub (eds.). Clifton, NJ: Humana Press.

Women of Color*/ Health/ Poverty/ Discrimination/ Reproductive Rights/ Federal Legislation/ Abortion/ State Legislation/ Health Hazards in the Workplace/ Laws/ Low Income Households

0933 Reinharz, Shulamit
(1988) "Controlling Women's Lives: A Cross-Cultural Interpretation of Miscarriage Accounts." Research in the Sociology of Health Care 7.
Women of Color*/ Reproductive Health/ Pregnancy/ Miscarriage/ Maternal and Infant Welfare/ Health Care/ Research Bias

0934 Savage, L. J.
Simpson, D. D. (1980) "Post-treatment Outcomes of Sex and Ethnic Groups Treated in Methadone Maintenance during 1969-1972." Journal of Psychedelic Drugs 12:pp. 55-64.
Women of Color*/ Drug Addiction/ Drug Rehabilitation/ Physical Health/ Racial and Ethnic Differences/ Sex Differences

0935 Snapp, Mary Beth
(1989) "Toward Race, Class and Gender Inclusive Research on Stress, Social Support, and Psychological Distress: A Critical Review of the Literature." Research Paper #10. Available: Center for Research on Women, Memphis State University, Memphis, TN 38152.
Women of Color*/ Race, Class and Gender Studies/ Mental Health/ Social Science Research/ Support Systems/ Research Methods/ Research Bias/ Psychological Stress/ Gender Bias/ Feminist Perspective/ Race Bias

0936 Sullivan, Deborah A.
(1989) "Conventional Wisdom Challenged: Trends in Infant Mortality of Minority Groups in Arizona, 1976-1986." Research in the Sociology of Health Care 8.
Women of Color*/ Health/ Families/ Maternal and Infant Welfare/ Infant Mortality/ Southwest/ Arizona

0937 Ulbrich, Patricia M.
Warheit, George J. et al. (1989) "Race, Socioeconomic Status, and Psychological Distress: An Examination of Differential Vulnerability." Journal of Health and Social Behavior 30(March):1:pp. 131-146.
People of Color*/ Mental Health Issues/ Stress/ Depression/ Economically Disadvantaged/ Socioeconomic Status

0938 Wilkinson, Doris
(1987) "Traditional Medicine in American Families: Reliance on the Wisdom of Elders." Marriage and Family Review II:pp. 65-76.
Women of Color*/ Health/ Folk Medicine/ Health Care Providers/ Home Remedies/ Traditions/ Older Adults/ Folk Healers

0939 Wilkinson, Doris
(1987) "Transforming National Health Policy: The Significance of the Stratification System." American Sociologist 18(Summer):pp. 140-145.
Women of Color*/ Race, Class and Gender Studies/ Health Care Policy/ Social Stratification/ National Health Insurance

0940 Zambrana, Ruth E.
(1988) "A Research Agenda on Issues Affecting Poor and Minority Women: A Model for Understanding Their Needs. Available: University of California at Los Angeles, School of Social Welfare, 405 Highland Ave., Dodd Hall 247E, Los Angeles, CA 90024-1425.
Physical Health/ Poverty/ Mental Health/ Disadvantaged/ Women of Color*

WOMEN OF COLOR*

0941 Zambrana, Ruth E.

(1990) "Bibliography on Maternal and Child Health Across Class, Race, and Gender." Available: Center for Research on Women, Memphis State University, Memphis, TN 38152.

Women of Color*/ Health/ Race, Class and Gender Studies/ Maternal and Infant Welfare/ Children/ Reproductive Health/ Bibliographies/ Research Resources

POLITICAL ACTIVISM/ SOCIAL MOVEMENTS

African American

0942 **Andrews, William L.**
(ed.) (1986) Sisters of the Spirit: Three Black Women's Autobiographies of the Nineteenth Century. Bloomington, IN: Indiana University Press. ISBN 0253287049. pp. 256.
African American/ Julia Foote/ Women of Color/ Religious Movements/ Autobiographies/ 19th Century/ Writers/ Authors/ Activism/ Feminism/ Jarena Lee/ Organizing/ Zilpha Elaw/ Women's History/ Social Change

0943 **Andrews, William L.**
Jackson, Mattie J. et al. (1988) Six Women's Slave Narratives. New York: Oxford University Press. pp. 384.
Women of Color/ Social Movements/ African American/ Women's History/ Autobiographies/ Personal Narratives/ Slavery/ Oppression

0944 **Angelou, Maya**
(1990) The Heart of a Woman. New York: Bantam. pp. 304.
Women of Color/ Personal Narratives/ African American/ Performing Arts/ Autobiographies/ Singers/ Maya Angelou/ Political Activism/ Writers/ Authors/ Social Movements/ Life Histories/ Women's History/ Social Change

0945 **Aulette, Judy**
(1987) "It's a Fight for Humanity's Sake: An Interview with Geraldyne Sawyer, First Black 'Woman' Mayor in the South." Humanity & Society 11(November):4:pp. 486-497.
Women of Color/ Social History/ South/ African American/ Civil Rights Movement/ City Government/ Racial Discrimination/ Political Office/ Geraldyne Sawyer/ Mayors/ Elected Officials

0946 **Brady, Mary Dell**
(1987) "Organizing Afro-American Girls' Clubs in Kansas in the 1920's." Frontiers: Journal of Women's Studies 9:2:pp. 63-73.
Women of Color/ Kansas/ African American/ Social Activities/ Women's History/ Organizing/ Girls/ Clubs/ Voluntary Organizations

0947 **Bumiller, Kate**
(1987) "Victims in the Shadow of the Law: A Critique of the Model of Legal Protection." SIGNS: Journal of Women in Culture and Society 12(Spring):3:pp. 421-439.
Women of Color/ Protective Legislation/ African American/ Civil Rights Movement/ Racial Discrimination/ Sex Discrimination/ Institutional Discrimination/ Legal Services/ Political Activism/ Social Movements

0948 **Carter, Gregg**
(1986) "In the Narrows of the 1960's Black Rioting." Journal of Conflict Resolution

30(March):1:pp. 115-127.
People of Color/ Civil Rights Movement/ African Americans/ Riots/ History/ Violence/ Protest Actions/ Political Activism/ Social Movements

0949 Carter, Gregg
(1986) "The 1960's Black Riots Revisited: City-Level Explanations of Their Severity." Sociological Inquiry 56(Spring):2:pp. 210-228.
People of Color/ Civil Rights Movement/ African Americans/ Urban Areas/ City Government/ Riots/ Protest Actions/ Violence/ Social History/ Political Activism/ Social Movements

0950 Carter, Gregg
(1987) "Local Police Force Size and the Severity of the 1960's Black Rioting." Journal of Conflict Resolution 31(December):4:pp. 601-614.
People of Color/ Police Officers/ African Americans/ Social Control/ Riots/ Protective Service Occupations/ Violence/ Civil Rights Movement/ Protest Actions/ Employment/ History

0951 Collins, Patricia Hill
(1987) "Black Women's Resistance: An Analysis of the Dialectics of Oppression and Activism." Presented: National Women's Studies Association Meeting, Atlanta, GA.
African American/ Women of Color/ Resistance/ Oppression/ Activists/ Activism/ Social Movements

0952 Crawford, Vicki L.
(1987) "We Shall Not Be Moved: Black Female Activists in the Mississippi Civil Rights Movement, 1960-1965." Dissertation: Emory University, Atlanta, GA.
Women of Color/ Race, Class and Gender Studies/ African American/ Protest/ Civil Rights Movement/ Political Participation/ History/ Social Movements/ South/ Mississippi/ Resistance/ Liberation Struggles

0953 Crawford, Vicki L.
(1987) "Black Female Grassroots Leadership in Rural Mississippi: Strategies of Resistance." Presented: National Women's Studies Association, Atlanta, GA.
Women of Color/ Rural Areas/ African American/ Social Change/ South/ Mississippi/ Resistance/ Grass Roots/ Organizing/ Political Participation

0954 Duffy, Susan
(1988) Shirley Chisolm: A Bibliography of Writings by and about Her. Metuchen, NJ: Scarecrow Press.
Women of Color/ Political Activism/ Bibliographies/ Elected Officials/ Shirley Chisolm/ African American/ Research Resources

0955 Filler, Louis
(1989) The Rise and Fall of Slavery in America. Englewood, NJ: Jerome S. Ozer.
Slaves/ African Americans/ Slavery/ Social Change/ Plantations/ Social Movements/ Freedom/ Emancipation/ People of Color

0956 Garland, Anne Witte
(1988) "Good Noise: Cora Tucker." in Women Activists: Challenging the Abuse of Power. Anne W. Garland (ed.). New York: Feminist Press.
Women of Color/ Community Service/ African American/ Biographies/ South/ Virginia/ Political Activism

0957 Gilkes, Cheryl Townsend
(1988) "The Margin as the Center of a Theory of History: Afro-American Women, Social Change, and the Sociology of W. E. B. DeBois." Presented: American

Sociological Association Annual Meeting, Atlanta, GA.
Women of Color/ Politics/ Race, Class and Gender Studies/ Social Status/ African American/ Economic Dependency/ Social Change/ Feminist Issues/ Marginality/ Social Movements

0958 Gooley, Ruby L.
(1989) "The Role of Black Women In Social Change." Presented: Southern Sociological Society Annual Meeting, Norfolk College, VA.
Women of Color/ Political Activism/ African American/ Social Change/ Civil Rights Movement/ Images of Women/ Resistance/ Liberation Struggles

0959 Grant, Jacquelyn
(1989) White Women's Christ and Black Women's Jesus: White Feminist Christology and a Womanist Response. Atlanta, GA: Scholar's Press.
African American/ European American/ Religion/ Feminism/ Christianity/ Religious Beliefs/ Religious Groups/ Comparative Religion/ Social Movements /Women of Color

0960 Grant, Joanne
(1980) "Fundi: The Story of Ella Baker." Distributor: University of California at Los Angeles Instructional Media Laboratory, 46 Powell Library, Los Angeles, CA 90024. Phone: (213) 825-0755.
Women of Color/ African American/ Political Activism/ Ella Baker/ Civil Rights Movement/ Organizing

0961 Grewel, Sabnam
et al. (eds.). (1988) Charting the Journey: Writings by Black and Third World Women. London: Sheba Feminist Publications.
Women of Color/ Third World/ African American/ Personal Narratives/ Women's History/ Social Movements

0962 Halvey, Lois Mark
(1989) The Education of a WASP. Madison, WI: University of Wisconsin Press. pp. 344. ISBN 0299119742.
European American/ Social Change/ African American/ Urban Areas/ Discrimination/ History/ 1960-1969/ Social Movements/ Civil Rights Movement/ Women of Color/ Education

0963 Herring, Cedric
(1989) "Deja Vu All Over Again: Wilson's Analysis of the Black 'Underclass'." Presented: Herman Sweatt Symposium on Civil Rights, Austin, TX.
People of Color/ Poverty/ Structural Discrimination/ Lower Class/ Economically Disadvantaged/ African Americans/ Civil Rights Movement

0964 Honey, Michael K.
(1987) "Labor and Civil Rights in the South: The Industrial Labor Movement and Black Workers in Memphis, 1929-1945." Dissertation: Northern Illinois University. DAI (April/May), Vol. 49, 1989.
People of Color/ Labor Movement/ African Americans/ Employment/ South/ Tennessee/ Labor History/ Civil Rights Movement/ Social Movements

0965 Hooks, Bell
(1988) Talking Back: Thinking Feminist, Thinking Black. Boston: South End Press. pp. 200. ISBN 0896083527.
African American/ Social Movements/ South/ Equality/ Women of Color/ Black Feminism/ Education/ Discrimination

0966 Jackson, Muriel
(1985) "The Maids." Distributor: Women Make Movies, Inc., 225 Lafayette, Suite

212, New York, NY 10012. Phone: (212) 925-0606 or Fax: (212) 925-2052.
Women of Color/ Socialization/ African American/ Social Movements/ Employment/ Cultural Influences/ Domestic Services/ Household Workers/ Working Class/ Blue Collar Workers

0967 King, Deborah Karyn
(1986) "Race, Gender and Class Salience in Black Women's Feminist Consciousness." Presented: Annual Meeting of the American Sociological Association, New York, NY.
Women of Color/ Social Movements/ African American/ Feminist Movement/ Black Feminism/ Race, Class and Gender Studies/ Social Class

0968 King, Deborah Karyn
(1987) "In Dialogue with our Mothers: Black Women's Tradition of Struggle and Survival." Presented: Series on Women's Culture, Middlebury College, Middlebury, VT.
Women of Color/ Survival Strategies/ African American/ Traditions/ Resistance/ Women's History/ Women's Culture/ Liberation Struggles

0969 Kopasci, Rosemarie
Faulkner, Audrey Olsen. (1988) "The Powers that Might Be: The Unity of White and Black Feminists." AFFILIA: Journal of Women and Social Work 3(Fall):3:pp. 33-50.
Women of Color/ Empowerment/ European American/ Feminism/ African American/ Feminist Theory

0970 Lanker, Brian
(1989) I Dream A World: Portraits of Black Women Who Changed America. New York: Stewart, Tabori and Chang. pp. 167. ISBN 1556700636.
African American/ Social Change/ Social Action/ Activists/ Women's History/ Women of Color/ Social Movements

0971 Laue, James H.
(1989) Direct Action and Desegregation, 1960-1962: Toward a Theory of the Rationalization of Protest. New York: Carlson Publishing. pp. 440.
People of Color/ Civil Rights Movement/ African Americans/ Voting/ Social History/ Desegregation/ Protest Actions/ Political Activism/ Social Movements

0972 Lorde, Audre
(1988) " I Am Your Sister: Black Women Organizing across Sexualities. " in The Psychopathology of Everyday Racism and Sexism. Lenora Fluani (ed.). New York: Harrington Park Press, Inc. pp. 25-35.
Women of Color/ Lesbians/ African American/ Sisterhood/ Black Feminism/ Organizing/ Grass Roots/ Feminist Organization/ Racial Discrimination/ Sex Discrimination/ Political Activism

0973 Marshall, Susan E.
(1990) "Equity Issues and Black-White Differences in Women's ERA Support." Social Science Quarterly 71(June):2:pp. 299-314.
Women of Color/ Belief Systems/ African American/ Racial and Ethnic Differences/ European American/ Equality/ Social Movements/ Racial Equality/ Activism/ Feminism/ Sexual Equality/ Economic Factors/ Equal Rights Amendment

0974 McKenzie, Maxine
(1987) "You Mean, I Still Ain't?" Breaking the Silence 5(Spring):3: pp. 8-10.
Women of Color/ Race, Class and Gender Studies/ African American/ Racial Discrimination/ Women's Movement

0975 Moyers, Bill
(1990) "Anne Wortham: Parts I & II." Distributor: PBS Video, Public Broadcasting Service, 1320 Braddock Place, Alexandria, VA 22314-1698. Phone: 1-800-424-7963.
Women of Color/ Affirmative Action/ African American/ Racial Discrimination/ Anne Wortham/ Social Movements/ Reverse Discrimination/ Social Change/ Civil Rights Movement/ Organizing/ Welfare State

0976 Murray, Pauli
(1989) Pauli Murray: The Autobiography of a Black Activist, Feminist, Lawyer, Priest and Poet. Knoxville,TN: University of Tennessee Press. pp. 464. ISBN 0870495968.
African American/ Higher Education/ Women of Color/ Pauli Murray/ Civil Rights/ Activism/ Feminism/ Women's Rights/ South/ North Carolina/ Social History/ Autobiographies/ Employment

0977 New York Center for Women in Government
(1984) "Black Women Achievers in America: Biographical Highlights." Available: Center for Women in Government, SUNY, Albany, NY.
Women of Color/ Political Activism/ African American/ Leadership/ Biographies/ Achievement

0978 Nelson, Barbara J.
Hummer, Alissa. (1989) "The Origins of the YWCA's Anti-Racism Campaign." Case Study in the Policy Process. Available: Hubert H. Humphrey Institute, University of Minnesota, Minneapolis, MN 55455.
African American/ Social Movements/ Social Relations/ Racial Discrimination/ Racial Equity/ Social Organizations/ YWCA/ Organizing

0979 Ohm, Rose Marie
(1985) "Current Trends in Black-American Experience." Presented: American Sociological Association Honors Program Session, Washington, DC.
People of Color/ Social Trends/ African American/ Minority Experience/ Social Movements/ Race Relations

0980 PBS Video
(1987) "Eyes on the Prize: America's Civil Rights Years Series." Distributor: PBS Video, 1320 Braddock Place, Alexandria, VA 22314.
People of Color/ Organizing/ African Americans/ Documentaries/ European Americans/ Civil Rights Movement/ Social Change/ Political Activism/ Social Relations

0981 PBS Video
(1987) "Eyes on the Prize II Series." Distributor: PBS Video, 1320 Braddock Place, Alexandria, VA 22314.
People of Color/ Organizing/ African Americans/ Documentaries/ European Americans/ Social History/ Civil Rights Movement/ Social Change/ Political Activism/ Social Relations/ Liberation Struggles

0982 Peats, Maureen
(1989) "Feminist or Black?" Daughters of Sara 15(March/April):2:pp. 15-16.
Women of Color/ African American/ Feminism/ Black Feminism/ Social Movements

0983 Penn State Audio-Visual
(1988) "Daughters of the Black Revolution." Distributor: Penn State Audio-Visual Services, Special Services Building, University Park, PA 16802. Phone: (814) 865-6314 or 1-800-826-0132.
African American/ Political Activism/ Social Movements/ Civil Rights Movement/ Daughters/ Political Leaders/ Malcolm X/ Martin Luther King, Jr./ Medgar Evers/ Father Daughter Relationships/ Resistance/ Women of Color

0984 **Perkins, Jerry**
(1986) "Political Ambition among Black and White Women: An Intragender Test of the Socialization Model." Women & Politics 6(Spring):1:pp. 27-40.
Women of Color/ Career Aspirations/ African American/ Educational Patterns/ European American/ Sex Role Stereotyping/ South/ Georgia/ Socialization/ Political Participation/ Activism

0985 **Pohlmann, Marcus D.**
(1989) Black Politics in Conservative America. White Plains, NY: Longman, Inc.
Race Relations/ Legislation/ Structural Discrimination/ Education/ Politics/ Racial Discrimination/ Public Policy/ Social Movements/ African Americans/ Welfare State/ People of Color

0986 **Rouse, Jacqueline Anne**
(1989) Lugenia Burns Hope, Black Southern Reformer. Athens, GA: University of Georgia Press. pp. 182. ISBN 0820310824.
African American/ Biographies/ Women of Color/ Social Organizations/ Segregation/ Women's Groups/ Discrimination/ Social Movements/ Women's History/ South/ Lugenia Burns Hope/ Social Change/ YWCA

0987 **Rutledge, Essie M.**
(1989) "Black/White Relations in the Women's Movement." Minority Voices 6(Fall):1:pp. 53-62.
Women of Color/ Race/ African American/ Gender/ European American/ Relationships/ Women's Movement/ Race Relations/ Racial Discrimination/ Sex Segregation

0988 **Scott, Patricia Bell**
(1981) "Some Thoughts on Black Women's Leadership Training." Working Paper #90, Wellesley College Center for Research on Women.
Women of Color/ Leadership/ African American/ Leadership Training/ Political Activism

0989 **Smith, Barbara**
(1986) "Black Lesbian/Feminist Organizing: A Conversation." in All American Women: Lines that Divide, Ties that Bind. Johnnetta B. Cole (ed.). New York: The Free Press.
Women of Color/ Barbara Smith/ African American/ Jameelah Waheed/ Lesbianism/ Homosexuality/ Tania Abdulahad/ Feminism/ Gwendolyn Rogers/ Social Movements/ Political Acitvism/ Organizing

0990 **Solomon, Irvin D.**
(1989) Feminism and Black Activism in Contemporary America: An Ideological Assessment. Westport, CT: Greenwood Press.
Feminism/ Women of Color/ Black Feminism/ Political Activism/ Feminist Scholarship/ Feminist Perspective/ Feminist Theory/ African American

0991 **Spelman, Elizabeth V.**
(1982) "Theories of Race and Gender: The Erasure of Black Women." Quest: A Feminist Quarterly 5:4.
Women of Color/ Research Bias/ African American/ Feminism/ European American/ Feminist Theory/ Social Movements/ Invisibility

0992 **Stoper, Emily**
(1989) The Student Nonviolent Coordinating Committee: The Growth of Radicalism in a Civil Rights Organization. New York: Carlson Publishing. pp. 351.
People of Color/ African Americans/ Civil Rights Movement/ Students/ Activism/ Politics/ Radicals/ Liberation Struggles

0993 Terborg-Penn, Rosalyn
(1987) "Discontented Black Feminists: Prelude and Postscript to the Passage of the Nineteenth Amendment." in Decades of Discontent: The Women's Movement, 1920-1940. Lois Scharf et al (ed.). Boston: Northeastern University Press.
Women of Color/ Discrimination/ African American/ Women's History/ Suffrage/ Nineteenth Amendment/ Feminism

0994 Terrelonge, Pauline
(1989) "Feminist Consciousness and Black Women." in Women: A Feminist Perspective. Jo Freeman (ed.) Mountain View, CA: Mayfield Publishing.
Women of Color/ Black Feminism/ African American/ Feminist Thought/ Women's Movement/ Social Movements

0995 Towns, Emilie M.
(1989) "Black Women and Social Evil: Ida B. Wells-Barnett's Social and Moral Perspectives as Resources for Contemporary Afro-Feminist Social Ethic." NWSA Journal 1(Spring):3:pp. 568-569.
African American/ Racial Discrimination/ Ida B. Wells-Barnett/ Women of Color/ Women's History/ Ethics/ Interviews/ Social Values/ Letters/ Religion/ Christianity/ Political Activism

0996 White, E. Frances
(1984) "Listening to the Voices of Black Feminism." Radical America 18:2,3.
Women of Color/ Feminism/ African American/ Feminist Theory/ Social Movements/ Black Feminism

0997 Women Make Movies, Inc.
(1982) "Never Turn Back: The Life of Fannie Lou Hamer." Distributor: Women Make Movies, Inc., 225 Lafayette, Suite 212, New York, NY 10012. Phone: (212) 925-0606 or Fax: (212) 925-2052.
African American/ Civil Rights/ Women of Color/ Fannie Lou Hamer/ Social Movements/ Organizing/ Resistance/ Voting Rights/ Mississippi/ South/ Social Change

0998 Yellin, Jean Fagan
(1990) Women and Sisters. New Haven, CT: Yale University Press. pp. 248.
Women of Color/ Harriet Jacobs/ African American/ Feminism/ European American/ Abolition/ Angelina Grimke/ Social Movements/ L. Maria Child/ Social Change/ Sojourner Truth

Asian American

0999 Asian Women United of California
(1989) Making Waves: An Anthology of Writings by and about Asian American Women. Boston: Beacon Press.
Women of Color/ Immigration/ Asian American/ War/ Historical Analysis/ Employment/ Memoirs/ Family/ Families/ Oral Histories/ Identity/ Activism/ Discrimination

1000 Chai, Alice Yun
(1988) "Global Feminism and Hawaiian Feminist Politics." Presented: Conference on Exploration in Feminist Ethics: Theory and Practice, University of Minnesota, Duluth, MN.
Women of Color/ Ethics/ Asian American/ Global Feminism/ Pacific Islander/ Political Theory/ Hawaii/ Social Movements

1001 **Chow, Esther N.**
(1987) "The Development of Gender Consciousness among Asian American Women." Gender & Society 1(September):3:pp. 4-10.
Women of Color/ Feminist Movement/ Asian American/ Consciousness Raising/ Race, Class and Gender Studies/ Social Issues/ Social Studies

1002 **Chow, Esther N.**
(1989) "The Feminist Movement: Where are All Asian Women?" in Making Waves: Writings by and about Asian American Women. Diane Yen Mei Wong and Judy Yung (eds.). Boston: Beacon Press.
Women of Color/ Social Problems/ Asian American/ Women's Roles/ Social Movements/ Consciousness Raising/ Feminist Movement/ Social Issues

1003 **Hohri, Sasha**
(1986) "Are You A Liberated Woman?: Feminism, Revolution, and Asian American Women." in All American Women: Lines That Divide, Ties That Bind. Johnnetta B. Cole (ed.). New York: The Free Press.
Women of Color/ Asian American/ Feminism/ Social Movements/ Liberation Struggles/ Images of Women/ Sexual Revolution

1004 **Ling, Susie**
(1989) "The Mountain Movers: Asian American Women's Movement in Los Angeles." Amerasia Journal 15:pp. 51-67.
Women of Color/ Social Movements/ Asian American/ Women's Movement/ Feminism/ Activism/ Feminist Movement/ California/ Pacific

1005 **Toy, Fran**
(1989) "Cutting through the Double Bind." Daughters of Sara 15(March/April):2:pp. 18-19.
Women of Color/ Social Movements/ Asian American/ Religion/ Chinese American/ Episcopalian/ Feminist Movement/ Double Bind

Latina

1006 **Azize-Vargas, Yamila**
(1990) "The Roots of Puerto Rican Feminism: The Struggle for Universal Suffrage." Radical America 23:1:pp. 71-80.
Women of Color/ Social Movements/ Latina/ Puerto Rican/ Colonialism/ Voting Rights/ Suffrage/ Women's Suffrage/ Women's History/ 19th Century/ Feminism/ Education/ Equal Access/ Activism/ Employment

1007 **Baver, Sherrie L.**
(1989) "Political Participation of Puerto Rican Women: Mapping a Research Agenda." AFFILIA: Journal of Women and Social Work 4:1.
Women of Color/ Political Participation/ Latina/ Puerto Rican/ Politics/ Socioeconomic Status/ Poverty/ Voting Behavior/ Political Activism

1008 **Cortez, Carlos E.**
(1980) Cuban Exiles in the United States. New York: Arno Press.
People of Color/ Exile/ Immigration/ Latinos/ Cubans/ Political Activism/ Public Policy

1009 **Diaz, Ada Maria Isasi**
Tarango, Yolanda. (1988) Hispanic Women: Prophetic Voice in the Church. New York: Harper and Row.
Latina/ Religious Reforms/ Religion/ Religious Movements/ Social Movements/ Churches/ Social Change/ Leadership/ Liberation Struggles/ Women of Color

1010 Diaz, Leticia
(1989) "Activism is Learned Behavior, and the Resources Section Provides a List of Publications and Organizations Dedicated to this Purpose." Intercambios: A Publication of the National Network of Hispanic Women 4(Summer):1:pp. 15-16.
Women of Color/ Latina/ Research Resources/ Women's Organizations/ Feminist Publications/ Political Activism/ Learned Behavior

1011 Garcia, Alma M.
(1989) "The Development of Chicana Feminist Discourse, 1970-1980." Gender & Society 3(June):2:pp. 217-238.
Women of Color/ Social Movements/ Latina/ Feminist Movement/ Chicana/ Feminist Scholarship/ Feminist Theory/ Feminist Perspective/ Race, Class and Gender Studies/ Racial Discrimination

1012 Garland, Anne Witte
(1988) "We've Found the Enemy: Gale Cincotta." in Women Activists: Challenging the Abuse of Power. Anne W. Garland. (ed.). New York: Feminist Press.
Women of Color/ Community/ Latina/ Working Class/ Political Activism/ Biographies/ Personal Narrative/ Feminism

1013 Moraga, Cherrie
(1986) "From a Long Line of Vendidas: Chicanas and Feminism." in Feminist Studies Critical Studies. Teresa deLauretis (ed.). Bloomington, IN: Indiana University Press.
Women of Color/ Sex Discrimination/ Latina/ Chicana/ Patriarchy/ Feminism/ Feminist Theory/ Women's Movement/ Social Movements

1014 Munoz, Carlos, Jr.
(1989) Youth, Identity, Power: The Chicano Movement. New York: Haymarket Press. pp. 200. ISBN 0860919137.
Latinos/ People of Color/ Political Activism/ Social Movements/ History/ Organizing/ Local Politics

1015 Orozco, Cynthia
(1989) "Women in the Mexican American Civil Rights Movement." NWSA Journal 1:1:pp. 163-164.
Women of Color/ Civil Rights Movement/ Latina/ Chicana/ Social Change/ Community/ Women in Politics/ Balancing Work and Family Life/ Women's History

1016 Ramos, Juanita
(1987) Companeras: Latina Lesbians. New York: Lesbian Herstory Archives Project.
Women of Color/ Feminist Theory/ Latina/ Chicana/ Feminist Movement/ Homosexuality/ Lesbians/ Sexuality/ Homophobia

1017 Weil, Connie
(1988) Lucha: The Struggles of Latin American Women. Minneapolis, MN: Prisma Books. pp. 200.
Latina/ Life Histories/ Social Structure/ Liberation Struggles/ Women's Rights/ Social Movements/ Women of Color

1018 Zaval-Martinez, Iris
(1988) "En la Lucha: The Economic and Socioemotional Struggles of Puerto Rican Women." Women and Therapy Journal 6:4:pp. 3-24.
Women of Color/ Life Histories/ Latina/ Liberation Struggles/ Coping Strategies/ Puerto Rican/ Survival Strategies/ Economic Factors/ Mental Health/ Political Factors

1019 **Zavella, Patricia**
(1986) "Reconciling 'Difference' in the Feminist Movement: A Latina Perspective." Presented: Conference on Perspectives on Feminism: Past Present and Future, Sponsored by the National Women and the Law Association, Washington, DC.
Women of Color/ Social Movements/ Latina/ Feminist Movement/ Feminism/ Diversity

Native American

1020 **Babcock, Barbara A.**
(1988) "At Home, No Womens are Storytellers: Potteries, Stories, and Politics in Cochiti Pueblo." Journal of the Southwest 30(Autumn):pp. 256-389.
Women of Color/ Folk Literature/ Native American/ Sex Roles/ Southwest/ New Mexico/ Political Activism/ Craft Art/ Politics/ Pueblo

1021 **Bernstein, Alison**
(1984) "A Mixed Record: The Political Enfranchisement of American Indian Women during the Indian New Deal." in Indian Leadership. Walter Williams (ed.). Manhattan, KS: Sunflower University Press. pp. 13-20.
Women of Color/ Tribal Customs/ Native American/ Politics/ History/ Voting Rights/ Political Participation/ Leadership/ Political Activism/ Enfranchisement

1022 **Bolt, Christine**
(1987) American Indian Policy and American Reform: Case Studies of the Campaign to Assimilate the American Indians. Winchester, MA: Unwin Hyman. pp. 228.
People of Color/ Native Americans/ Social Movements/ Assimilation Patterns/ Public Policy/ Social Change/ Case Studies/ Social Reform/ Legislation/ Socialization

1023 **Hauptman, Lawrence**
(1979) "Alice Jemison: Seneca Political Activist." Indian Historian 12:2:pp. 15-40.
Women of Color/ Women's History/ Native American/ 20th Century/ Iroquois/ Social Movements/ Political Activism/ Culture Conflict/ Alice Jemison/ Biographies

1024 **Jensen, Joan M.**
(1977) "Native American Women and Agriculture: A Seneca Case Study." Sex Roles 3:5:pp. 423-431.
Women of Color/ Iroquois/ Social Status/ Native American/ Division of Labor/ Agriculture/ History/ Political Power/ Social Movements/ Women's Work/ Social Change/ Assimilation Patterns/ Sex Roles/ Economic Power/ Missionaries

1025 **Kasee, Cynthia R.**
(1989) Let Your Women Hear Our Words: The Rights of Cherokee Women before the 19th Amendment." Available: Department of Sociology & Anthropology, Miami University, Oxford, OH 45056.
Women of Color/ Voting Rights/ Native American/ 19th Amendment/ Cherokee/ Women's History/ Social Movements/ Sex Roles

1026 **Knack, Martha C.**
(1989) "Contemporary Southern Paiute Women and the Measurement of Women's Economic and Political Status." Ethnology 28(July):pp. 233-248.
Women of Color/ Socioeconomic Status/ Native American/ Political Status/ Paiute/ Women's Roles/ Political Activism

1027 **Koester, Susan H.**
(1988) "'By the Words of Thy Mouth Let Thee Be Judged': The Alaska Native

Sisterhood Speaks." Journal of the West 27(April):pp. 35-44.
Women of Color/ Activism/ Native American/ Women's Organizations/ Alaska/ Social Movements

1028 LaDuke, Winona
(1983) "The Morality of Wealth: Native American and the Frontier Mentality." Radical America 17:pp. 69-79.
People of Color/ Mining Industry/ Native Americans/ Activism/ Environment/ Ecology/ Economics/ Navajos

1029 LaDuke, Winona
(1983) "Native America: The Economics of Radioactive Colonization." Review of Radical Political Economy 15:pp. 9-19.
People of Color/ Mining Industry/ Native Americans/ Activism/ Environment/ Political Economic System/ Ecology/ Economics/ Navajos

1030 Loren, Barbara
(1987) "Native American Writers: Survival and Transformation." Belles Lettres 2(May/June).
People of Color/ Reviews/ Native Americans/ Writers/ Poetry/ Authors/ Fiction/ Liberation Struggles

1031 Lynch, Robert N.
(1986) "Women in Northern Paiute Politics." SIGNS: Journal of Women in Culture.and Society 11:1:pp. 352-366.
Women of Color/ Sex Roles/ Native American/ Politics/ Leadership/ Political Participation/ Political Power/ Activism

1032 Mathes, Valerie Sherer
(1987) "Helen Hunt Jackson and the Campaign for Ponca Restitution, 1880-1881." South Dakota History 17(Spring):pp. 23-41.
Women of Color/ Helen Hunt Jackson/ Native American/ Women's History/ Biographies/ Social Movements/ Social History/ Political Activism

1033 Mathes, Valerie Sherer
(1990) Helen Hunt Jackson and Her Indian Reform Legacy. Austin, TX: University of Texas Press. pp. 256.
Women of Color/ Organizing/ Native Americans/ Social Change/ Biographies/ Helen Hunt Jackson/ Social Movements/ Political Activism

1034 Navajo-Hopi Task Force
(1982) "Navajo Relocation Review." A Special Report by the Navajo-Hopi Task Force, the Land Dispute Commission, and the Navajo Times. Window Rock, Navajo Nation.
Social Movements/ Public Policy/ People of Color/ Relocation/ Native Americans/ Navajos/ Hopi

1035 Osawa, Sandra Sunrising
(1988) "In the Heart of Big Mountain." Distributor: Sandra Sunrising Osawa, 1st Avenue West, Seattle, WA 98119. Phone: (206) 281-9177.
People of Color/ Government/ Native Americans/ Public/ Organizations/ Political Activism

1036 Smith, Andy
(1989) "Beyond the Pow-Wow." Off Our Backs 19(July).
Women's Organizations/ Women of Color/ Political Activism/ Native Americans/ Social Movements

1037 Thornton, Russell
(1987) American Indian Holocaust and Survival: A Population History Since 1492. Norman, OK: University of Oklahoma Press. pp. 352.
People of Color/ Native Americans/ Demography/ Population Trends/ Population Growth/ Liberation Struggles/ Social History/ Holocaust/ Survival Strategies

1038 Todd, Judith
(1986) "Opposing the Rape of Mother Earth." in All American Women: Lines That Divide, Ties That Bind. Johnnetta B. Cole (ed.). New York: The Free Press.
Women of Color/ Native American/ Hopi/ Strip Mining/ Feminism/ Social Movements/ Environmentalism/ Political Activism/ Extractive Industry

1039 Wallace, Michelle
(1988) Wilma Mankiller: Principal Chief of the Cherokee Nation." Ms. 16(January):pp. 68-69.
Women of Color/ Political Office/ Native American/ Political Activists/ Cherokee/ Political Power/ Biographies/ Politics/ 20th Century/ Leadership

1040 Weeks, Philip
(1990) Farewell My Nation: The American Indian and the United States, 1820-1890. Arlington Heights, VA: Harlan Davidson. pp. 250.
People of Color/ Colonialism/ Native Americans/ Oppression/ History/ Discrimination/ 19th Century/ Land Settlement/ Migration/ Liberation Struggles/ Relocation

1041 Welch, Deborah
(1985) "An American Indian Leader: The Story of Gertrude Bonnin, 1876-1939." Dissertation: University of Wyoming, Laramie, WY
Women of Color/ Leadership/ Native American/ 19th Century/ Biographies/ 20th Century/ Reformers/ Women's History/ Sioux/ Activists

1042 Willard, William
(1984) "Gertrude Bonnin and Indian Policy Reform, 1911-1938." in Indian Leadership. Walter Williams (ed.). Manhattan, KS: Sunflower University Press. pp. 70-75.
Women of Color/ Activists/ Public Policy/ History/ Biographies/ 20th Century/ Reformers/ Sioux/ Leadership

Southern

1043 Aulette, Judy
(1987) "It's a Fight for Humanity's Sake: An Interview with Geraldyne Sawyer, First Black 'Woman' Mayor in the South." Humanity & Society 11(November):4:pp. 486-497.
Women of Color/ Social History/ South/ African American/ Civil Rights Movement/ City Government/ Racial Discrimination/ Political Office/ Geraldyne Sawyer/ Mayors/ Elected Officials

1044 Crawford, Vicki L.
(1987) "We Shall Not Be Moved: Black Female Activists in the Mississippi Civil Rights Movement, 1960-1965." Dissertation: Emory University, Atlanta, GA.
Women of Color/ Race, Class and Gender Studies/ African American/ Protest/ Civil Rights Movement/ Political Participation/ History/ Social Movements/ South/ Mississippi/ Resistance/ Liberation Struggles

1045 Crawford, Vicki L.
(1987) "Black Female Grassroots Leadership in Rural Mississippi: Strategies of Resistance." Presented: National Women's Studies Association, Atlanta, GA.
Women of Color/ Rural Areas/ African American/ Social Change/ South/ Mississippi/ Resistance/ Grass Roots/ Organizing/ Political Participation

1046 Effland, Anne Wallace
(1985) "Exciting Battle and Dramatic Finish: The West Virginia Woman Suffrage Movement Part I: 1867-1916." West Virginia History 46:1,4:pp. 137-158.
Suffrage Movement/ West Virginia/ South Atlantic/ Women's History/ Social Change/ Women's Rights/ Voting Rights/ Feminism/ Suffrage

1047 Garrow, David J.
(1989) The Walking City: Montgomery Bus Boycott, 1955-1956. New York: Carlson Publishing. pp. 662.
Women of Color/ African American/ Boycotts/ Protest Actions/ Civil Rights Movement/ History/ Social Change/ Resistance/ Liberation Struggles/ South/ Alabama

1048 Gerster, Patrick
Cords, Nicholas (eds.). (1989) Myth and Southern History Vol. II: The New South. Champaign, IL: University of Illinois Press. pp. 208.
Women's History/ 20th Century/ Social Movements/ Social Change/ South

1049 Gimelli, Louis B.
(1989) "Louisa Maxwell Cocke: An Evangelical Plantation Mistress in the Antebellum South." Journal of the Early Republic 9(Spring):pp. 53-71.
European American/ Louisa Maxwell Cocke/ Evangelism/ South/ Women's History/ Religious Movements/ Plantations/ Antebellum

1050 Jacoway, Elizabeth
(1988) Behold, Our Works Were Good: A Handbook of Arkansas Women's History. Little Rock, AR: Arkansas Women's History Institute in association with August House. pp. 112.
South/ Women's Organizations/ Arkansas/ Women's Studies/ Women's History/ Biographies/ Oral History/ Social Movements/ Bethal May Stockburger/ Women of Color*

1051 Jacoway, Elizabeth
(1988) "Redefining Our Past: The Work of the Arkansas Women's History Institute." in Behold, Our Works Were Good: A Handbook of Arkansas Women's History. Elizabeth Jacoway (ed.). Little Rock, AR: Arkansas Women's History Institute in association with August House.
South/ Arkansas/ Social Movements/ Women's Organizations/ Women's History/ Self Esteem/ Pride

1052 Janiewski, Dolores
(1987) "Flawed Victories: The Experiences of Black and Women Workers in Durham during the 1930's." in Decades of Discontent: The Women's Movement, 1920-1940. Lois Scharf et al (eds.). Boston: Northeastern University Press.
Women of Color/ Women's Movement/ South/ Labor Laws/ Employment/ Labor History/ Unions/ Organizing

1053 Lawson, Stephen F.
(1990) Black Ballots: Voting Rights in the South, 1944-1969. New York: Columbia University Press. pp. 474.
People of Color/ Social Movements/ African Americans/ Social History/ South/ Voting Rights/ Political Activism

1054 Maggard, Sally Ward
(1989) "Eastern Kentucky Women on Strike: A Study of Gender, Class, and Political Action in the 1970's." Dissertation: University of Kentucky (Order No. DA8914910).
South/ Kentucky/ Labor Disputes/ Employment/ Labor History/ 1970-1979/ Factory Workers/ Politics/ Unions/ Political Activism/ Women's History/ Class/ Strikes/ Social Movements/ Gender Studies

1055 McMillen, Neil R.
(1989) Dark Journey: Black Mississippians in the Age of Jim Crow. Champaign, IL: University of Illinois Press.
People of Color/ Discriminatory Practices/ African Americans/ Racial Discrimination/ South/ Mississippi/ Antebellum/ Social History/ Segregation/ Liberation Struggles/ Social Movements

1056 Pharr, Suzanne
(1988) Homophobia: A Weapon of Sexism. Inverness, CA: Chardon Press. pp. 91
Women of Color*/ South/ Homophobia/ Lesbians/ Patriarchy/ Oppression/ Women's Movement/ Sex Discrimination/ Racial Discrimination

1057 Rable, George C.
(1989) Civil Wars: Women and the Crisis of Southern Nationalism. Champaign, IL: Universtiy of Illinois Press. pp. 384.
South/ European American/ Women's History/ Social Movements/ Civil War/ Stereotypes/ Plantations/ Nationalism

1058 Rosenberg, Ellen M.
(1989) "Serving Jesus in the South: Southern Baptist Women under Assault from the New Right." in Women in the South: An Anthropological Perspective. Holly F. Mathews (ed.). Athens, GA: University of Georgia Press. pp. 122-135.
South/ Traditionalism/ Religion/ Baptist/ Conservative Movement/ Church Work/ Separate Spheres/ Religious Movements/ Religious Reforms

1059 Rouse, Jacqueline Anne
(1989) Lugenia Burns Hope, Black Southern Reformer. Athens, GA: University of Georgia Press. pp. 182. ISBN 0820310824.
African American/ Biographies/ Women of Color/ Social Organizations/ Segregation/ Women's Groups/ Discrimination/ Social Movements/ Women's History/ South/ Lugenia Burns Hope/ Social Change/ YWCA

1060 Salmond, John A.
(1988) Miss Lucy of the CIO: The Life and Times of Lucy Randolph Mason, 1882-1959. Athens, GA: University of Georgia Press. pp. 240.
South/ Biographies/ Labor Movements/ Unions/ Activism/ Suffrage/ Voting Rights/ History/ 20th Century

1061 Wilson, J.
(1989) "Public Work and Social Participation: The Case of Farm Women." Presented: American Sociological Association Annual Meeting, San Francisco, CA.
South/ Labor Force Participation/ Employment/ Farm Families/ North Carolina/ Family/ Rural Areas/ Social Activism

1062 Wolfe, Margaret Ripley
(1987) "Feminizing Dixie: Toward a Public Role for Women in the American South." Research in Social Policy: Critical, Historical, and Contemporary Perspectives 1.
South/ Social Policy/ Roles/ Public Sphere/ Public Roles/ Political Activism

1063 Young, Mary E.
(1989) "Racism in Red and Black: Indians and Other Free People of Color in Georgia Law, Politics, and Removal Policy." Georgia Historical Quarterly 73(Fall):pp. 492-518.
People of Color/ Politics/ Native Americans/ Relocation/ African Americans/ Interracial Relations/ Liberation Struggles/ Political Repression/ Racial Discrimination/ Law/ Georgia/ South

1064 Women Make Movies, Inc.
(1982) "Never Turn Back: The Life of Fannie Lou Hamer." Distributor: Women Make Movies, Inc., 225 Lafayette, Suite 212, New York, NY 10012. Phone: (212) 925-0606 or Fax: (212) 925-2052.
African American/ Civil Rights/ Women of Color/ Fannie Lou Hamer/ Social Movements/ Organizing/ Resistance/ Voting Rights/ Mississippi/ South/ Social Change

*Women of Color**

1065 1989 Vote 70 Project, Inc.
(1989) "Vote 70." Distributor: Shepard Productions, 578 Center Dr., Memphis, TN 38112.
Women of Color*/ Civil Rights/ Women's History/ Women's Rights/ Social Movements/ Voting Rights/ Suffrage/ Feminism

1066 Allen, Paula Gunn
(1986) "Angry Women Are Building: Issues and Struggles Facing American Women." in All American Women: Lines that Divide, Ties that Bind. Johnnetta B. Cole (ed.). New York: The Free Press.
Women of Color*/ Consciousness Raising/ Liberation Struggles/ Social Movements/ Activism/ Feminism/ Coping Strategies/ Survival Strategies

1067 Ashmore, Harry S.
(1989) Hearts and Minds: A Personal Chronicle of Race in America. Cabin John, MD: Seven Locks Press. pp. 532.
Women of Color*/ Discrimination/ South/ History/ Slavery/ Reagan Administration/ Racial Discrimination/ Civil Rights Movement

1068 Brooks, Suzanne R.
et al. (1984) "Moving Mountains Past, Present, and Future: The Role of Women of Color in the American Political System." Working Paper: The Brown Papers #1, The National Institute for Women of Color.
Women of Color*/ Political Systems/ Women's History/ Power/ Political Activism

1069 Evans, Sara
(1989) Born For Liberty: A History of Women in America. New York: Free Press. pp. 400. ISBN 0029029902.
Native American/ Slaves/ African American/ Immigration/ Women's History/ Social Change/ Women's Movement/ Resistance/ Women of Color*

1070 DuBois, Ellen Carol
Ruiz, Vicki L. (eds.) (1990) Unequal Sisters: A Multicultural Reader in U.S. Women's History. New York: Routledge. pp. 496.
Women of Color*/ Women's History/ Sisterhood/ Wages/ Income/ Employment/ Family Life/ Community Development/ Political Activism/

1071 Garland, Anne Witte

(1988) "Education's the Thing: Maria Fava and Mildred Tudy." in Women Activists: Challenging the Abuse of Power. Anne W. Garland (ed.). New York: Feminist Press.

Women of Color*/ Social Movements/ Feminism/ Personal Narrative/ Political Activism/ Maria Fava/ Poverty/ Mildred Tudy/ South/ Education

1072 Gould, Ketayun H.

(1987) "Feminist Principles and Minority Concerns: Contributions, Problems, and Solutions." AFFILIA: Journal of Women and Social Work (Fall).

Women of Color*/ Feminist Theory/ Diversity/ Double Bind/ Social Change/ Social Movements

1073 Gunew, Sneja

(1990) Reader in Feminist Knowledge. New York: Routledge. pp. 432.

Women of Color*/ Feminist Perspective/ Social Movements/ Feminist Studies/ Radical Feminism/ Feminist Theory/ Socialist Feminism/ Feminist Scholarship/ Sisterhood/ Feminist Differences

1074 Hamilton, Roberta

Barrett, Michele. (1987) Politics of Diversity: Feminism, Marxism, and Nationalism. New York: Routledge. pp. 360.

Women of Color*/ Diversity/ Culture/ Social Movements/ Politics/ Feminism/ Nationalism/ Marxism

1075 Hewitt, Nancy A.

(1983) "The Social Origins of Women's Antislavery Politics in Western New York." in Crusaders and Compromisers: Essays on the Relationship of the Antislavery Struggle to the Antebellum Party System. A. M. Kraut (ed.). Westport, CT: Greenwood.

Women of Color*/ Social Movements/ Slavery/ Abolition/ Political Activism/ New York/ Northeast/ Politics/ Antebellum/ Antislavery

1076 Hewitt, Nancy A.

(1986) "More than Suffrage: The Early Women's Movement." Presented: National Women's Law Conference, Washington, DC.

Women of Color*/ Empowerment/ Women's Movement/ Suffrage/ Women's History/ Social Movements/ Women's Rights

1077 Hewitt, Nancy A.

(1987) "The Feminist Frontier: Women and Community Activism." Presented: Diane Weiss Memorial Lecture, Center for the Humanities, Wesleyan University, Middletown, CT.

Women of Color*/ Feminism/ Social Movements/ Community Action/ Activism/ Political Participation

1078 Kramarae, Cheris

(1989) "The Language of Multicultural Feminism." Center for the Study of Women in Society (Newsletter-University of Oregon). pp. 3-5.

Women of Color*/ Lesbians/ Social Movements/ Feminism/ Homophobia/ Racial Discrimination/ Language/ Diversity

1079 Loescher, Gil

Monahan, Laila. (1989) Refugees and International Relations. New York: Oxford University Press. pp. 448.

Women of Color*/ Oppression/ Public Policy/ Political Activism/ Churches/ Sanctuaries/ Refugees

1080 Ostrander, Susan A.
(1989) "Feminism, Volunteerism and the Welfare State: Toward a Feminist Sociological Theory of Social Welfare." The American Sociologist 20(Spring):1:pp. 29-41.
Women of Color*/ Race, Class and Gender Studies/ Feminist Movement/ Sociology/ Volunteer Work/ Welfare/ Social Welfare/ Feminist Theory

1081 Plaskow, Judith
Christ, Carol P. (1989) Weaving the Vision: New Patterns in Feminist Spirituality. New York: Harper & Row. pp. 366.
Feminist Perspective/ Women of Color*/ Feminist Scholarship/ Black Feminism/ Feminist Studies/ Spirituality/ Feminist Movement

1082 Pope, Jacqueline
(1986) "Organizing Women on Welfare: Planning at the Grass Roots Level." Dissertation: Columbia University, New York, NY. DAI Vol. 47(03A).
Women of Color*/ Activism/ Public Welfare/ Public Policy/ Social Change/ Organizing/ Public Assistance/ Social Movements/ Women Living in Poverty/ Grass Roots/ Religion/ Political Action

1083 Schecter, Susan
(1982) Women and Male Violence: The Visions and Struggles of the Battered Women's Movement. Boston: South End.
Women of Color*/ Racial Discrimination/ Social Movements/ Crisis Shelters/ Violence Against Women/ Battered Women/ Home Life/ Race, Class and Gender Studies

1084 Simon, Barbara Levy
(1988) "Social Work Responds to the Women's Movement." AFFILIA: Journal of Women and Social Work 3(Winter):4:pp. 60-68.
Social Work/ Women of Color*/ Welfare/ Women's Movement/ Feminist Movement/ Female Intensive Occupations/ Consciousness Raising

1085 Stein, Eileen
(1988) "Perseverance, Growth Cornerstones of Pay Equality Movement in 1988." Newsnotes 9(December):2.
Women of Color*/ Employment/ Pay Equity/ Sexual Equality/ Earnings/ Wages/ Social Movements

1086 Trask, Haunani Kay
(1983) Fighting the Battle of Double Colonization: The View of a Hawaiian Feminist. Honolulu, HI: University of Hawaii Press.
Women of Color*/ Colonization/ Feminism/ Political Activism/ Hawaii/ Pacific/ Resistance/ Double Bind

AUTHOR INDEX

(refers to citation number)

D

E

F

G

H

KEYWORD INDEX

(refers to page numbers)

U

V

W

Y

Z

DATE DUE
